Ibsen's lively

Ibsen's lively art

A PERFORMANCE STUDY OF THE MAJOR PLAYS

Frederick J. Marker and Lise-Lone Marker

The right of the
University of Cambridge
to print and sell
all manner of books
was granted by
Henry VIII in 1534.
The University has printed
and published continuously
since 1584.

CAMBRIDGE UNIVERSITY PRESS

Cambridge

New York   New Rochelle

Melbourne   Sydney

PUBLISHED BY THE PRESS SYNDICATE OF THE UNIVERSITY OF CAMBRIDGE
The Pitt Building, Trumpington Street, Cambridge, United Kingdom

CAMBRIDGE UNIVERSITY PRESS
The Edinburgh Building, Cambridge CB2 2RU, UK
40 West 20th Street, New York NY 10011–4211, USA
477 Williamstown Road, Port Melbourne, VIC 3207, Australia
Ruiz de Alarcón 13, 28014 Madrid, Spain
Dock House, The Waterfront, Cape Town 8001, South Africa

http://www.cambridge.org

© Cambridge University Press 1989

First published 1989
First paperback edition 2005

A catalogue record for this book is available from the British Library

Library of Congress cataloguing in publication data
Marker, Frederick J.
Ibsen's lively art: a performance study
of the major plays/
Frederick J. Marker, Lise-Lone Marker.
p.   cm.
Bibliography.
Includes indexes.
ISBN 0 521 26643 2 hardback
1. Ibsen, Henrik, 1828–1906 – Stage history.   2. Ibsen, Henrik,
1828–1906 – Criticism and interpretation.   I. Marker, Lise-Lone,
II. Title
PT8899.M37 1989
839.82′26 – dc 19   88–18675   CIP

ISBN 0 521 26643 2 hardback
ISBN 0 521 61924 6 paperback

Contents

Illustrations

Preface

It should, one hopes, be a truism that a play is fundamentally a text for performance, which, by definition, is capable of achieving its fullest degree of expression only in the direct encounter between actor and spectator, when the apparent statement of the text is transformed, by mutual consent, into living representation. This is what Peter Brook means when he says that "no play can speak for itself." What is more, Brook reminds us, the process of theatrical interpretation must of necessity take place in an active, sometimes even a revolutionary mode – for the simple reason, as he explains, that "if you just let the play speak, it may not make a sound. If what you want is for the play to be heard, then one must conjure its sound from it." Seen in these terms, the plays of Henrik Ibsen have stimulated just such an active and regenerative search for theatrical forms and images capable of accommodating and amplifying his vision on the stage. During the course of more than a century and a quarter, this search has resulted in the broadest conceivable spectrum of practical responses on the part of actors, directors, and stage designers – responses which, taken together, make up an essential dimension of the critical attitude adopted toward Ibsen, whether in our time or in his own. Henry James once referred to him as "a sort of register of the critical atmosphere, a barometer of the intellectual weather." Each succeeding generation seems to discover – or rediscover – elements in his work that renew the dialogue in which the past and the present continue to meet. Theatrical performance is the true meeting place where these elements in a dramatist's work are tested.

It should be made clear at the outset that this book is not intended as a comprehensive survey or a chronological tabulation of the stage history of Ibsen's plays in any particular country or period. Even were an all-inclusive production calendar of this sort feasible, it would not serve our principal critical objective. Rather, the aim here is to offer

ix

more detailed, comparative analyses of certain key productions and clusters of productions, in an effort to shed fresh light on the problems of interpretation governing each of the plays discussed and on some of the ways in which these problems have been tackled in different periods and different theatrical contexts. The main emphasis is thus placed on the nature and continuity of the theatrical response to specific kinds of Ibsen play, from a romantic work like *Peer Gynt* to a so-called symbolic one like *John Gabriel Borkman*. Of course, as Georg Brandes quickly came to recognize, to Ibsen of all men such catchwords as "realism" and "symbolism" meant little in themselves: "although devotion to reality characterises both his nature and his poetry, yet he is poet and thinker enough always to let a deeper meaning underlie the reality he represents" (from Brandes' Third Impression, 1898). This deeper meaning manifests itself in Ibsen's theatrical syntax (in what Brandes calls the "almost broad obviousness" of his "emblematic tendency"), yet the precise manner of its expression is the lively variable that continues to give his major plays their abiding fascination in performance.

In fact, of course, each one of Ibsen's twenty-six plays possesses a performance history of some kind, however slight. Even the mighty *Emperor and Galilean* was at last performed in its entirety in a seven-hour production at Det Norske Teatret in Oslo in 1987. In the interests of readability and synthesis, however, we have inevitably had to select and to concentrate on six of the most representative and most frequently performed works, which provide the nucleus of this study. Each reflects a distinct aspect of Ibsen's dramaturgy and (sooner or later) a consequently altered pattern of theatrical response to the new challenge. In turn, the detailed performance studies of these six key works contribute to the development of a broader conceptual framework to which some significant productions of other plays in the canon (*Rosmersholm*, *An Enemy of the People*, *Little Eyolf*, and *The Master Builder*, to name four) are then related, at least in passing.

In a book that ventures to range in scope from Ibsen's own early productions of his work in the 1850s to the most recent reinterpretations and theatrical paraphrases of our own day, the issue of selection and emphasis becomes even more crucial when it involves choosing the productions and individual performances that seem usefully conceptual or broadly representative or (preferably) both. In the last analysis this process depends upon individual judgment, but it is hoped that the result in this case has been a selection that mingles tradition and experiment in a manner that may stimulate readers to consider and develop their own comparisons. (For reference purposes, a concise chronological index to the 200-odd productions included here is provided at the back of the book to guide the reader through the study's time-frame, but this apparatus is hardly a substitute for the far more comprehensive production calendars found elsewhere.) Above all, a study whose methodology is consistently reconstructive is quite obviously dependent for its success upon the gathering of the objective factual evidence that constitutes the basis for all theatre research – annotated texts, promptbooks, rehearsal records, set and costume designs, photographs, reviews, and whatever else has not already perished. The availability of such evidence, together with our conscious determination to push beyond the familiar and limited confines of English Ibsen into the less commonly traversed territory of German, Russian, Scandinavian and (in the earlier period) French theatre culture, has given the volume the shape it has – and, we hope, the basis for its usefulness as well. With a few exceptions, productions of Ibsen in other media (film, television, and radio) have remained outside the scope of our discussion, as have the many ballet and opera adaptations of the plays – in themselves, a fascinating subject for a study of its own.

Because of the comparative approach taken, a great deal of newly translated material has been incorporated here. In all but the instances noted, the authors themselves are responsible for the translations in this volume.

The modest genesis of this book was a paper read at a conference at the University of British Columbia, held in honor of Ibsen's sesquicentennial in 1978; it subsequently appeared in *Modern Drama* (December 1978) with the title "Ibsen's Theatre: Aspects of a Chronicle and a Quest." Some of the observations about the first American productions of Ibsen were initially published in *Scandinavian Review* that same year, in an article entitled "Early Ibsen Performances in America." A few of the major productions given prominence in this book (notably William Bloch's *Wild Duck*, Ingmar Bergman's *Hedda Gabler*, *Nora*, and *The Wild Duck*, and the world premiere of *A Doll's House*) have been discussed by us in various other contexts before, but in each case the material has been thoroughly revised on the basis of a fresh look at the sources. Otherwise, all other material in the volume appears in print for the first time.

The complexity of the source-gathering which a study such as this entails has required the assistance and occasionally tried the patience of a good many individuals and institutions. In particular, it is a pleasure to acknowledge the active help and cooperation of the following: the staff of the Bibliothèque Nationale in Paris; the Residenztheater, the Kammerspiele, and Dr. Heinrich Huesmann and the staff of the Deutsches Theatermuseum in Munich; the Max Reinhardt Forschungs- und Gedenkstätte in Salzburg; Dr. Klaus Völker and Ilse Buhs in Berlin; Det Kongelige Teaters bibliotek, Statsbiblioteket, Universitetsbiblioteket, and Ida Poulsen and Lisbet Grandjean of Teatermuseet in Copenhagen; Drottningholms Teatermuseum and Dr. Tom J. A. Olsson and the staff of the library of the Kungliga Dramatiska teatern in Stockholm; the Helsingin Yliopisto Pääkirjasto in Finland; the Harvard Theatre Collection and the Theatre Collection of the Museum of the City of New York; the Theatre Museum, the Royal Shakespeare Company, and the National Theatre in London; and in Oslo, Jan Johansen and Gerd Stahl of Nationaltheatret, Edward Baro of Det Norske Teatret, and Universitetsbiblioteket and Trine Næss of its Theatre Collection.

On the editorial side, we are grateful to Victoria L. Cooper and Sarah Stanton of Cambridge University Press for their helpful advice and encouragement.

Not least, we acknowledge our gratitude to the Social Sciences and Humanities Research Council of Canada for its sustained financial support and encouragement of our research for this project.

1

Becoming Ibsen

During the early years of his career in Norway, as a stage director in Bergen and later in Christiania (now Oslo), Henrik Ibsen acquired and developed that keen sense of the practicalities of performance that is such a prominent characteristic of his dramaturgy. Although *Catiline*, his first play, was politely refused by Christiania Theatre, its successful production of his one-act saga drama *The Warrior's Barrow* in 1850 earned the twenty-two-year-old playwright a free pass and thus gave him his first real opportunity to study live theatre, by watching a variety of plays that constituted a representative cross-section of the romantic repertory. Only one year later, at the invitation of the renowned violinist and composer Ole Bull, he took up the post of playwright-in-residence at Bergen's Norske Teater, where, for the next few years, a new Ibsen play was performed annually on the theatre's founding day. At the end of his first season in Bergen, Ibsen was also offered the job of stage director and was given a three-month travel grant to Copenhagen and Dresden for the purpose of acquiring, as his contract stated, "such knowledge and experience as will enable him to assume the position of *Instructeur* at the theatre, which embraces not only the instruction of the actors and actresses, but also the management of everything pertaining to the equipment and properties of the stage, the costumes of the players, etc."[1] Both at the Court Theatre in Dresden and especially at the Danish Royal Theatre in Copenhagen, the young apprentice director was exposed to the methods and materials that gave him the practical basis for his own management of the Bergen Theatre.[2]

During the period when Ibsen took up his new directorial responsibilities, the theatre in general was on the threshold of a profound transition. Despite the increasing concern at mid-century with the ideal of ensemble acting, the modern conception of a director as the guiding artistic force behind a production, coordinating all details of the performance and integrating them into a unified whole, was not fully formed until the 1880s. Around 1850, the personal influence of the director was still governed by the principles and aesthetics of a theatrical system based on relatively few rehearsals, the observance of recognized rules and conventions for positioning on the stage, and the preservation of the individual actor's independence in preparing his role. Nor were the responsibilities of stage direction necessarily vested in one person. In Bergen, this task was (very typically) divided into two distinct parts, stage arrangement, which was assigned to Ibsen, and role instruction, which was the province of Herman Laading, a well-educated schoolmaster whom we might call a dramaturge today. At least in theory, Laading took charge of preparatory play analysis and role elucidation, while Ibsen, as stage director, was asked: "(1) to organize the scenic arrangements, including the costumes and scenery, of each play, and generally to direct it (groupings, entrances, exits and poses, etc.); (2) to watch the mime and gestures of each player, to ensure that the physical expression is appropriate to the words and the character of the part; and (3) to achieve the necessary coordination and show each of the performers which part, in terms of the scenes, he is to play in the overall action."[3] At times, notably when his own plays were being staged, Ibsen extended his mandate to embrace not only the creation of a suitable physical *mise-en-scène* but the supervision of the actors' interpretations as well. Nevertheless, the nature of his influence remained decisively different from that exerted by a succeeding generation of naturalistic directors like Bjørn Bjørnson, William Bloch, and their more famous contemporaries in France, Germany, and Russia. "There was no question," recalled Lucie Wolf, who acted under Ibsen both in Bergen and in Christiania, "of his ever giving us instruction as Bjørnson did."[4]

Rather, the young director's chief preoccupation was with the visual effects of setting and costuming and with picturesque patterns of movement and grouping – effects and patterns that reflect the fundamental character of the romantic theatre as a colorful "living picture gallery" (to borrow Schinkel's apt phrase). The rich pictorial beauty of this style of theatre held a profound fascination for Ibsen the dramatist as well as for Ibsen the director. Having eventually also assumed the supervisory task of stage-managing each night's performance, he kept a careful record of the sets, floor plans, crowd positions, props, and other matters pertaining to each production in the repertory. As scholars have demonstrated, these production notes (for thirty-three of the 121 plays performed during his five-year tenure in Bergen) provide a convincing impression of an able director's readiness to experiment

1 Water-color sketch by Ibsen from his Bergen years, perhaps meant for a rustic landscape setting.

with new and unconventional approaches to practical problems of stage arrangement.[5] The real significance of these notes, however, is as evidence of Ibsen's developing sensitivity to the importance of setting, lighting, and costuming as dramatic values – large-scale metaphors capable of concretizing the drama's theme and mood. Furthermore, of the hand-colored costume sketches and stage designs we are told he customarily prepared for his productions, enough iconographic evidence has survived to confirm this sense of Ibsen's decisive responsiveness to the visual aspects of theatrical expression.[6] The manner in which he utilized this visual component in his work would change radically – and more than once – during his career, but its central importance to his conception of a play never diminished.

Hence, far from being hampered, as critics have sometimes maintained, by the so-called "artificiality" and "unreality" of the theatrical context in which he found himself at the beginning of his career, Ibsen – who during this period regarded a measure of abstraction as a *sine qua non* for the theatrical art – exploited the flamboyantly pictorial and totally theatricalized theatre of the romantic era to the fullest, in his effort to bring an added dimension of dramatic suggestiveness to the performance of his own plays. Although the technical and financial resources of the Bergen Theatre were sorely limited, the five saga dramas he wrote and staged there are fortified with an ambitious and demanding series of atmospheric stage environments upon which the dramatic action depends. Thematic affinities between a play like *Lady Inger of Østeraad* (1855) and Ibsen's later work have often been pointed out, but the conceptual use of setting and lighting in this early historical drama, with its sombre Gothic interiors illuminated by moonlight, firelight, or the flickering glow from a branched candlestick, provides an indirect but equally significant foretaste of that strong visual consciousness which becomes so characteristic of the dramatist's mature work. In the medievalized ballad play *The Feast at Solhaug* (1856), the first Ibsen play to be acted outside Norway and the only one of his works to enjoy unqualified popular success in Bergen, it was again the author-director's powerful visual imagination and his ability to exploit the resources of the theatre to underscore theme and mood that made the strongest impression. Hence, although these early literary products of Ibsen's stage apprenticeship have had little or no subsequent performance history, their importance as signposts in his maturation as a theatre poet should not be overlooked.

In the summer of 1857, Ibsen resigned his post in Bergen to take up a new and, he hoped, a more visible position in the Norwegian capital as "stage instructor and artistic director" at Christiania Norske Teater, the distinctly unprestigious rival of the established "Danish" theatre on the Bank Square. Located in an unfashionable street and patronized by a predominantly working-class audience, this playhouse had an artistic reputation that was none too high, and Ibsen's five-year directorship there ended with the theatre's financial collapse in 1862. As we know, the Christiania years were in general a time of great personal hardship and self-doubt for Ibsen, during which his dramatic output faltered and even threatened to cease altogether. For five years between *The Vikings of Helgeland* (1857) and *Love's Comedy* (1862), he wrote nothing at all for the stage. On the other hand, his involvement in practical theatre – and in the ongoing debate over its true nature and purpose as a cultural force – continued unabated. In particular, his views on the function of stage direction reflect a wider attitude being voiced on many sides in the 1850s and after: the director's art can be compared to the art of the painter; in both cases, once the pervading tonal coloring of the work has been established, the task then is to place the individual figures in the composition in an harmoniously integrated and meaningful relationship to the whole.[7] While hardly original in themselves, such views remind us of Ibsen's steadily developing concern with total theatrical effect, as an indispensable aspect of the *dramatist*'s thinking about his play.

The Vikings of Helgeland, which Ibsen directed with great success at the Norske Teater (24 November 1858), proved to be a crucial turning-point in dramaturgical terms – away from the contrived style and improbable situations of the earlier plays, toward a concept of dramatic action shaped by Hermann Hettner's insistence (in *Das moderne Drama*, which Ibsen read with profit during his early Bergen years) that great historical tragedy must concern itself primarily with character rather than with mere intrigue. In theatrical terms, meanwhile, the play's elemental characters and larger-than-life action drawn from the Iceland-ic sagas locate it unequivocally in the older tradition of romantic pic-turesqueness. Ibsen makes skillful use of costumes, setting, and light-ing to accentuate the underlying vision and atmosphere of a stark, rough Viking age. From the turbulent, wintry seacoast of the opening act, the drama moves to a banquet-hall interior, at first dimly lighted by a log fire burning on a stone hearth in the center of the floor and later (in Act Three) seen by daylight, before returning in the final act to the rocky, barren shore. This coast, illuminated by the sombre glow of torches, a log fire, and the moon ("occasionally seen through dark and ragged storm clouds"), is the stern arena for the final tragic events that end with a vision of black horses and the avenging valkyrie Hjørdis riding through the sky – "the last ride of the dead on their way to Valhalla." Similarly bold contrasts in the color and texture of the costumes – described in unusual detail in the stage directions because Ibsen had at first hoped to have the play produced at Christiania Theatre itself, rather than by his own company – lend added force to the picturesque impact upon which the effect of Ibsen's ambitious saga pastiche depends. It is not surprising that the singular attempt made by Edward Gordon Craig in 1903 to transfigure *Vikings*, in somewhat the same spirit as that in which Appia sought to simplify and trans-figure Wagner, found no imitators in the modern period.[8] Rather, this once-popular play is inseparably linked to the nineteenth-century taste for pictorial illusionism and ethnographic detail exemplified so well in Eugen Quaglio's painted scenery for the craggy, fateful seacoast, evidently designed by him for a production of the play in Prague in 1884.

By the time Ibsen staged *The Pretenders* at Christiania Theatre almost six years later (17 January 1864), the long apprenticeship he had served in this older theatrical tradition was at its end. The dramatist, by now thirty-six years old, desperately needed – and soon found – a new and less constrictive artistic climate for his development. As a play, his first incontrovertible masterpiece is only superficially similar to his earlier work, for it now uses the action and spectacle of medieval history – the

2   The wild, rocky seacoast in *The Vikings of Helgeland* (Acts I and IV) as designed by Eugen Quaglio in 1884, probably for a production in Prague.

struggle of Haakon and Skule for the Norwegian throne – as a metaphor for the underlying spiritual (and deeply personal) dichotomy between the irresistible power of a great calling and the paralyzing impotence of self-doubt and anguished self-scrutiny. While Ibsen's own production of his sprawling epic drama adopted a style (reflected in his stage directions and in P. F. Wergmann's surviving stage design) rooted in a traditional attention to historical "accuracy" and "authenticity," the play's subsequent production history, which has been recounted in detail elsewhere, is in itself a vivid chronicle of the changing theatrical styles and forms adopted to accommodate and amplify Ibsen's vision on the stage.[9] From this moment on, in other words, Ibsen's plays belonged to the theatre at large.

The fact that the dramatist himself was rarely satisfied with the interpretations of others may be the inevitable outcome of his method. "Ibsen dislikes watching performances of his plays – I understand that it is in fact directly painful for him," writes Emil Poulsen, one of the greatest of Ibsen's early interpreters, in an article that may be among the first, but is certainly not the last, to question the playwright's "intrusion" into the actor's and the director's territory, through the medium of prescriptive stage directions: "It is said that he works out his plays in his head, down to the minutest detail; only when everything is completely finished is the play written down. Thus he lives

3 The only surviving design for one of Ibsen's productions of his own plays:
P. F. Wergmann's setting for the moonlit convent yard in the last act of *The
Pretenders* (1864).

with his characters in the most intimate relationship – knows every
feature of their faces, every intonation in their voices, virtually every
fold in their garments. How then can he expect to see precisely this
image reproduced on the stage? Every moment will be a struggle
between the actor's picture and his own – a continual effort on the
actor's part to erase the picture that has been stamped on Ibsen's mind
for so long. It is for this reason I think it must be painful for him."[10]

   The Christiania production of *The Pretenders* in 1864, the last performance Ibsen ever directed, thus marks the end of his active involvement in the practical theatre. Nevertheless, countless letters to those
engaged in producing his plays, dealing with casting, role interpretation, and even specific staging suggestions, demonstrate that he never
lost touch with the living theatre and wrote with concrete performance
conditions in mind (rather than, as Poulsen suggests, for the reader
and the printed page). The intimate knowledge of the stage and its
conventions which he gleaned from his early experiences as a director
sharpened his extraordinary sensitivity to the poetry of environment
in the theatre, that is, to the use of theatrical elements that create a
specific mood capable of strengthening the spiritual action of the
drama. Directing the first productions of his early saga dramas, he

taught himself to write a carefully visualized, highly charged physical *mise-en-scène* into his plays, aimed at concretizing the psychological states and spiritual conditions of the characters. Costumes, settings, props, and lighting effects remained throughout his career the syntax of his dramatic poetry. In turn, this inherent theatricality in his work has been the source of its continued vitality, long after the specific theatrical conditions for which a given play seems intended have changed or vanished altogether.

2

In the hall of the Mountain King:
Peer Gynt

When Ibsen at last left Norway behind him and journeyed south in the spring of 1864, he felt that he had escaped, as he later recalled, "from the darkness into the light, from the mists through a tunnel out into the sunshine."[1] A distinct new phase in his growth as a playwright began. Both *Brand* and *Peer Gynt*, the first two plays that he completed during his long, voluntary exile, were conceived as dramatic poems, unfettered as such by the technical limitations of existing theatrical practice and intended, at least initially, to be staged only in the activated imaginations of the reading public. *Peer Gynt*, its author wrote to the critic and translator Edmund Gosse (30 April 1872), "is wild and formless, recklessly written in a way I could only dare to write when far from home." Five years earlier, its publication had met with considerable hostility on the part of those critics who regarded the play as a work in which the blend of light-hearted fantasy and biting satire lacked any ideal element and, as such, any poetic validity.

It was the influential Swedish director Ludvig Josephson who first recognized the great theatrical potential inherent in the new, freer, "reckless" style of these monumental reading dramas. During Josephson's enlightened leadership of Christiania Theatre in the mid-1870s, he was responsible for a cluster of significant Ibsen experiments. His pioneering stage version of *Peer Gynt*, presented for the first time on 24 February 1876 and retained in the Christiania repertory for an unprecedented run of thirty-seven performances, was thus the high-point in a succession of achievements by Josephson that had previously included the premieres of both the revised version of *Lady Inger of Østeraad* (1875), starring Laura Gundersen as the intense, troubled Inger, and *Love's Comedy*, the vigorous satire of the institution of marriage that Ibsen finished in 1862 but did not see produced until Josephson staged the play in Christiania in 1873.

Far more than these earlier endeavors, however, this director's

9

mammoth production of *Peer Gynt*, which required four and three-quarter hours to perform, stretched the resources of the conventional theatre of *trompe l'œil* illusion to the limit. "When the director is entrusted with staging a play," Josephson writes in his book *Teater-Regie* (1892), "he must nowadays approach this task in the most painstaking way through the study of detail – or, we might rather say, scientifically."[2] In somewhat the same spirit of pictorial fidelity as that which animated the work of the Meininger troupe, Josephson's precise and colorful *mise-en-scène* for Ibsen's drama pressed into service not only the theatre's own capable designers, Wilhelm Krogh and Olaf Jørgensen, but also a corps of landscape painters that included the gifted young naturalist Fritz Thaulow. Their common task was to create a pictorial background for *Peer Gynt* that was rich in local color and "authentic" ethnographic detail. As a result, Peer's progress through the world was presented here as a series of realistically conceived episodes and striking (if quite literalized) pictorial stage effects. Henrik Klausen was a lyrical and sprightly Peer in an interpretation in which – despite the amusingly trollish Mountain King created by the celebrated comic actor Johannes Brun – the lyrical element far outweighed the satirical. In this respect, Josephson's concept was inextricably bound up with the commissioned musical score composed for the occasion by Edvard Grieg – that charming but inappropriately rhapsodic excrescence of which the play has never fully succeeded in ridding itself. Ibsen's Peer, the fraud and self-deceiver who goes roundabout, remained, in this first ambitious production of the work, primarily the dreamer of romantic dreams that crystallized into a dream vision of the redemptive Solveig, who appeared before him as he slumbered in the Moroccan desert in the fourth act.

When *Peer Gynt* again came to the stage, after an interval of nearly a decade, at the more cosmopolitan Dagmar Theatre in Copenhagen, the romantic, pictorialized style of production still held sway and seemed to the theatre's director–manager, Theodor Andersen, the only feasible alternative for such a work. His lavish Dagmar production, in which Grieg again assisted personally and Henrik Klausen re-enacted his playful and distinctly lyrical interpretation of Peer, holds considerable interest because Ibsen himself contributed detailed written advice about the performance and subsequently expressed his enthusiastic approval of it.[3] ("You would have been amused at me during rehearsals," he wrote to his friend Franz Beyer a week after the opening on 15 January 1886. "I was so happy at being able to express my intentions that I put my oar in everywhere.")[4] In general, the Copenhagen revival of *Peer Gynt* affords a perfect example of the emphasis on the creation of a vivid and colorful but also fundamentally believable stage environment which would retain its hold on the production history of this play for decades to come. For the more simplified, dematerialized, and suggestive approach that such a work seems so obviously to invite, *Peer Gynt*, like Strindberg's later dream plays, had to wait until the post-naturalistic period.

At Dagmar Theatre in 1886, however, the implicit objective was to create an unmitigated conviction of reality in the settings, costumes, and lighting – a reality remarkable at once for its "authentic" ethnographic flavor and for the pictorial intensity of its visual appeal. Reviewing the production in *Politiken* the next day, Edvard Brandes commended it as being "of great significance" precisely because "it peels off, so to speak, the play's outward symbolism and reveals Ibsen's work as a poem about our own lives." Little effort was made in this nineteenth-century *Peer Gynt* to discern any distinction between the realms of the real and the unreal, nor did it concern itself, as a modern production might naturally be expected to do, with the articulation of a web of symbolic resonances in the work. Thirty-nine actors were used and hence some doubling occurred – but purely for practical reasons rather than as part of a director's thematic or even psychoanalytical design (as, for instance, in Michael Elliott's 1962 Old Vic production, in which Leo McKern was both Peer *and* his shapeless nemesis, the Boyg – or, to take an even more ambiguous illustration, in the notable Danish revival staged by Line Krogh at Aarhus Theatre in 1977, in which Aase and Solveig, mother and madonna, were played by the same actress).

Such intellectual gymnastics belong, however, to a more restless and tradition-weary age. In the nineteenth century, even the grotesque and fantastical elements in *Peer Gynt* – the trolls, elves, and goblins whom Peer encounters in the abode of the Mountain King – appeared to be as "real" in their own world as Mother Aase, Solveig, and the wedding guests at Haegstad Farm were in theirs. Rather than inhabitants of a symbolic and disturbing dream world, these "entertainingly grotesque" figures (to borrow Brandes' phrase) were the comfortably familiar elves of the *eventyr* tradition of adventure and romance – a tradition of which the plays and stories of H. C. Andersen, the folk ballets of August Bournonville, and, for that matter, an early Ibsen play like *Midsummer Eve* all partake.

In Theodor Andersen's stage version, the play was shortened (with Ibsen's approval) to eighteen scenes, each one of which depended on a suitably atmospheric setting and hence required a correspondingly complicated change of scene. The strong appeal which this four-and-a-

half-hour spectacle exerted for its first Danish audiences was, as reviews of it clearly reveal, dependent on the impression of immediacy and reality which it conveyed. Both the director's notes and Ibsen's own remarks and cuts are preserved in a surviving promptbook that amply demonstrates this concern with credible characters and situations and with a recognizably Norwegian milieu. The focal point of the opening scene, for example, was an impressively three-dimensional Norwegian log house, upon the roof of which Peer deposited his angry, shouting mother when their quarrel was over. (A drawing by the playwright, depicting Peer in full flight after having performed this feat, is accompanied by his own typically precise and practical suggestions for how to accomplish it.) For the episode of Aase's death – the only portion of Ida Aalberg's performance of the role that actually met with Ibsen's approval – the setting was a comparably faithful replica of a "simple Norwegian room," corresponding in detail to the printed stage directions. Kari's old cat sat on a wooden chair, as it had been wont to do in days gone by, watching the poignant scene.

Some of the play's other Norwegian scenes were endowed with even more graphic picturesqueness. Peer's newly-built cabin in the forest, decorated with reindeer's antlers above the door, stood in the midst of a snowy clearing, and the faithful Solveig reached it in exactly the manner described by Ibsen in his text – on skis. Such an effect, unusual though it might seem to us, posed no problem whatever for a nineteenth-century director or designer who knew his craft. The promptbook notes show us how adroitly it was done: "To the right [of Peer's cabin] a long track with blocks, to which are fastened a pair of skis with bindings . . . Solveig steps out of these as soon as the blocks reach the ground."

While realistic details of this kind were included to strengthen the illusion of a concrete milieu and culture, far more exotic and spectacular touches were also distributed liberally throughout the production. Both a whimsical pantomime of capering animals, trolls, and other preternatural creatures in the Troll King's palace and Peer's fourth-act adventures in Morocco afforded satisfying opportunities for elaborately staged romantic tableaux. In the desert, outfitted in rich oriental robes and complacently smoking a hookah outside the tent of an Arab

4   Impressions from Theodor Andersen's production of *Peer Gynt* at Dagmar Theatre, Copenhagen, in 1886: (a) design by Bernhard Olsen for the Troll King, the Troll Courtier and a troll child; (b) Solveig's arrival at Peer's cabin on skis (Act III), as sketched by Poul Fischer.

chieftain, Peer watched a primly Victorian Anitra (complete with peacock-feather fan) perform with her decorous bevy of dancing girls. This romanticized rendering of the highly ironic encounter between the self-made "Prophet" and his rather tawdry idea of "das Ewig-Weibliche" thoroughly delighted the critic for *Nationaltidende* (16 January 1886), who liked the episode mostly for its "beautiful groupings and fine lighting effects." The Anitra sequence also reiterated the sympathetic image of Peer established by Henrik Klausen in the world premiere of the play at Christiania Theatre a decade before. As Klausen's disillusioned dreamer slept in the oasis, the protective dream-vision of a forgiving Solveig again hovered before him.

Shipwrecks were a favorite stock-in-trade of the managers and machinists of the last century, and the prospect of staging the sinking of not one but two vessels in *Peer Gynt* was a challenge to be welcomed by nineteenth-century producers of the play. The spectacular high-point of the Dagmar production was the wreck that opens the last act, in which the ship carrying the now aged Peer back home to Norway founders and he saves himself (at the expense of the hapless Cook) by clinging to the keel of an overturned dinghy. Although primitive by comparison with the mighty shipwrecks and scenes of naval combat that were a speciality of the Parisian theatres at mid-century, Theodor Andersen's resourceful solution made it plain that Peer's narrow escape from drowning was to be regarded as a real occurrence (as distinct from, say, a symbolic enactment of his death). A gauze scrim drawn across the proscenium opening endowed the wreck scene with the atmosphere of a foggy, storm-tossed night on the North Sea. The entire stage floor around the ship was covered with a large "sea cloth," beneath which a squad of "wave boys" were deployed. Their job was to facilitate the disappearance of the stricken vessel, while at the same time their energetic movements under the cloth created the illusion of a violently agitated sea. "When the ship sinks [into the large trap in the stage floor]," explains the promptbook, "the mast falls and the sea cloth is pulled over the trap" by the unseen stagehands. The "singular realism" and "shattering effect" for which this scene was praised by the Danish critics drew added force from Grieg's turbulent musical introduction to Act Five, "a very stirring tone painting" which, in the words of the music reviewer assigned to describe the score to the readers of *Politiken*, presented "the whole orchestra . . . in agitation, whining like the howling storm, raging with muffled reverberations."

Grieg's familiar music for *Peer Gynt*, used in these early productions to illustrate key episodes and heighten their emotional impact, did much to reinforce the traditional "romantic" conception of the play that the Dagmar performance so vividly exemplifies. In turn, the richly melodious and nationalistic coloring of Grieg's popular stage music – seen by him as a first step toward a national Norwegian opera that he never completed – inevitably imparted to a production such as this a basic tone of unmitigated lyricism and even sentimentality. Its use casts an aura of romance over the play that obscures the ironic and anti-sentimental aspects of Ibsen's ambiguous hero, the poetic dreamer who is *also* the clever braggart, the vain egoist, the self-deceiver who shirks responsibility and evades reality – in brief, "the true agonist" (to borrow Ezra Pound's felicitous description of Ibsen himself) gripped by the sense of life as "a combat with the phantoms of the mind."[5] (Pound's image evokes in turn Michael Elliott's interpretation of the play as a work which, like life itself, describes a struggle "between man's deeper self . . . and his surface, animal self, his troll self.")[6] Not unexpectedly, however, it was the conciliatory atmosphere of folklore and romance which continued to color productions of *Peer Gynt*, both within Scandinavia and elsewhere, well into the present century.

Even those transitional interpretations that inclined, in different ways, toward a more abstract, deromanticized approach still retained many elements of the traditional picture-book mode of representation in which Ibsen's dramatic poem seemed to be anchored. In the Moscow Art Theatre production of the work in 1912, for example, Stanislavski sought to introduce stylized scenery and symbolic stage effects, without thereby sacrificing that "more refined and deeper realism" which was the hallmark of his directorial method. For this production – the ninth and last in the impressive cycle of Ibsen plays staged by the M.A.T. – the symbolist painter Nikolai Rerich created a sequence of vividly stylized decors, including a fantastical landscape of mountain formations and a widely admired silvan setting for Peer's final reunion with Solveig. "The sight of those flaming firs, that blue brook, and the tall hut will remain within me and with me forever," the poet Sergei Gorodetski wrote to the designer after the premiere on 9 October 1912. "Yesterday as I watched Peer Gynt return to Solveig, I could not hold back the tears of longing and delight."[7] Yet in its retention of Grieg's music (and the attendant undertone of pathos implicit in Gorodetski's comment), its reliance on pictorial illustration and multiple changes of scene, and its emphasis on spectacular effects (including a particularly fine shipwreck conjured up "with the help of shadows swaying on the walls and the spray of sea foam on the portholes")[8], Stanislavski's production concept surely reflects the ruling idea of the play that had previously persisted in Christiania, Copenhagen, and elsewhere.

(Taken to its most literalistic extreme, the tendency to portray the

5 Program cover designed by Edvard Munch for Lugné-Poë's production of *Peer Gynt* in Paris, 1896.

subjective emotional and spiritual experiences of a play like *Peer Gynt* in terms of overt pictorial illustration and explanation is perhaps best exemplified in the severely criticized film of the play which the intrepid Moresco Company concocted in 1915 – possibly inspired by the very popular touring performances given a few years before by the late Richard Mansfield. On celluloid, even Peer's supremely imaginative fictional "ride" to the gates of Soria-Moria Castle with his dying mother was translated into a painfully literal trip in a reindeer sled. "The poor camera man attempted to photograph it and achieved something supremely ridiculous," commented a disgusted Walter Prichard Eaton at the time.)[9]

Richard Mansfield's own ambitious production of *Peer Gynt* in 1906, while quite conventional in terms of its episodic staging and illustrative use of Grieg, represents in some ways an interesting new approach, particularly in the actor's interpretation of the role of Peer. By the time of Ibsen's death in that same year, most of the dramas of his post-romantic period had already been competently produced in New York City. Florence Kahn had given pioneering performances in such "difficult" works as *The Master Builder* (1900), *Rosmersholm* (1904), and *When We Dead Awaken* (1905), Mary Shaw had electrified Manhattan audiences in *Ghosts* (1903), Elizabeth Robins, Blanche Bates, Mrs. Fiske, and Nance O'Neall had all won favor in *Hedda Gabler*, and *A Doll's House* had become a play that turned up almost every week in the repertory of one stock company or another throughout the country. Coming as it did at the height of this Ibsen insurgency, Mansfield's English-language premiere of *Peer Gynt*, which opened at the Grand Opera House in Chicago on 29 October 1906 but quickly reached New York (four months later), revealed to American audiences a new but no less unsettling aspect of the playwright's art. Despite Mansfield's undisputed personal success as Peer, the contemporary response to the play itself was uncomfortable; the *New York World* (26 February 1907), to take a single example, judged it "vague and puzzling at times, and always sordid in its view of man's baser nature."

At the core of this controversial production was a portrayal of Peer that came several steps closer to the perplexed and suffering non-heroic hero familiar in many modern readings of the play. Mansfield, who was over fifty and very near the end of his life when he acted the part, seems to have been an unyouthfully sardonic, at times even critically detached interpreter of Peer. His aim was, in his own words, an amalgamation of "pathos and sorrow – the eternal heritage of man – in the first acts" with "satire, playful humor, and, finally, great sadness" in the final movement of the work. Act Four was, in accordance with Ibsen's own suggestions for cutting the play, almost entirely omitted in Mansfield's version, and the weight of his emphasis seems clearly to have been placed on the final act, in which fantasy and irony achieve free rein. "I propose playing *Peer Gynt* in a spirit of travesty, and to present it as a 'phantasmagoria,'" the actor wrote to his bewildered friend and biographer, William Winter. "I shall leave it to the people to find out the fun."[10]

Even Winter, an astute theatre critic but perhaps the most biased and obstinate Ibsen opponent of his day, was able to appreciate the unusual power of "the actor's revelation of himself" in this role – a revelation that proceeded from Mansfield's layered, self-reflective attitude toward the "preposterous vagabond" and impersonator he enacted. The dominant quality of this performance, Winter observes, was its total saturation in "the airy complacence of indurated selfishness." The point is well exemplified in the critic's description of Mansfield's ironic, arrestingly "modern" desentimentalization of Aase's death:

His conduct in the death scene – the best scene in the play – expertly simulated wild passion and acute suffering, combined with self-pity and theatrical delirium; the whole showy, extravagant outburst, however, being suffused with that attentive, observant, obvious self-consciousness which is inseparable from the endeavor, whether made in speaking or writing, or anything else, to express something that is unreal or unfelt.[11]

Fully a decade before Mansfield's remarkable performance, another transitional stage interpretation of a radically different kind was contributed by Aurélien Lugné-Poë and his Théâtre de l'Œuvre in Paris, whose *Peer Gynt* (12 November 1896) became the first important production of this play staged outside of Scandinavia. As the foremost exponent of the symbolist movement in the French theatre of the 1890s, this influential young actor–director applied his defiantly anti-naturalistic approach to no fewer than ten Ibsen productions in the brief course of five years. In the very first of these, *The Lady from the Sea* (1892), the distinctive and controversial Ibsen style that was to become Lugné-Poë's trademark was already clearly defined, fully half a year before l'Œuvre came into being. His chief inspiration was obviously Maeterlinck's belief in unseen forces and unspoken meanings as the true wellsprings of tragic (symbolist) drama, linking the characters to a hidden and transcendent realm beyond everyday existence – epitomized in this play by Ellida Wangel's strange community with the sea. Convinced of the power of language to create "spoken" scenery, Lugné-Poë created what he called *décors de suggestion* to evoke an appropriate mood by means of color, line, and light.[12] These shadowy, starkly simplified settings, comprised largely of primitive painted backdrops and a bare minimum of furniture and properties, were dreamscapes cloaked in semi-darkness, devoid of clear-cut lines and precise details. No drawings or sketches of them survive, if indeed any were ever made for the non-specific decorative backgrounds which l'Œuvre required for its experiments.

Lugné-Poë's acting company, encouraged to emulate his personal example in such roles as Doctor Wangel, Rosmer, Solness, and a gallery of other Ibsen protagonists, adopted a system of slow, trance-like gestures and a portentously intoned, even chanted delivery in order to intensify the desired atmosphere of strangeness, enigma, and dream. In a sarcastic review of *The Master Builder* in *Le Temps* (9 April 1894), the staunchly conservative Francisque Sarcey maliciously pretended to have "discovered" the real origins of Lugné-Poë's symbolist style of performance:

After the first act I met in the corridor one of the best informed men in Paris on the subject of the German theatre. We chatted together about how Lugné-Poë had interpreted the role of the master builder, Solness.
– "On the German stage," he told me, "it is traditional; when Ibsen is produced the actors aim to make the spectator forget that these are human beings of flesh and blood that he sees before him on the stage; they make few movements, almost no gestures at all, and then only grand, almost hieratic ones; their delivery takes the form of a slow chant that seems to fall from supernatural, symbolic lips . . ."
– "And," I asked him, "does symbolism amuse the Germans?"
– "They are less resistant to it than you are. But they don't go to the theatre to amuse themselves. They eat sausages and drink beer between a couple of symbols: that sustains them."

The fact remains, meanwhile, that Ibsen himself, seeing the same production of *The Master Builder* when it was given in Christiania in October 1894, appears to have pronounced it "the resurrection of my play," while in his turn George Bernard Shaw, reviewing the French tour when it reached London the following spring, described Lugné-Poë's Solness as "amazingly true to life," robustly like "a person he had met a dozen times in ordinary life" (*Saturday Review*, 30 March 1895). Some have taken these differences of opinion as evidence of a change of heart and style on Lugné-Poë's part, brought on quite suddenly by Ibsen's remark (after he had seen *Rosmersholm* on the same tour) that his work should "be played passionately and not otherwise." Although not enough solid information exists to resolve the question of a changed performance style, certain it is that the 1896

Peer Gynt at the Théâtre de l'Œuvre was still firmly rooted in the symbolist aims and methods of this organization. Even the haunting drawing made by Edvard Munch for the cover of the program for Lugné-Poë's production provides a graphic intimation of the suggestive, somnambulistic mood which this director invariably sought to invoke, irrespective of which Ibsen play he was presenting. In this particular Munch sketch, we see the ravaged, sorrowful countenance of an old woman lost in thought, significantly juxtaposed with the figure of a young girl with long, flowing hair who stands gazing – as figures in symbolist dramas were wont to gaze – into the far distance, across a dream-like landscape of deep valleys and distant mountains.

Although far tamer than the tumultuous opening of Alfred Jarry's savage comedy *Ubu Roi*, which was acted at the Théâtre de l'Œuvre only a month later, the premiere of *Peer Gynt* (in which Jarry appeared as the Troll King) provoked its full measure of critical confusion and dissension. Leading the delegation of French traditionalists, Sarcey professed himself (again) bewildered both by the disjointedness and obscurity of Ibsen's play and by the mingling of modes in its production: "What remains of *Peer Gynt* (for us, at least) are the first two scenes which are so full of life, and these other two scenes [Aase's death and the end] where the idea and execution are those of a master. The rest is fog, and the thickest of fog, symbolic fog." Especially galling to Sarcey was the fact that "one segment of the audience" – what he elsewhere calls "the holy battalion of Ibsenites at their posts" – so vociferously disagreed with him: "Nothing exasperates me so much as to see people swoon with pleasure at scenes which seem to me either perfectly unintelligible or absolutely puerile," he grumbled.[13] Jules Lemaître, writing in *Revue des Deux-Mondes*, dismissed the whole affair even more brusquely, as a pretentious and unremarkable example of "the philosophico-symbolico-dramatic genre" that contained "about as much philosophy as some vaudeville by Labiche."[14] In the wake of these highly unsatisfactory verdicts, Georg Brandes came to Ibsen's defence. In a coolly argued – and hotly contested – manifesto published in *Cosmopolis* early in 1897, the eminent Danish critic openly rebuked his French colleagues for their literary chauvinism, their inadequate comprehension of Ibsen's native culture and language, and their consequent tendency to grope for hidden symbolic meanings where only concrete reality was intended. On the whole, however, Brandes was inclined to excuse the French critics on the grounds that they had been grossly misled by the aura of spurious mysticism that invariably surrounded the performance of Ibsen's plays on the Paris stage. Without actually naming Lugné-Poë and his Théâtre de l'Œuvre, he unequivocally denounced their use of shadowy symbolist settings and their artificial style of acting ("une espèce de plain-chant monotone qui psalmodie les rôles au lieu de les jouer").[15]

Writing for the Norwegian press, Bjørn Bjørnson addressed himself more clearly than any of the French reviewers to the actual production itself. Bjørnson, who had staged and starred in his own robustly "authentic" revival of *Peer Gynt* in Christiania in 1892, tended to regard Lugné-Poë's *mise-en-scène* as primitive and even amateurish, rather than deliberately symbolic. The unfamiliar style of staging seemed a far cry from the pictorial splendor of the play's Scandinavian productions. "The curtain rose on a setting of sorts, a faded birch grove with light-green stones and violet set-pieces," he observed drily; the subsequent decor for the wedding at Haegstad Farm "presented a light concoction of winter and midsummer."[16] In terms of the acting itself, however, Bjørnson was impressed rather than troubled by the lyrical approach to Peer taken by Abel Deval, a gifted young actor whom Sarah Bernhardt had launched three years before. "His acting style was not new – it was French in declamation and manner – but he was commanding, he knew what he wanted, and he never lost self-control even though he often expressed himself with warmth and passion." Above all, it was the suppressed pathos of Deval's interpretation of Peer that differentiated him from the sprightly, barefooted rogue–hero delineated by Henrik Klausen and, subsequently, by Bjørn Bjørnson himself. "There was sorrow and silence where we imagine wild defiance, quiet joy where we see him storming the gates of Heaven," Bjørnson concluded. "But his Peer succeeded. With a wise smile, more gentle than satirical, he went quietly about his business. As a broken old man he was the Peer we know. He reached the same goal by other paths."

In these descriptive comments, we discern more than a hint of an elegiac, predominantly sentimental tone that prevailed throughout Lugné-Poë's production. Its implicit thematic focus, in the opinion of many reviewers, was the indelible memory of a pure, forgiving Solveig whom Peer had never forgotten. Shaw, who came across from London to cover the event for the *Saturday Review*, was quite taken aback (for he had, of course, not seen the play on stage before) to encounter the intrusion of the already familiar tableau in which Peer lies dreaming in the Moroccan desert – at which moment, Shaw writes, Solveig was "exhibited . . . to him as a dream vision in the conventional Drury Lane fourth-act style." This romantic cliché illustrates a general tendency on this director's part to sentimentalize the deadly earnest and grim humor of Peer's ordeal, by subordinating it to what Shaw calls "the

pretty middle-class doctrine that all moral difficulties find their solution in love as the highest of all things."[17]

Hence, "Solveig's Song" by Grieg came to be, from the outset, this
production's emotional anthem. Each fresh appearance or reminder of
Solveig herself – played by Suzanne Desprès, Lugné-Poë's faithful
partner in his Ibsen campaign – was greeted by the audience with
jubilant approval. Evidently oblivious to the problem represented by
the Button Moulder (whose crucial explanation to Peer of what "being
oneself" really means was cut!), the lovers were reunited in the final
scene in a manner that pleased even the sternest critics. Peer "finds
Solveig, now white-haired, waiting for him, just as Fortune in La
Fontaine's story waited at home for the restless traveller who had
searched far and wide for her," Sarcey was moved to declare. "He lays
his head on his fiancée's lap; she caresses him and he dies [sic]
consoled."[18] Shaw was inclined to view this tender moment with
greater skepticism, and probably with greater accuracy as well: "In the
last scene, which [Desprès] chanted in a golden voice very much à la
Bernhardt, she did not represent Solveig as blind, nor did her make-up
suggest anything more than a dark Southern woman of about forty-
two, although Peer was clearly at least ninety-nine, and by no means
young for his age." On the whole, Shaw's attitude toward this scene
was colored by the grave reservations he had concerning Lugné-Poë's
radical abridgement of the entire fifth act, in which the episode with
the drowning Cook, most of the Strange Passenger's part, the funeral
of the man who cut off his finger, and Peer's encounter with the Thin
Person were all eliminated. This drastic surgery was designed, Shaw
decided, to allow *Peer Gynt* to appeal to "a congenitally unmetaphysical
nation, to which the play seems as much a mixture of sentiment and
stage *diablerie* as *Faust* seemed to Gounod."

The unresolved critical controversy that surrounded this production
suggests an uneasy marriage of styles in Lugné-Poë's ostensibly "symbolist" interpretation. Grieg's romantic music, endlessly encored at
the Théâtre de l'Œuvre, played its usual dominant role in determining
the atmosphere and tone of the performance. One Norwegian reviewer was even prompted to report that it was solely the "precision and
delicacy" of the orchestral contribution that "carried the entire production through the hazards that unmistakably threatened it on every
side."[19] Seen in this light, then, even Lugné-Poë's *Peer Gynt* remained,
despite its experimental leanings, closely linked to the work's original,
solidly romantic stage tradition, committed to a view of the play that
would accord with Grieg's harmonious musical illustrations of it.

THE ANTI-ROMANTIC REACTION AND ITS AFTERMATH

Although the nineteenth century and its aesthetic attitudes retained a firm and enduring hold on *Peer Gynt* in performance, a change of outlook was bound to occur, albeit belatedly, in the modern period. In the Italian premiere of the play at the Teatro di Torino in 1928, for example, Grieg's popular music was still a dominant feature of the production, but critics had by then begun to point to an essential "incompatibility between Grieg's intentions and Ibsen's" (Luigi Cocchi in *Il Momento*, 11 October 1928).[20] By 1944, when the Danish Royal Theatre in Copenhagen produced a traditionally spectacular revival of the play, directed and designed by Svend Gade and once again ornamented with Grieg's score, a discernible reaction to this approach had at last set in – as indeed it had in England, where Tyrone Guthrie brought the Old Vic company back to London with a Grieg-illustrated *Peer Gynt* that same season.

In Copenhagen, the predominantly romantic tone and pictorial style of the original Dagmar production had remained cherished traits of each successive revival of the play, from Karl Mantzius' monumental production starring Johannes Poulsen in 1913 to Svend Methling's two similarly conceived revivals, seen at the New Theatre in 1926 and again at the Royal Theatre in 1933. To a more thoughtful critic like Frederik Schyberg, however, Methling's lavish *mise-en-scène* merely reemphasized the inadequacy of conventional pictorial illusion used in conjunction with a work of "pure poetry" such as *Peer Gynt* or Goethe's *Faust*. "At any rate, a production such as this demonstrates clearly how wrong *they* are who demand literature instead of theatre in the theatre," Schyberg declared in *Dagens Nyheder* (26 September 1933). "For all its abundance of talent and personalities, a production of *Peer Gynt* at the Royal Theatre today is no more than *a reminder to the audience of a significant work of literature* – a little more, but not much more, than a film version of a famous novel." The root of the problem, for Schyberg, was a shared failure to recognize *Peer Gynt* as a conscious critical comment on the romantic ethos, rather than a charming and rather naive illustration of it. As such, the swelling, virtually Wagnerian pathos which Eyvind Johan-Svendsen brought to the title role in this production epitomized the misapprehension that Schyberg attempted to describe: "The great monologue on the mountain, which he built up to a truly formidable climax, called forth wild applause and was an admirable achievement – but it was *wrong*. For a moment, Peer Gynt was transformed before our eyes into a Faust."

Much more clearly and precisely formulated was this same critic's influential assessment of the Svend Gade revival eleven years later. The best of Gade's settings, Schyberg observed in *Politiken* (15 September 1944), "amount to scenic poetry, the rest to richly varied toy theatre, to Jules Verne, to the ideal realization of a production of *Around the World in Eighty Days* or *Captain Grant's Children*." This heavy emphasis on pictorial illusion was now seen, in turn, as the direct – and undesirable – consequence of the play's traditional musical accompaniment. Grieg's score ("concert music, not theatre music, and there is *far* too much of it," Schyberg insisted) was blamed specifically for glossing over the work's more disturbing dissonances and hence robbing it of its ironic force. Again, the acting interpretations, including the soaring, lyrical performance of the title role by the young Mogens Wieth, seemed guided (much as opera singers might be guided) by the meaning of the music, rather than by the wit and savagery of the text. Nowhere is this discrepancy between the surging pathos of Grieg's music and the bitter, anti-heroic irony of Ibsen's poetry more apparent than in Peer's frenzied, fantastical flight from the harsh and inconvenient reality of his mother's death agony. "Mogens Wieth acted Aase's death scene according to the music, not the intent of the words," Schyberg declared. "It was excusable, it was beautiful, and it will become popular – but it was wrong." The broader conclusion drawn by this critic was to have far-reaching implications for the future: "There is no doubt that the popularity of *Peer Gynt* is due chiefly to Grieg's music," he argued. "There is no doubt either that precisely this music helps to distort the play and make it 'beautiful': Grieg makes *Peer Gynt* romantic – but *Peer Gynt* is an anti-romantic work!"[21]

Some three years later, reappraising his own estimable, all-star revival (with Ralph Richardson as Peer, Laurence Olivier as the Button Moulder, and Sybil Thorndike as Aase) in 1944, Tyrone Guthrie virtually reiterated several of Schyberg's reservations about the use of music and solid scenery for the play, despite the fact that he himself had used both these elements effectively in his New Theatre production. "If I ever have the opportunity of staging *Peer Gynt* again, I shall hope to feel free to jettison Grieg, to jettison any 'realistic' scenery," he admits in an essay entitled "Some Afterthoughts on *Peer Gynt*," published in 1947. "If it is to be presented at all, it must be with great simplicity, even austerity." Guthrie's objection to the stylistic straitjacket imposed by traditional "Victorian" music directly parallels Schyberg's argument: "If Grieg's intention is to succeed, Ibsen's must fail" – painfully so when the ending becomes "the apotheosis of Radiant Womanhood [in which] the Button Moulder's last speech has either been cut, or drowned in warm treacle from the band-pit."[22] Too intelligent a theatre reformer to heap the entire blame on Grieg, meanwhile, this director also repudiates both time-wasting scene changes and that constrictive "quality of literalness and weight" which even light and sketchy scenery will impose on the imaginative fabric of such a work. Above all, Guthrie's afterthoughts on the play emphasize his belief – largely unrealized (perhaps unrealizable) in his relatively conventional Old Vic endeavor – that "given almost no visual 'illusion,' the imagination of an audience would be more free to roam with Peer from farm to mountain, from mountain to forest, from Norway to Africa and back again to Norway, from youth to age, from fact to symbolism, from light fantasy to deep philosophy."[23]

The process of reassessment and renewal advocated in theory at this time by Guthrie, Schyberg and others was, in fact, already under way in practice, especially in Scandinavia. As early as 1934, a notable production of the play presented at Kungliga teatern in Stockholm, directed by Per Lindberg and starring the brooding Gösta Ekman as a serious and poetic Peer, had, for example, gone some distance toward deromanticizing the work. Traditional musical accompaniment, if not abandoned entirely as Lindberg himself had originally wanted, was at least eliminated by him at key moments. The conventional, Christmas-pantomime style of realistic staging was likewise banished and replaced by simplified back projections that transformed the troll scenes into "shadowy dream visions."[24]

In 1948, a far more decisive step was taken by Hans Jacob Nilsen, who both directed and played the title role in a controversial, defiantly "anti-romantic" Peer Gynt, translated for the first time into New Norse, at Det Norske Teatret in Oslo. In an eloquent defense of his approach, Nilsen singles out a story told him by Svend Methling, who had directed the play at the Royal Theatre in Copenhagen fifteen years earlier. Having been informed by his designer that any production of Peer Gynt must be presented as "a journey through Norway," Methling reportedly answered: "Peer Gynt is no journey through Norway; it is a journey through a human mind." Shaped by precisely this point of view, Nilsen's innovative production (2 March 1948) was, in his words, intended to send the audience from the theatre "shaken but fortified, more aware of the power the trolls have over us but more prepared to fight them."[25] The incongruous nationalism and romanticism inherent in Grieg's Suite were conclusively set aside. Instead, the stark, dissonant tones of a new musical score by Harald Sæverud (Opus 28) sought to impart a unifying pattern of "musical–psychological development" to the play.

The fulcrum of Nilsen's revolutionary experiment was Arne Walentin's supple but by no means entirely abstract design concept, which drew on the familiar Reinhardt combination of a turntable stage and simplified, softly colored back projections, screened across the full width of a cyclorama. On the revolving stage stood stylized rock formations that were seen from a variety of angles as the play progressed and the stage rotated. Otherwise the only "scenery" consisted of a minimum of simplified, easily movable set-pieces. By utilizing the values of space, light, color, and form in varying combinations, Walentin's technique succeeded in evoking an atmosphere of dream and fantasy that would have been unattainable with conventional painted scenery. As a result of this flexible arrangement the play, divided into thirty-one scenes, could be acted almost in its entirety – substantially, in this form, still as a kaleidoscope of colorful episodes held together by the picaresque hero and his quest. (When Walentin designed *Peer Gynt* again at Det Norske Teatret fourteen years later, this time under the direction of Tormod Skagestad, his approach to the design problem, although basically unchanged, had undergone some interesting modifications. This time, viewed against a flat backcloth rather than a full cyclorama, the two-dimensional projections were smaller, more abstract and symbolic in character, and – deliberately – less illusionistic. In the 1962 production, the rapid changes of scene no longer took place in darkness but became instead part of the visual experience, as one projection dissolved cinematically into the next.)

It can be argued that the earliest productions of *Peer Gynt*, by directors such as Josephson and Theodor Andersen, concentrated their efforts on a literal, virtually cinematographic rendering of the lyrical and romantic elements evident chiefly in the first and third acts of the play. By contrast, a modern reformer like Hans Jacob Nilsen turned his attention, and ours, to the psychological implications of the uglier, more grotesque elements (the trolls within) in the second act. Nilsen was well aware of the thematic centrality of the last two acts, without which "that harshness and cruelty which give deeper perspective to Peer's character" are lost. It remained, however, for Ingmar Bergman to forge a total and coherent theatrical image of the play that would penetrate beyond the limits of the first three acts into the dark and disturbing recesses of the work's final movement.

The conscious aim of Bergman's mammoth, ninety-actor production, which opened at the Malmö City Theatre on 8 March 1957, was to lay bare the inner, deromanticized essence of Ibsen's drama, removing it decisively from the realm of amiable but confused pantomime and cleansing it – before the very eyes of the audience – of all the sentimental stereotypes and consoling idealizations that had been built up

6   The millhouse and "Castle rises on castle": two of Arne Walentin's most imaginative designs for the revolutionary *Peer Gynt* presented by Hans Jacob Nilsen at Det Norske Teatret, Oslo, in 1948.

around it over the years. "The effect," declared one reviewer, "is astonishing: it is like seeing a painting cleansed of its yellowed exhibition varnish."[26] Enthusiasts and skeptics alike seemed ready to agree that here, at last, was Ibsen's poem liberated in word and picture from the lyrical and musical trappings of its earlier stage tradition. Bergman "has placed Ibsen back in the poet's seat and closed the orchestra pit," wrote Martin Strömberg in *Stockholms-Tidningen* (9 March 1957). "The inner logic of the drama, carried through to the final scene, has never been made as clear on stage as it is here."

As this remark indicates, the rival claims of Grieg and Sæverud were at last put aside and almost all musical accompaniment was eliminated in Bergman's interpretation. Solveig (Gunnel Lindblom) sang her song to a simple, unoperatic Norwegian folk melody; Anitra (Ingrid Thulin) did a sexy dance (false rump and all) to the harsh beat of a drum solo. The standard view of the play as a spectacular kaleidoscope of more or less realistic pictures was likewise definitively overturned. Max von Sydow, fresh from his screen success as Antonius Block, the anguished Knight in *The Seventh Seal*, was a pilgrim again – a rootless, opportunistic, doubt-ridden Peer whose inward, spiritual journey toward final disillusionment and nothingness was the ruling concept which the entire visual strategy of the production was designed to express. As the journey of Peer's life progressed, the bits and pieces of tangible realistic detail that supported the opening scenes were gradually and deliberately pared away. Eventually, only stylized projections of black-chalk sketches were used to establish, in a purely nonrepresentational manner, the prevailing mood of a particular scene (as distinct from its geographical location). At last, as Peer's progress neared its end, even these signposts were removed and the stage was left completely stripped and empty. In the fifth act, as Peer roamed near the last crossroads of life, all theatrical paraphernalia had vanished and the vast expanse of the Malmö stage (a spectacular thirty-six meters in width) became an apparently endless, vacant, darkness-enshrouded space that accentuated the old man's isolation and despair and defined the impasse he now faced.

In von Sydow's dark, driven Peer Gynt (so clearly "With the mark of destiny on his brow," as he tells Solveig in the final scene), critics recognized a bold departure from the accepted archetype of Norwegian blondness and roguishness. "There is demon blood in Peer, scapegoat blood, pirate blood," wrote Per Erik Wahlund. "And it is this strange flavor which both attracts and repels the settled folk, and makes him take up with trolls and wander far beyond the secure bounds of human society."[27] In this sense, Peer's three principal "social" scenes stood out in this production, obviously comprising a triptych of associated images. His first, disastrous encounter with his society, at the wedding feast at Haegstad Farm, was played in a basically realistic setting that was, however, hemmed in by a vaguely sinister and menacing view of mountains in the distance. The effect conveyed an unmistakable sense of this director's unidyllic interpretation of the wedding scene as an ugly, drunken, violent brawl that culminates in the brutal abduction of the bride by Peer, the embittered outsider. His subsequent initiation into King Brose's brutish troll court then became an orgastic, hideously deformed replay of the raucous Haegstad revels. The Greenclad One, adorned with pouting red nipples painted on her skin-tight tulle, was a grotesque caricature of Peer's lascivious desires. Caught in a weird, Hieronymus Bosch vision of hell, the candidate for trolldom seemed literally on the verge of being swallowed up by an anti-world that rolled forward in a block "like an infestation of vermin, fluttering and waving in uniform reactions until it breaks up, like an avalanche of lava-colored rocks, and sucks itself firmly around Peer, a sticky mass of hair and snouts that already is half-way the Boyg."[28]

The third panel in the triptych depicted the most harrowing experience of all in Peer's journey through a hostile world: the mocking coronation of the egoist in the Cairo madhouse. In this nightmare realm, where "Absolute Reason passed away at eleven o'clock last night," a procession of "nodding, staring, yawning, sleepwalking, aimlessly revolving and grimacing monsters, dressed in the same baggy, khaki-colored institutional outfits," emerged out of empty space.[29] Neither the barred windows nor the cages mentioned in Ibsen's stage directions (and prominently evident in, for example, Guthrie's performance) were to be seen on Bergman's stage. Nor were they needed, for "scenery" as such consisted mainly of the static or animated figure compositions that were, throughout this production, its most important decorative feature. In the darkness of the vast, empty stage, bare except for some simple benches, the figures of the inmates were isolated in pools of light to form a macabre tableau around Peer and Begriffenfeldt, his mad guide to this chamber of horrors. A few of them demonstrated their personal fixations in practice, to the utter unconcern of their fellows. As the Fellah, weighed down with the burden of King Apis' past greatness, hanged himself before Peer's horrified eyes, a neighboring inmate leaned his weary head against the corpse. When Hussein, wearing an Einstein mask, cut his throat to illustrate his frustration at being forever an unsharpened pen, the rest of the contorted company marched around the stage in a stately polonaise in honor of their new-found Emperor, Peer. Both the topical social satire that preoccupied Ibsen in this scene and the tone of black comedy that marked Hans Jacob Nilsen's approach to it were subordinated to Bergman's grimly serious interpretation of the mad-house episode as a concrete and frightening glimpse of an inferno of madness, absurdity, and despair that was the outermost station on Gynt's long spiritual pilgrimage in search of his true self.

"Forward and back is equally far," Peer is fond of saying, but in this instance his homeward journey was far bleaker and more lonely. It took him through an endlessly dark and empty universe of a stage, where menacing presences threatened him at every turn and he was unable any longer to fantasize himself away from the reality and finality of death. Awaiting him in the deep shadows was the heavy, sinister figure of the Button Moulder (Toivo Pawlo), crouched over his ladle, his bellows, and his doomsday book. From out of this same darkness Solveig emerged, but Peer's reunion with her was cleansed of any trace of sentimentality. Instead, the concluding moments of the play resolved themselves on a bleak and extremely subdued note of loneliness and of ultimate reckoning. The final picture that confronted the audience, observed Nils Beyer in *Morgon-Tidningen* (9 March 1957) was simply that of "two human beings on the immense stage, and in the background the mute, bent figure of the Button Moulder, his casting ladle in his hand and his box of tools upon his back." The actual presence of the Button Moulder produces, of course, an effect quite unlike that created by the mere sound of his voice heard "behind the house," as the stage directions suggest. In this respect, Bergman's ending was less ambiguous than Ibsen's: Pawlo's brooding silhouette made it plain that Peer was very near the third and final crossroads and could no longer escape.

Broadly speaking, the starkly dematerialized, existentialist approach so well represented by Bergman's *Peer Gynt* finds its direct antithesis in the work of contemporary directors who have viewed Peer's crisis not as an image of personal human suffering but as the reflection of the false values of a corrupt and corrupting society. Although probably the most prominent exponent of the latter view has been Peter Stein, whose widely discussed *Peer Gynt* opened at his new Schaubühne am Halleschen Ufer in Berlin in 1971, ideological inter-pretations of the play, or parts of it, have not been uncommon, espe-cially in the German theatre. While perhaps not always as radical as Stein's comprehensive critique of Peer as the archetypal "*petit bourgeois* adventurer," such interpretations have attempted to bring a Brechtian spirit of active social criticism and a correspondingly "epic" style of production to bear on Ibsen's fantasy and its underlying mythology.

It is not difficult to understand why the trolls and the colorful inhabitants of the fourth act might seem particularly adaptable to such a purpose. In Werner Egk's operatic version of *Peer Gynt* (1938) – an imaginative decomposition and exploration of Ibsen's text in musical terms – a more general tendency is clearly reflected. The trolls, Egk insists in his libretto, must be seen not as fantastic creatures in fur suits but as grotesque distortions of humanity, "the frightening incarnations of human debasement. We must imagine ourselves set down in an assembly of social climbers, pedants, fools, bullies, sadists, and gangsters of all shades."[30] Egk's score, austerely cleansed of the complacent romantic harmonies of Grieg, rings in the troll passages with the strident, mocking jazz rhythms of Kurt Weill at his best. In Kurt Horres' 1982 revival of Egk's work at the Bayerische Staatsoper in Munich, the troll kingdom was a glittering, garish crystal palace of interior-decorator chrome and plexiglass, capable of revolving at times like an outlandish merry-go-round. The troll courtiers were ladies and gentlemen of polite society, the women bedizened with feathers and jewels, the men laden with medals won in some unknown war. Only their zombie countenances, revealing subtle hints of animal features, distinguished them (one hopes) from the elegant spectators seated in the stalls of the opera house. Their dance was, of course, a tango, pranced with the affected dignity of an Offenbach travesty. The Old Man of the Mountains was, in this instance, a savage Idi Amin of a Troll King, covered with military decorations, crippled in body as well as in spirit.

In the middle movement of Egk's opera, which takes its inspiration from episodes in Ibsen's fourth act, the "Brechtian" tone becomes even more pronounced. The action is transferred from the exotic coast of Morocco to a sleazy port city in Central America – a corrupt and brutal Mahagonny populated by parasites and swindlers, where money is the only virtue and power the only law. Gynt, whose ship laden with gold lies at anchor in the harbor, is now scarcely a step away from achieving his egocentric goal of becoming Emperor of the World – but the price for his success has been the sacrifice of all human compassion ("Die Welt regiert nicht Mitleid, nur die Tat!"). Dressed in Horres' revival in the gaudy white outfit and glittering tie of some banana-republic Onassis, he proclaims his cynical gospel of ruthless exploitation from a hanging bridge suspended high above his listeners – three dehumanized and unscrupulous money-brokers who promptly take the capitalist at his word and rob him of his precious cargo.

Ultimately, however, Egk's *Peer Gynt* remains something of a theatrical and conceptual hybrid, in which elements of epic theatre and expressionism mingle and irony is mixed liberally with a sense of compassion for Peer, the prodigal whose nightmare odyssey of self-discovery returns him, for a short time at least, to the safety of Solveig's world. In Horres' new production of the music-drama, however, this final reunion was undercut by the visual note of menacing uncertainty which, in one form or another, is found in so many contemporary performances of the play as well. The conventionalized gestures and attitudes of a phony mother-and-son Pietà, so mercilessly pilloried by Stein in Berlin, were studiously avoided. Instead, as the final chords of Egk's score sounded and Peer reached out his hands to Solveig across the bare cottage table that separated them, six lifeless mannequins, stiffly mounted on rods, materialized out of the shadows in the background. These apparitions – ghosts, perhaps, of Mads, Ingrid, Aase, and other victims of Peer's selfish inhumanity – made no sound, but their eerie presence bespoke the inevitability of retribution.

A quite different, much harsher approach to the character of Peer Gynt emerges in the type of production that finds its logical culmination in Stein's famous interpretation, which divided Peer's life into eight segments, played by six different actors. One of these same actors, Michael König, had previously appeared as Peer in a 1968 production at the Theater am Goetheplatz in Bremen, which is, in many respects, surely the direct precursor of Stein's theatrical experiment. In Bremen (where Stein was also directing at this time), König's violent, acrobatic portrayal delineated not "a passive Kaspar Hauser figure moving in a fantasy world [Peter Handke's *Kaspar* had just been seen in Bremen], but an equally unrealistic, recklessly aggressive character chasing after false paradises."[31] The Peer Gynt of this performance, wrote Reimar Hollmann in *Süddeutsche Zeitung* (11 June 1968), "is more than merely the negative hero, the indecisive dreamer, the labile egoist, the incarnation of Norwegianism. He becomes the virtual denunciation of the whole concept of the romantic hero, which folklore seeks to propagate but which reality neither knows nor has any use for." Aspects of Stein's critical, demythologized conception of the Peer figure – as a character more akin to Jarry's obscene egomaniac Ubu than to Goethe's Faust – were clearly prefigured in König's explosive performance.

"In a world such as this, the silvan landscapes of romantic scenery and the Biedermeier plush of Grieg's music automatically disqualify themselves," Hollmann's review of the ambitious Bremen production continues. Directed by Kurt Hübner, this virtually uncut, five-hour spectacle made use (as had, for example, Heinrich Koch's more streamlined productions of the play in Berlin and Frankfurt a decade before) of a simplified unit setting that eliminated the need for scene changes and provided a large, flexible space that could be used to comment visually on the thematic flow of the play. The expressive spatial arangement designed by Wilfried Minks allowed the action to proceed on three separate levels, thereby achieving an evocative scenic rhythm with a bare minimum of actual scenery. At the front of the main, semi-circular acting area, four steps on either side led down into an "underworld" created by a sunken forestage. Above this, suspended high over the stage, a steel bridge coldly illuminated by neon tubes provided a third, "heavenly" sphere where Peer indulged himself in his airy visions and lofty flights of fancy.

It was across this suspension bridge that Peer dashed dramatically at the beginning of the play, hotly pursued by Aase (played by Edith Clever, who recreated the role for Stein in Berlin three years later). As his half-skeptical, half-fascinated mother listened, the fabulist spun his tale of riding the buck over the Gjendin Edge – and then suddenly vaulted over the railing of the bridge and dropped to the floor of the stage below, leaving his enraged parent to continue her protests aloft. "It was a plunge of some ten or twelve feet," observed Jost Nolte in *Die Welt* (10 June 1968), "and it was the first in a series of countless shocks to the audience, as they watched [Peer] do his balancing act on the edge of the abyss."

The most startling visual aspect of Minks' set, however, was a strange frieze of grotesque, sub-human figures that encircled the principal playing area. This comic-strip background of huge, squat, baby-faced gargoyles was the first thing the audience saw when it entered the theatre, and Peer's odyssey was overseen by these grimacing, rubber-doll monsters from start to finish. This graphic enigma touched off the usual guessing-game among the critics, who saw in it everything from "a satire of the fatheaded bourgeoisie" to a symbol of Peer's self-acknowledged inability to distinguish between trolls and human beings. Viewed more simply, however, the device functioned as a visual reminder of the menacing atmosphere of Peer's dark world, which reviewers of this production felt was epitomized in the "unbearably violent cruelty of the hara-kiri scenes in the madhouse: these were the manifestation of the inwardly repressed, escapist character traits in Peer's own personality" (Hollmann).

Despite its neck-breaking pursuit of contemporary relevance, Hübner's *Peer Gynt* incorporated its share of somewhat incongruously old-fashioned choices. Chief among these was the director's decision ("an act of reverence toward the Meininger," one critic suggested wryly) to send Peer, as the self-styled Prophet, galloping in with Anitra (iv.viii) on a real horse. Comparatively minor though it might seem, the incident reveals a crucial distinction between Hübner's approach and Stein's, related though their two productions may be in other respects. Stein's insistence on the use of an immense stuffed horse, mounted on wheels and pushed by four harem girls, for Peer's entrance in this same scene reflects more than simply a modernist's conviction that a live horse in the obviously fictive context of a theatrical performance does more to undermine illusion than to foster it. More to the point, Stein's choice succinctly illustrates his strong ideological view of the play itself as an anachronism – a dramatic taxidermist's specimen, as it were, demonstrating the obsolescence of the *petit bourgeois* myth of individualism and realization of "self." Accordingly, in this director's eyes the objects and properties in the play "are like exhibits in a museum." His audiences must never be allowed to forget "that the horses that appear are completely fake – they're stuffed horses." Like the lion that pursued Peer in the desert and the four-wheeled pig he rode into the troll kingdom, "they are only authentic in that they are genuinely stuffed." "Everything that is used, or let's rather say quoted, creates an illusion to a certain extent but it does so almost in passing," he explained to an interviewer. "We have to approach these things like pictures, objects and mummies which are displayed in museums."[32] These "second-hand things and objects" exist, for Stein, as the very emblems of the second-hand, bankrupt *Weltanschauung* that underlies Peer's hopeless search for a "true self" and Ibsen's depiction of it.

Ostensibly, Stein's Schaubühne collective undertook *Peer Gynt* solely in order to "attempt to develop an understanding of our own bourgeois origins."[33] However, it is worth remembering the rather precarious reputation previously held by the play in the German theatre. "*Peer Gynt* is no holy gospel," declared *Frankfurter Allgemeine* in connection with the Hübner revival. "There are things in this long dramatic poem – weighed down as it is by references to a specific time and place – which, like seeds stored too long, do not repay the effort of cultivating them." *Die Welt* was blunter on this occasion: "Ibsen's play has outlived itself." Comparable opinions are to be found throughout the reviews of the earlier German productions of the play by Heinrich Koch and others. Hence, whether Stein intended it or not, his determination to bill the work as a charming but outdated museum-piece – "A Play of the Nineteenth Century," as loudspeakers proclaimed it at the start of his performance – effectively forestalled unfavorable critical comment on this score.

As it turned out, meanwhile, the mammoth, story-book production by the Schaubühne, which required two full evenings to perform and which opened to ecstatic notices on 13 and 14 May 1971, utterly transcended ideological considerations by carrying the spectator, willy-nilly, back to the palmiest days of nineteenth-century scenic spectacle. The deromanticizing of *Peer Gynt* had, in effect, come full circle. "The triumph of this *mise-en-scène*, I fear, is due entirely to the fact that it once more satisfies those feelings of hunger for total theatre," observed the highly regarded critical authority Günther Rühle. "For the simple reason that characters are developed, scenes are permitted to evolve as if they were plays in themselves (for example: the wedding at Haegstad, the troll wedding, the homecoming) . . . The whole obsolete, illusionistic way of doing things experienced a grandiose return, despite the fact that the dramaturgical intent was decidedly to prevent this from happening." Anyone wishing to measure the force of the appeal this critic describes can readily do so by viewing the widely distributed videotape record of the event, which was shown in German movie-houses at the time. Like Max Reinhardt's great experiments in the Grosses Schauspielhaus half a century earlier, Rühle continues, Stein's production "creates the perfect impression that one is in a museum – one where the art of illusion is carried to such heights that the figures there seem to come alive once more."[34]

Rather than attempting to squeeze this colorful pageant into the limited confines of the Schaubühne am Halleschen Ufer itself, it was presented, before an audience of 700 spectators seated on bleachers, in one of Berlin's large exhibition halls. The overall result was a mardi gras atmosphere, a carnival of pantomime effects that were, in themselves, intended as an ironic commentary on the heights to which the *petit bourgeois* imagination can attain. "Step right up! The nineteenth-century circus is here! Henrik Ibsen's world view in Peter Stein's Super-Total-Show!" began Rolf Michaelis' review in *Frankfurter Allgemeine*, aptly headlined "Picture Book of the Bourgeoisie" (17 May 1971). "This is the story of Peer and his bourgeois century: life lived at second hand, as a reproduction, a kitsch picture for a photograph album – a critical history of the human race."

The heart of this spectacle was Karl-Ernst Herrmann's ingenious unit set, a sprawling, undulating platform reminiscent of the popular medieval tradition of a polyscenic stage of juxtaposed localities. Helmuth Karasek's review in *Die Zeit* (21 May 1971) paints an especially lively picture of Herrmann's versatile playing-field, as seen from the stands where the spectators sat along either side of the eighty-two-foot oblong platform:

7 Peer before the massive, cutout Sphinx in Peter Stein's open-stage production at the Schaubühne am Halleschen Ufer, West Berlin, in 1971.

One looked down on a hilly panorama that, at one end of the traverse, ascended to the Nordic mountain where Solveig waited, throughout the second part, singing outside her hut (a grotesquely lovely image of the male fantasy of an unshakably faithful beloved who, should the need arise, can attest to the fact that he has not lived his life in vain – a woman to be exhibited in a glass display-case). Located at the opposite end was, in the first part, the idyllic setting for the rustic wedding and, on the second evening, a splendid expanse of canvas sea in which [Peer] risked drowning and upon which, shining in the unreal brilliance of a theatre sun, a toy yacht sailed and then exploded. Thus was our grandparents' canvas dream-world of adventures on land and sea brought to life.

For winter-time, a white cloth covered this hilly landscape; were we in the desert, then a yellow cover lay outstretched in the glittering light of the projectors. In addition, this stage structure was continually ready with ingenious surprises. The mountain opened on the troll world, which looked like a nice old-fashioned dusty parlor. Or, at the touch of a button . . . a Sphinx rose up from the stage floor, leaving an indentation deep enough to house Professor Begriffenfeldt's madhouse.

Stein and his ensemble had decided well in advance that they wanted to preserve the play's fantastic, fairy-tale elements and the whole naively evocative picture-book quality associated with nineteenth-century theatre. As dramaturge Dieter Sturm had warned the group a year ahead of time: "The line described by the play must be realized on stage. If you denounce everything point by point the moment that it arises, nothing will be achieved."[35] Hence, the core of Stein's approach was the ironic doubleness inherent in the concept of "quotation" which he and others have borrowed from Brecht's theory of dialectical theatre (specifically, the statement in Brecht's "Short Description of a New Technique of Acting" that the epic actor "speaks his part not as if he were improvising it himself but like a quotation"). Applied to *Peer Gynt*, the "quoting" style meant the maintenance of a critical attitude toward the work and the events in it – such as Peer's entry into the troll kingdom, mounted on a stuffed pig pushed by masked and singing trolls in shabby Victorian dress – without thereby dissipating the incident's intrinsic imaginative appeal.

Nowhere in the production was this technique of quotation more effectively employed than in the brief adventure-story narratives which, delivered over the loudspeakers by an unseen master of ceremonies, introduced each of the "chapters" in the epic chronicle of Peer's life. The eight titled episodes of this version (with the name of the actor who played Peer in each) are as follows:

Part One
"The Bride Abductor" Act I (Heinrich Giskes)
"The Lord of the Mountains" Act II i–iv (Michael König)
"The Realm of the Trolls" Act II v–vii (Bruno Ganz)
"Free as the Birds and Fugitive in the Woods" Act II viii and Act III (Wolf Redl)

Part Two
"A Yankee in the Desert" Act IV i–iv (Dieter Laser)
"The Prophet in the Harem" Act IV v–viii (Wolf Redl)
"On the Track of the Past" Act IV ix–xiii (Werner Rehm)
"Under the Sign of the Onion" Act V (Bruno Ganz)

At the conclusion of the first part, the narrator's spiel, laced with the cliffhanger clichés of pulp fiction, offered a catalogue of the wonders yet to come ("Everywhere danger threatens. Will Peer reach his goal? Will he find his own true self? . . ."). Similarly, the second evening, itself entitled "In Foreign Parts and the Voyage Home," began with a narrative synopsis of what had gone before, during which the four Peers who had been involved in the preceding evening's episodes re-enacted key moments from each of them.

The aim of this novelistic "serialization" of Peer's life history was clearly to redirect the focus from the inner struggles of the individual (the traditional view of the role in the theatre) to the social and economic circumstances that condition Peer at given stages. In breaking up the part and distributing it among six actors (all perceptibly different in build and appearance), more was obviously at stake than the lesser motives mentioned by Stein – the need to honor the democratic principles of his collective and the wish to lighten the severe demands which this particular part places on a single actor. Far more significant, surely, is the fact that this deconstructive process renders the title character itself a "quotation," from which audience sympathy is detached and to which its critical scrutiny is instead directed. This sense of "epic" awareness was further encouraged by the distinctive manner in which one Peer exchanged places with the next. For example, after Giskes succeeded in carrying off Ingrid (depicted here as more of an *economic* conquest than a sexual one), König simply appeared and lifted the expensively dressed bride off his mate's shoulders. In turn, after König's understated, thoroughly anti-lyrical delivery of Peer's great second-act monologue ("Castle rises on castle"), he knocked himself out against an imaginary rock, to the comic accompaniment of a Walt Disney sound effect. The third Peer in the series, Bruno Ganz, then entered and lay down nearby in the same position; a follow-spot swung over to pick up his prostrate form, and the theatrical relay race went on.

The end result of this dissection of Peer's character was not, however, a cold or emotionally unaffecting performance (nor of course does Brecht's own theory of epic acting presume any such outcome). Indeed, the restraint of Stein's style was at times perforated completely. Peer's horrified encounter with Begriffenfeldt's naked, bleeding lunatics, enacted at the foot of the massive, cutout Sphinx that was hoisted up from the stage floor, took on the emotionally lacerating proportions of Peter Brook's trend-setting production of *Marat/Sade* in 1964. Yet even in Stein's violent rendering of the madhouse scene, the political dimension did not become obscured: the excessive preoccupation of the lunatics with themselves and their personal obsessions was merely an extreme example of the selfishness of capitalism – "the cold-blooded madness of naked, self-immolating individualism," as Karasek phrased it in his review.

In general, then, Stein and his actors worked to develop a performance style for *Peer Gynt* in which – as was the case with the production concept as a whole – the maintenance of critical distance did not preclude an emotional impact. "They act the role *and* criticize it," Volker Canaris wrote with enthusiasm in *Theater heute*. "The bourgeois aesthetic of 'embodying' a role has here been so perfected that it becomes a new style in itself, a critical dialectic, an aesthetic means of knowledge." There was no "distancing" involved in the individual actor's portrayal of Peer, this critic felt, "no difference established between what is said and what is meant, between character and actor. Instead the character has at one and the same time the magic power of the story-teller who casts a spell over his listeners and the boastfulness of the charlatan whom no one believes."[36] In this respect at least, Stein's approach reveals a striking sensitivity to that peculiar doubleness which is an essential facet of Peer's character as Ibsen conceived it – and, for that matter, as Richard Mansfield played it, with "expertly simulated" passion and suffering, at the very beginning of this century.

It was only in the final section of Stein's version that a wholesale revision of the original text, undertaken for ideological rather than theatrical reasons, radically altered Ibsen's dramatic concept. Wishing to use this closing segment "to show the reason why we have per-

formed this extensive spectacle," Stein found (predictably enough)
that the work's dark final movement – Peer's journey through the
kingdom of the dead – was utterly unsuited to his utilitarian purposes.
"The ending provided by Ibsen, the morality play which is appended,
and above all the sentimental closing image with Solveig and Peer are
passages where we cannot remain faithful to the text. But the production should not treat the ending ironically or destroy it but use and
adapt it meaningfully."[37] With this in mind, Botho Strauss, who edited
the script for Stein, set about rewriting the fifth act to provide a clearer
denunciation of Peer's *petit bourgeois* selfishness and insensitivity to the
struggles of others. The eulogy over the grave of the man who chopped
off his finger (politically an unsatisfactory alternative to Peer's solip-
sism) was cut and a funeral procession for Ingrid, the abducted bride,
was substituted. Peer's metaphysical encounter with the Thin Person
was likewise eliminated, and the questions put to him by the Strange
Passenger, as they struggle in the sea after the shipwreck, were rewrit-
ten to emphasize Peer's social failings ("Have you at any time in your
life felt any concern about one or more of your fellow men? Have you
ever tried to find out the facts about social conditions in Norway?").

   The retention of the monologue which Peer speaks when grubbing
for onions in the forest on the eve of Pentecost was, however, crucial to
Stein's purpose. "In the image of the onion," he had decided at an
early stage, "a basic attitude of the bourgeosie is revealed: search for
identity, permanent self-castration, the longing to return to the
womb."[38] The immediate aftermath of Peer's anagnoric soliloquy was
his encounter with a reborn Button Moulder – a futurist technocrat
surrounded by his assistants, curiously out of place in the "quoted"
but charming museum-world which Stein had created. Introducing
himself as "Engineer Buttonmoulder," he explained to Peer that he
represented a firm which was starting a comprehensive program of
clearance and redevelopment in this region of Norway. His assign-
ment: to gather and recycle all those elements standing in the way of
progress – insignificant individuals, unworldly poets, persons of independent means, and the entire retrogressive middle class! "You and
your sort," he told Peer, "will go into the melting pot to be converted
into new raw material," in order to become "the lubricating oil that
keeps the wheels of our economy turning smoothly."[39] As Peer pon-
dered his sentence, the Engineer's worker-assistants began to clear the
ground of debris and spray it with disinfectant.

   Despite Stein's earlier decision not to "treat the end ironically or
destroy it," the closing moments of his production were steeped in the

trenchant tone of Brechtian satire. Peer's problematic reunion with Solveig was treated with all the mock solemnity of Macheath's scaffold reprieve in *The Threepenny Opera*. Coldly ordered by the Button Moulder to put his house in order, Peer crawled up into the lap of the blind, aged woman who had waited for him all this time – to form a fitting tableau for what both Stein and Brecht would call a "happy" ending. The workers then carried the pair down to the main playing area and deposited them, still joined in their touching Pietà pose, amidst the play's other museum exhibits. Here, these quaint relics of the obsolete bourgeois cult of individualism were photographed with an old-fashioned tripod camera. Had there been time, Stein had in fact planned to set up a mechanical assembly-line on stage which would turn out small, plastic-packaged replicas of the Pietà tableau, for distribution to the audience.

In the confrontational context of the Schaubühne production, the atmosphere of mystery and dread surrounding the final act was plainly irrelevant – as was the sense, emphasized in so many productions of *Peer Gynt*, that the play ends on a suspended, ambivalent note. In Stein's reinterpretation, the very idea of Peer's "redemption" through the magnanimity of Solveig's love was a perfunctory moralistic coda that he reduced to a hollow romantic fiction – an ideal metaphor for the kitsch (pop art) industry which, Stein observes sarcastically, continues to flourish by "propagating, in millionfold reproductions, empty myths about the individual genius." With the caustic finality of his closing image, the director distanced himself from the play and "reduced it to a souvenir." "The cold use of this melancholy pose made us recognize how worn out such stylizations are," Rühle commented in a later piece in *Frankfurter Allgemeine* (28 April 1978). "Reflected in the dead eyes of Jutta Lampe (Solveig) the drama suddenly seemed like a ghost, while up until then it had, because of its new-found freshness, seemed such fun."

Although the mammoth Schaubühne *Peer Gynt* was, in some respects, an extreme example of the use of Ibsen's text as pretext for a Marxist analysis of cultural history, the intellectual clarity and force of Stein's metatheatrical style were incontrovertible. As a result, the production has been widely influential. In particular, Stein's method of quotation addresses itself usefully and appropriately to the complex problem of the play's spirit of irony and its own self-conscious references to itself as a work of theatre ("No need to worry," the Strange Passenger assures Peer after the shipwreck: "You won't die in the middle of the last act"). Whether Stein's method can work *in nuce*, stripped of the socio-analytical premises that fostered it, was a question answered only inconclusively by the similarly styled, two-evening revival performed at the Guthrie Theater in Minneapolis in 1983.

Directed by Liviu Ciulei, this opulent, picture-book spectacle (visually so engaging that one critic declared himself "enraptured by it like a child watching a pantomime for the first time")[40] incorporated many images and impressions that observers found familiar from the Schaubühne production. Yet the shabby respectability of the trolls in porcine masks and Victorian dress was, in this case, only an incidental parody of middle-class values, in an otherwise unparodic interpretation. The Pietà imitation with which the second evening at the Guthrie ended, suffused in a blaze of white light, was left to stand as a sentimental conclusion to the play, not, as Stein wanted, as a harsh critical comment that questioned the waste of Solveig's life – and Peer's. The whole technique of quotation was perhaps most profitably applied, however, in Santo Loquasto's flexible design concept, in which "quoted" reminiscences of Victorian theatre – floor planks and traps patterned after nineteenth-century construction-site materials, for instance – were introduced into a highly contemporary, open-stage setting characterized by the use of steel scaffolding and moving mirror panels. For the shipwreck scene, Loquasto and Ciulei resurrected a particularly choice example of Victorianism that carried their audience, had they known it, back in time and space to the play's heyday at the Dagmar Theatre in Copenhagen, a hundred years before. In this scene the stage was covered with what older theatre practice called a "sea cloth" of billowing parachute silk, into whose undulating waves the stricken ship eventually disappeared. To produce the billowing effect, electric fans were supplemented by the efforts of a squad of stagehands moving beneath the cloth and around its edges. Had the ghost of Theodor Andersen been watching from the wings of the Guthrie, he might have recognized these helpers instantly as "wave boys."

A much more misconceived attempt to resurrect the theatrical past was seen in the ostentatious "triple" Peer Gynt with which National-theatret in Oslo reopened, after five years of work to repair fire damage, in 1985. Conceived and directed by Edith Roger, this unusual project's aim was to present a triptych of three productions of the play, each one beginning at a different point in Peer's life: after the shipwreck, in the Moroccan desert, and at the opening of the first act. Each production showed the audience a different constellation of actors in the major roles of Peer, Aase, and the Button Moulder, who also doubled as Begriffenfeldt. Unfortunately, whatever deeper intention had prompted this experiment was obscured by the heavy, literalistic pictorialism of the stage design (by Tina Schwab) and the direction. Thus, a purling mountain stream ran with real water, in which one of the three Saeter girls bathed her feet. Solveig once again arrived at Peer's newly-built cabin in the hills on her skis (equipped, by now, with modern release bindings). Mother Aase drew her last breath in a small, rustic interior that seemed virtually a replica in miniature of the "authentic" rough-hewn cabin designed by Jens Wang for Bjørnson's naturalistic production of the play in 1892. Ultimately, however, it was the now blatant inappropriateness of the Grieg score – played in this instance by a full forty-man pit orchestra and chanted by an operatic chorus of musical-comedy trolls and peasants – that reduced this ponderous spectacle to what the veteran Swedish critic Björn Nilsson coldly dismissed as "grandiose tastelessness."

Despite such renewed interest in Victorian pictorialism (whether "quoted" or not) in the play's more recent performance history, *Peer Gynt* remains a work that lends itself at least as well to the simplest and most non-representational style of setting: some ladders and scaffolding, for example, which – as in the Royal Shakespeare Company's chamber-theatre production at The Other Place (Stratford) in 1982 and in the Barbican's Pit in 1983 – can let the audience create, in its own imagination, the troll palace and the madhouse, the mountain hut and Peer's tent in the desert. In the case of the Ron Daniels production by the RSC, which featured Derek Jacobi as Peer, the announced aim was to enable the actors to "feel beneath their feet not a plasterboard, 'poetic' Norway, but a living, authentic terrain with its own culture, communal demons, hardships, and code of laws."[41] The means used to achieve this end, however, was largely the texture of the language the actors were given to speak (in a spare translation that experimented with the intermittent use of a stylized rural Ulster speech) rather than the cumbersome reproduction of a series of "authentic" regional settings.

In general, quite unlike the prose plays that follow it, *Peer Gynt* is characterized by a virtually Shakespearean expansiveness and a correspondingly broad spectrum of possible performance choices. Far more open and associational in its structure and hence less confined to a specific theatrical mode, it has (Peter Stein's museum metaphor notwithstanding) seemed to grow more modern, rather than less so, as twentieth-century theatre has evolved. The "blemishes" that disturbed literary critics when the work first appeared in print – "the misanthropy and self-hatred" that bothered Brandes, the "general sense of incongruity and disjointedness" that distressed even a staunch Ibsen supporter like Gosse – have often been precisely the

8   Peer (Derek Jacobi) acquires a tail in the palace of the Troll King (Act II), in the Royal Shakespeare Company's chamber-theatre production in 1982–3.

traits that have appealed to directors and performers in the modern period. Ibsen himself, of course, was stung by the initial criticism of his play – particularly by Clemens Petersen's somewhat vague objections to it as unpoetic and lacking in "idealism." The playwright's angry reaction ("If I am not a poet, what have I to lose? I shall try my hand as a photographer") is as universally familiar as its epoch-making consequences. By the end of the 1870s, Ibsen had left his "poetic" period behind and had begun to forge an entirely new and different mode of dramatic expression, a mode that translated the stifling atmosphere of contemporary prejudices and bourgeois moral hypocrisy into a metaphor for an all-inclusive tragic fate.

3

One Nora, many Noras

Although *The Pillars of Society* had caused its fair share of controversy when first produced in 1877, *A Doll's House* shook the very foundations of contemporary society and its supporting ethical structure. The world premiere of Ibsen's new play, staged at the Royal Theatre in Copenhagen on 21 December 1879, enjoyed what even the dramatist himself agreed was "unparalleled success," readily apparent in its exceptional run of twenty-one performances in repertory during the first season. Its popular appeal aside, however, the original production of *A Doll's House* ignited a firestorm of critical debate and dissent. This discussion is of special interest because it was, in this case, so obviously influenced by impressions drawn from the actual performance and in particular from the persuasive portrayal of Nora by Betty Hennings. Although the first edition of the text had been brought out by Gyldendal, Ibsen's Copenhagen publisher, some two weeks earlier, the theatre management had shrewdly persuaded most of the critics to save their principal review for the production. Perhaps as a result, the critical reaction to the play itself in performance did not, as one might suppose, focus on such abstract issues as the "problem" of women's rights or the moral validity of Nora's accusations in the famous discussion scene. Indeed, this scene, so prominent in Shaw's interpretation of the technical novelty in Ibsenism, provoked surprisingly little comment among the play's first theatrical reviewers. Instead, the real questions at issue became the dramatic motivation for Nora's behavior, the audience's reaction to what it perceived as an atmosphere of unrelieved pessimism, and, above all, the effect of Ibsen's disturbingly open ending – so unlike the more agreeably conventional resolution provided in *The Pillars of Society*, which had had its world premiere at this same theatre two years before. In fact, a number of commentators drew a direct parallel with the earlier play, comparing Nora's ethical dilemma to that of the selfish and fraudulent Karsten Bernick in

Pillars. Among the more sympathetic critical voices, Vilhelm Topsøe maintained stoutly in *Dagbladet* (22 December 1879) that Nora remains "childishly innocent" in her guilt, by reason of the fact that her character is composed of a "strange mixture of right and wrong, of comprehension and lack of comprehension, of ignorance and flashes of realization." In a rather condescending review in *Fædrelandet* (22 December), poet and politician Carl Ploug was prepared to agree that, although she has broken the law, Nora never really loses the audience's sympathy. Nevertheless, Ploug found it impossible to condone or understand the fact that "when she realizes that by concealing the matter from her husband too long she has placed herself in the power of a person who will and can prostitute her and him, she still does not overcome her cowardice and find an opportunity to confide the trouble to her husband." The pugnacious critic and theatre manager M. W. Brun was more outspoken, vigorously denouncing as "psychologically false" the very idea that Nora does not confess to Helmer and obtain his forgiveness. Brun's harsh notice in *Folkets Avis* (24 December) set the tone of moral outrage which *A Doll's House* would continue to encounter during its first journey through the world. The play, this writer declared, "begins with small 'macaroon lies' which grow into 'white lies' and finally culminate in . . . a psychological–dramatic lie," perpetrated by the playwright himself in his desire "to produce something which no one has ever seen or heard before." The psychological essence of this "falsification" was felt, by Brun and others, to consist in Nora's unnatural rejection of maternal love, seen in her "impossible" desertion of her three children. As a result, Brun insisted,

we are left in the most painful mood, literally disgusted by a catastrophe which in the crudest manner departs from ordinary humanity in order to exalt the untrue, that which is equally outrageous in aesthetic, psychological and dramatic terms. I ask you directly: is there one mother among thousands of mothers, one wife among thousands of wives, who would behave as Nora behaves, who would desert husband, children and home merely in order to become a "human being"? I answer with conviction: no and again no!

Vilhelm Topsøe was among the few who disagreed: "With each line of dialogue exchanged between Nora and Helmer in the play's final scene, we feel the gulf between them widening more and more, and it creates a gripping effect to witness that bond being unravelled strand by strand." Although Topsøe's review in *Dagbladet* shared the opinion that Ibsen's rejection of maternal love constituted "the weak point" in his play, this critic asserted (rightly enough) that any reconciliation after such heightened suspense would have appeared "flat and fool-ish." If the critical response to Nora's final choice fluctuated, however, there was at least one dramaturgical point on which every reviewer of this production was in agreement: the "spiritual metamorphosis" which Nora undergoes in the third act was unanimously regarded as a glaring breach of dramatic logic. Conservative critic Erik Bøgh, who as the Royal Theatre's play reader coldly rejected *Ghosts* two years later, put it this way in *Dagens Nyheder* (22 December): "Nora has only shown herself as a little Nordic 'Frou-Frou' and as such she cannot be trans-formed in a flash to a Søren Kierkegaard in skirts." In one sense, this reaction to the improbable abruptness of Nora's transformation obviously reflects the specific performance given by Betty Hennings, whose characterization so profoundly influenced not only the recep-tion but also the comprehension of Ibsen's play. In broader terms, meanwhile, the Danish critics had put their collective finger on the most crucial problem facing any actress or director undertaking this particular play.

To her contemporaries – including Ibsen – Betty Hennings *was* Nora, the veritable personification of the dramatist's literary creation. Even the surly Brun was obliged to concede that she presented "such an attractive, natural, and beautiful picture of the young, inexperienced, naive, and carefree wife and mother that one truly envied Helmer the treasure which he possessed." The novelist, actor, and critic Herman Bang writes that she transformed "even readers to spectators because, after we have but once seen her, she follows us from scene to scene, we see her and not Nora, even as we read." This happens, Bang continues in his exceptionally fine analysis of her acting style, "because we continually place the stress where Fru Hennings has placed it, be-cause, influenced by her, we hesitate where she hesitates, we close our eyes where she closes them."[1] At twenty-nine Hennings was the period's ideal of the charming, graceful ingenue, and as such her Nora was the embodiment of youthfulness, unconcerned gaiety, and chil-dish caprice. Bang's impressionistic description captures perfectly the fundamental tone of childishness in her performance:

Follow her in the first scene, as she flutters about with childish officiousness, childish helplessness, childish rashness. Watch her opening the packages to show what she has bought, she displays her purchases with childish wonder . . .

In her first scene with Mrs. Linde, speaking with childish haste, she whispers, looks around her, whispers again – all with the eagerness of a child talking behind her teacher's back. Something about this obliterates the significance of the secret, makes it – what it of course ought not to be – one of the important secrets of children, the inexhaustible content of school confidences created by the tedium of the lessons and of interest during recesses.

The same child-like quality was accentuated in her scene with her own children:

One remembers her noise, her mobility, her extremely child-like manner of speaking, the rapidity of her gestures, the change in her diction, which takes on almost nervous speed during her long chatter with the children. For this monologue is chatter, and Fru Hennings' art, which once again has created an incomparable vignette out of this situation, gives speech to the children where the dramatist has left them silent.

Even in her first encounter with Krogstad she continued the same line of attack, moving from alarm to the childish defiance in which she seeks refuge with the declaration, "It was I who signed Papa's name."

This reading of Nora's initial character affected the ensuing development of the figure in several decisive ways. Looking back on Betty Hennings' performance in later essays, Edvard Brandes emphasized the total absence of eroticism in "this fine and chaste figure, who nonetheless is supposed to have had three children with Helmer in a rush of sensuality which at the end of the play she regrets." Although Hennings "struggled ably and successfully against the gulf which her temperament and personality placed between her and Ibsen's Nora," Brandes felt that, in particular, her technically skillful and vivacious tarantella lacked that "sensual abandon" which it requires as "the erotic high-point of the marriage."[2] In this respect at least, the virginal, asexual child-wife delineated by Hennings had perhaps more in common with the idealized heroines of romantic fiction than with the passionate young woman who frees herself with difficulty from her physical relationship with her husband at the end of Ibsen's play.

Another, quite different consequence of this actress's approach was that it served to redirect the principal dramatic emphasis to the first two acts of the play – filled, remarked *Berlingske Tidende* (22 December), with a series of "charming pictures" in which "the sun-drenched comfort and happiness of the 'Dolls' House' are depicted, and in which the lark cavorts with her children, decorates the tree, and plays hide-and-seek." In reading the play, Vilhelm Topsøe observed, the "cheerless" third act is the focus of attention, but in performance one's interest centers instead on the development of dramatic crises throughout the second act, from the first moment when Nora is alone with the stripped Christmas tree to the closing seconds when, after her hectic tarantella, she shouts for champagne. As a former ballerina with exceptional pantomimic ability, Hennings was ideally suited to the visually expressive moments around which the Royal Theatre production was concentrated – the children's game interrupted by Krogstad's sudden appearance in the doorway (considered by many as the actress's best scene), the tree-trimming punctuated by Nora's mimic reactions to her husband's recital of Krogstad's unsavory background, the tarantella rehearsal. Each of these vignettes seemed, in the words of the reviewer for *Dags-Telegrafen* (23 December), "to stop in a tableau effect for an instant, imprinting its picture indelibly on the mind of the spectator and then moving on again in the inexorable progress towards the fateful consequences of the conclusion."

The transition to the subdued and chilling mood of the final act precipitated a jarring break with Nora's previous personality that most of the reviewers ascribed to the writing itself. "The cold and quiet clarity and seriousness which replace Nora's gay frivolity and spineless despair cannot come so quickly. They must be prepared for with many thoughts and considerations which the playwright has simply skipped over," Carl Ploug argued in *Fædrelandet*, contending that Ibsen is too easily tempted "to place dramatic effect above the truth which he has endeavored with great success to depict throughout the foregoing action." As for Betty Hennings, although Ploug found her voice too subdued to be audible in this section and Brandes criticized her lack of authority in her confrontation with Helmer, most commentators were unreserved in their praise for her handling of this undeniably difficult transition from songbird to new woman. She rose, Topsøe declared, from confusion and disappointment to become "what she must become, the greater of the two, completely superior to her husband." Years later, a cosmopolitan observer like Maurice Baring still marvelled at the coherence she achieved: "I have seen many Noras: Eleonora Duse and Réjane and Agnes Sorma in Berlin; but Fru Hennings played the part as if it had been written for her," the English novelist-diplomat recalled. "The irony was indeed harrowing, and the disenchantment complete; but irony, disillusion, weariness, disgust were all merged into a wonderful harmony, as the realities of life gradually dawned . . . She made the transformation, which whenever I had seen the play before seemed so difficult to believe in, of the Nora of the first act into the Nora of the last act seem the most natural thing in the world."[3]

Yet the final emotional impression left by Nora's choice was, critics agreed, one of dissonance and confusion rather than triumph. The general feeling of disappointment and joylessness recorded by virtually every reviewer of the production was to a great extent the result of the fact that – as a spokesman for modernism like Edvard Brandes recognized – critics and audience alike harbored the views and sympathies of Torvald Helmer. As a consequence, his wife's decision to leave him seemed incomprehensible. As portrayed by Emil Poulsen he seemed, in the words of *Dags-Telegrafen*, "such a congenial, refined, professionally energetic and honest, domestically happy and likeable personality that his greatest offence seemed to be that he has chosen a frivolous little girl as his wife." His demands appeared, to this viewer and others, fully as reasonable as Nora's, whereas his faults were far less glaring. (Strindberg's famous attack on the play had, in other words, ample critical precedent.) In his review in *Ude og Hjemme* (4 January 1880), Edvard Brandes alone saw Helmer for what he is, "the intellectual aristocrat without intellect, arrogantly conservative partly by conviction and partly out of pragmatism, indifferent, but possessing all the opinions of good society."

Poulsen – a versatile actor whose Ibsen characterizations extended from his early Bishop Nikolas in *The Pretenders* (1871) to his restlessly grieving John Gabriel Borkman (1897) – was able, in Topsøe's view, to endow Helmer with "the right touch of vacillation, half educated, half amiable, a little arrogant, and cleverly ordinary." His finely detailed reading of the part was, Erik Bøgh observed, a remarkable filigree of contrasts and shadings that ranged from the "short-sighted, self-satisfied playfulness with his tormented wife" to the "exultant champagne mood that turns first to indignation and then at once to vapid jubilation" and on through "all the shifting moods of the closing scene, in which he must deliver the cues for Nora's divorce proceedings."

As to what Poulsen's characterization actually conveyed, however, opinions differed sharply. *Berlingske Tidende* saw him as the aesthete who shuns ugliness; beneath the aesthetic pleasure he takes in Nora lies deep and sincere love, manifested "in his sorrow when his lark is silenced in the last act and the sunlight seems to disappear from his home." By contrast, *Fædrelandet* was convinced that Poulsen conveyed the brutal, callous egoist behind the mask of the considerate and infatuated husband – sometimes too boldly underscored, as when "he staggers a little after returning from the ball: this makes the transition to seriousness and sorrow too intense." Herman Bang too, saw Ibsen's Helmer as an egoist, but he considered Poulsen's interpretation "excessively coarse" and hence incognizant of what Bang regarded as this character's "totally aesthetic nature." "Poulsen has wished to prepare from the outset for the brutality which is one of the determining features in Helmer's character, and which breaks out as early as the second act where, despite Nora's pleas, he sends off the letter to Krogstad." The actor would, maintained Bang (unseconded by any other critic), "have achieved much more in terms of truth and power if he had played Helmer as nobler, finer, far more elegant than at present."[4] Brandes disagreed, going so far as to assert that Emil Poulsen alone stood on a level with Ibsen's composition. However, Brandes' prediction that the shared philistine sympathy for Helmer and his ideas would cause the play to fail on the stage proved far from accurate.

Critical interpretations might conflict, but the artistic stature of the performances given by Betty Hennings and Emil Poulsen remained undisputed. Rather less effective were the characterizations of the other key figures in Nora's life-drama. As Mrs. Linde, Agnes Gjørling made little impression on the critics, while Sophus Petersen's melodramatic rendering of Krogstad convinced them that this shipwrecked sufferer was nothing more than a stock stage villain. The initial response to the presence of Doctor Rank in the play was utter bewilderment – ascribed by Brandes to Peter Jerndorff's inability "to reveal the various and eternally changing movements of mind and spirit through his rather dry, flat voice. Passion, bitterness, envy, malice were totally foreign to him," making the actor incapable of portraying "Death's certain prey, the victim of melancholy, hopeless love's bitter cripple: Dr. Rank."[5]

The first performance of a work that quite literally heralded the breakthrough of modernism in the European theatre was, perhaps inevitably, a hybrid, a transitional mixture of old and new methods. Throughout most of the nineteenth century, as we know, a director in the modern sense of the term was unknown. Hence, although the conservative and rather uninspired H. P. Holst was placed in charge of the "arrangement" of the Royal Theatre production of A Doll's House, one would search in vain for a director's script containing detailed instructions for movement, groupings, and line readings.[6] Such matters of interpretation were still, to a far greater degree than now, the sovereign responsibility of the individual actor. Accordingly, actual rehearsals were few in number: only eleven were held, including the dress rehearsal, for this important premiere. Seen in this light, the practical significance of the carefully visualized, precisely coordinated mise-en-scène which Ibsen now began to write into each of his "modern" plays becomes readily apparent.

As for the setting itself, most of its elements were simply borrowed from the earlier production of *The Pillars of Society*, which was still in the repertory. In its attempt to establish a convincingly realistic environment of solid walls, lighted lamps, and doors that shut and banged with a familiar sound, the Royal Theatre relied for the most part on the explicit and implicit directions found in the text itself. Of particular interest, therefore, are those touches presumably added by Holst and his stage-manager in an effort to deepen the desired sense of a life-like milieu. The busy bank manager's offstage study, for example, was furnished in painstaking detail: "a desk with papers, boxes, writing materials, two candlesticks (which Helmer lights in Act III), matchholder, paperweight. Above the desk a painting and a photographic portrait. Chairs and a bookcase." The hallway landing, likewise only fleetingly glimpsed by the audience, was furnished with an authenticity that would, twenty years later, be hailed as an innovation in Stanislavski's productions of Ibsen and Chekhov. In the living-room itself, a well-stocked sewing-basket and a woodbox placed beside the stoneware oven gave the actors additional opportunities to create an atmosphere of living reality on the stage. Such items as flowering plants, floral bouquets, and chairs with flowered seat-covers conveyed an air of middle-class refinement in the Helmer household. Two provocative objects commented (whether intentionally or not) on Nora's two principal functions in the marriage; on the bookcase, among sets of books in expensive bindings, stood a bust of Venus, while a reproduction of Raphael's Madonna with Child hung conspicuously in the middle of the rear wall, above the piano.

From the outset, critics responded to Ibsen's poetic use of lighting values in *A Doll's House*. The gradual transition – literal as well as figurative – from initial brightness to encroaching darkness seemed a process "as unnoticed but as certain as the work of Nature itself, when day is transformed into night" (*Dags-Telegrafen*). From the cheerful brightness of the first act, accentuated by the glittering decorations Nora hangs on the tree, the production modulated to the more somber mood of the second, underscored by such graphic details as the plundered Christmas tree, the torn and dishevelled masquerade costume, and the burnt-down candle stubs in the chandelier that hung over the middle of the room. During the intimate exchange between Nora and Doctor Rank at the very center of the play, the lights dimmed slowly until the crucial break-point in their scene ("And now you know you can confide in me as in no one else"); after it, Helene carried in the lamp at her mistress's bidding and the stage lights again brightened. In the final act, the return of the Helmers from the costume ball was illuminated only by the lights from the hallway and a small lamp on the round table (the battleground for the imminent confrontation). The atmosphere of bleakness and joylessness that affected many of the play's first reviewers in this final movement was intensified in theatrical terms by other elements as well: costume changes, as Nora lays aside her masquerade dress to reappear in "ordinary clothes with a small valise," and (live) sounds from beyond the room – music and distant voices from Consul Stenborg's party, steps heard softly on the stairs, and at last the punctuating slam of the street door below.

The actual physical staging of this influential premiere, closely tied as it was to Ibsen's own stage directions, typifies a pattern that varied little in the productions of *A Doll's House* that eventually followed elsewhere. (Even at the Royal Theatre, where the 1879 production stayed in the repertory for fully twenty-eight years, a well-acted modern revival directed by Gerda Ring in 1955 still relied to a surprising

9   A posed studio photograph of the tarantella scene in the world premiere of *A Doll's House* at the Danish Royal Theatre, Copenhagen, in 1879. Betty Hennings is Nora, Rank (Peter Jerndorff) is at the piano, and Helmer (Emil Poulsen) sets the beat, while Mrs. Linde (Agnes Gjørling) looks on.

degree on the traditional "points" and groupings established by the original *mise-en-scène*.) On the other hand, this quality of sameness has inevitably been modified by the infinite variety inherent in the character of Nora herself, to which virtually every notable actress of each succeeding generation has sought to bring a fresh approach or a new tone.

A significant variation was thus introduced almost at once by Johanne Juell, whose performance at Christiania Theatre barely a month after the Copenhagen opening (20 January 1880) brought a new sense of genuine mental anguish to Nora's frantic scene with Mrs. Linde in the second act, just before the tarantella rehearsal ("If I should lose my mind – and that could well happen"). Edvard Brandes observed that, despite the slapdash character of this production as a whole, the young Norwegian actress "showed us how madness lurked in poor Nora's confused brain, as the terrible fear crushed her spirit. One's heart beat at that moment with the same feverish haste as Nora's own."[7] Others were even more outspoken in preferring Johanne Juell to Betty Hennings, on the grounds that she seemed "the first to hold Nora's charac-

10 A sprightlier tarantella, arranged almost exactly as in the Copenhagen production for the Norwegian premiere of *A Doll's House* at Christiania Theatre in 1880. Here, Johanne Juell is Nora, Thora Neelson is the apprehensive Mrs. Linde, and Arnoldus Reimers marks time as Helmer.

ter together, so that the childish gaiety of the first act did not clash
incomprehensibly and crudely with the mature seriousness that follows the catastrophe. The admired Nora of Fru Hennings thus fell into
two parts, both equally striking in performance. But the gay little
squirrel held not the slightest hint of that Nora whose terror later
rouses her to seriousness."[8] (The problem of the role's apparent
bifurcation was, of course, by no means unique to Hennings' performance. When, for example, Beatrice Cameron undertook the part for the
first time in New York exactly ten years later, the principal and persis-
tent objection was that she "insist[ed] too strongly upon both extremes
of her character," thereby causing it to seem inconceivable "that the
weak and foolish creature of the first two acts . . . should be changed, in
the twinkling of an eye, into a self-possessed and resolute woman,
ready to fight her own way in the world rather than live in the same
house with the husband in whom she has been disappointed.")[9]

The great legendary Noras of this early period – Eleonora Duse,
Gabrielle Réjane, Vera Kommisarjevskaya, Agnes Sorma and Janet
Achurch – were all travelling stars who, in an age long before talking
films and television, brought their highly individualistic approaches to
the "problem" of Nora before mass audiences in every part of the
civilized world. The best-known and probably the most controversial
among them was Duse. Acting in a heavily cut Italian text, her restrained, quietly intense, and stubbornly anti-melodramatic interpretation of Nora seems to have caught most London critics by surprise and
disappointed their expectations when she first appeared there in 1893.
William Archer dismissed as "mere pedantry" her refusal "to give the
slightest start" when Krogstad exposes her clumsy forgery, and he
deplored the omission in her *Casa di Bambola* of such "touching" moments as Nora's scenes with Anne-Marie and with the children.[10]
Archer was satisfied, however, that at least the feverish tarantella,
hich he had always abhorred as an unnecessary concession to theatricality on Ibsen's part, was reduced by her to a quiet sequence in
which she donned a crown of roses, seized the tambourine, danced a
few tentative steps, and then sank down exhausted in a chair. Other
critics were less tolerant of Duse's method. *Truth*, no champion of
Ibsenism, objected (15 June 1893) that "she treats the play in perfectly
straightforward fashion, not as a psychological study but as a domestic
drama," while the *Times* (12 June) described her Nora as "a shallow,
flighty, morbid, neuropathic creature upon whose course of conduct it
is impossible to reckon . . . In ten minutes, when she has had time for a
change of mood, nobody would be surprised to hear her returning
cab-wheels outside." Yet this curt rejection of her final choice as mere

caprice contradicts the evidence which Archer read in Duse's hollow-eyed, ashen face as she appeared at the beginning of the last act: "One felt that Helmer must indeed have drunk an incredible quantity of champagne not to see that the shadow of death lay over this woman."[11]

What Archer saw, of course, was what Arthur Symons has described in a fine passage as a "kind of melancholy wisdom which remains in her face after the passions have swept over it." For Duse, in other words, the very expression of emotion became "all a restraint, the quieting down of a tumult until only the pained reflection of it glimmers out of her eyes, and trembles among the hollows of her cheeks."[12] In the particular case of Nora, the underlying secret she seemed always to be holding back is best described by Gunnar Heiberg, a veteran Ibsen director who understood the challenge of his countryman's plays in a usefully practical way:

Duse cut those scenes at the beginning of the play (the game under the table with the children, for example) which did not suit her purpose, and thus she obtained that consistency in the character which she was able to reveal. Behind the clouded veil of infatuation which obscured husband and home and society for her, there waited, fully formed, the mature, wholly conscious woman, needing only an inducement to break through her veil. It became profound and simple. It was a symbol of the modern woman's passage from the home out into society. She concentrated first and foremost on the ruling idea upon which Ibsen, in her estimation, had built his play.[13]

In broader terms, this performance decision on Duse's part denotes a growing emphasis on the (dramatic) action of discovery and self-discovery in *A Doll's House*, and a corresponding de-emphasis of the (essentially novelistic) process of character "development" that literary critics, then as now, have so persistently stressed in this play. In the German Noras of Sorma and Irene Triesch, this sense of the outcome as a foregone conclusion reached more emphatic proportions. Triesch, who played Nora in Otto Brahm's distinguished company, introduced what Alfred Polgar calls in his first-hand account of the Lessing Theatre's performances "a peculiar change in tragic emphasis." This Nora, Polgar records with evident surprise, embodied from the very outset the maturity and self-awareness revealed by her at the end of the play. "With her, the dramatic development seems to be not a process of growth and maturation, but rather one of release from a latent, already existing condition; not an evolution but an awakening of a human being from a strange bondage." Hence the "happy" Nora of the first act seemed to this observer "not someone playing a carefree game, but a sleepwalker dancing on the edge of an abyss."[14]

This darker reading was in turn foreshadowed by Agnes Sorma's renowned interpretation of Nora, which she first created for Brahm at the Deutsches Theater in Berlin in 1894. By fusing the lightness and the strength in the character, Sorma seemed "the first to heal the Nora split," Siegfried Jacobsohn observed. "Her personality, which on the surface was all teasing and trills and flirtatiousness, revealed an undertone of such force that the mistake of her marriage, like its inexorably sudden end, became clear."[15] "Die Sorma's" electrifying performance colored the final, inevitable clash with Helmer with a savage, even Strindbergian tinge of satisfaction. "That love which turns to hatred, that antagonism toward the man which underlies every sexual relationship, that blood-lust which arises out of every struggle to be the stronger – all this was brought together in Sorma to become *contempt*," Gunnar Heiberg wrote of a touring performance she gave in Brussels in 1900. As the moment of the confrontation approached and Helmer eagerly incinerated the incriminating documents returned by Krogstad, Sorma's Nora stood quietly in the background, watching disdainfully. As her husband, "small and human, grovelled in his miserable joy and happiness and relief in the foreground," her ominous presence seemed to Heiberg "like the goddess of contempt on a giant pedestal":

Her hostile eyes follow him, her head gives a quick backward jerk to avoid smelling him, her wonderful mouth twists itself into a distorted smile – formed like an arch, with the corners of the mouth drawn far, far down.[16]

If such a moment of pent-up fury might seem somehow less unexpected in, say, the Allmers' home than in the ostensibly tamer Helmer household, we may want to remember that Sorma's Nora was indeed a kind of prelude to her robust and disturbing portrayal of Rita Allmers in the world premiere of *Little Eyolf* at the Deutsches Theater the following year (12 January 1895). It is even more interesting that this same confluence can be observed in the career of one of Sorma's greatest rivals, Janet Achurch, whose early Nora introduced Ibsen to the scandalized English theatre public in 1889. Gradually, however, Achurch's subsequent reappearances in the part during the nineties drew a darker, more troubled portrait of "the reckless child-wife" and "the macaroon-munching doll" she had begun by playing in Charles Charrington's first, pioneering production at the Novelty Theatre in London. Some critics, among them William Archer and George Bernard Shaw, regretted the change. Archer protested in 1892, after the Charringtons had returned from their world tour with *A Doll's House*, that the actress no longer depicted the sudden emergence of a new woman in the final act, but instead "shows us the old Nora in a resentful, argumentative humour."[17] Shaw took this argument further in 1897, objecting that Achurch's mature Nora had lost her previous "wonderful *naiveté*" and could "no longer content herself with a girl's allowance of passion and sympathy. She fills the cup and drains it ..."[18] In fact, the real essence of the change seems to have been the new vehemence and "impetuous, ungovernable strength" which Shaw himself, scarcely six months earlier, had lavishly praised in Achurch's portrayal of Rita Allmers in *Little Eyolf* – a richly faceted performance in which "her face was sometimes winsome, sometimes listlessly wretched, sometimes like the head of a statue of Victory, sometimes suffused, horrible, threatening, like Bellona or Medusa."[19] Thus, the marital clash of Nora and Torvald acquired, in her later performances, something of the same passionate anger and bitterness Achurch brought to the tortured relationship of Rita and Alfred Allmers. As described by Clement Scott in the *Daily Telegraph* (11 May 1897), her discussion scene opposite Courtenay Thorpe (who had also played Alfred to her Rita) seems strikingly akin to Sorma's intense "Strindbergian" rendering of this same moment: "The danger removed, cowardice disappeared and the egotist asserted himself once more. It left the man, however, not only weak, whimpering, and demoralized, but old, wretched, and scarred with the fury of that mental tempest," writes this otherwise implacable Ibsen antagonist. "The acting was so good that, if we may express it so, the man becomes the hysterical woman, and the woman becomes the silent, sullen, and determined man."

Other influential Noras of the Yellow Decade approached the challenge by entirely different paths. Coaxed out of early retirement to play Nora for a single benefit performance in 1894, the erstwhile comedienne Minnie Maddern, now the wife of Harrison Grey Fiske, gave Ibsen his first unequivocal success in the New York theatre. The ubiquitous Courtenay Thorpe, whom New Yorkers had seen as Osvald in *Ghosts* only a month before, also reappeared in this production as Helmer, but the undivided focus of attention was Mrs. Fiske's "new" acting. Her unexpectedly subdued mode of psychological naturalism, animated by what Lewis Strang felicitously termed "the inherent force of suppression," seemed to break fresh ground.[20] Enthusiastic critics compared her style to that of Eleonora Duse, who had made an American tour the previous year, but this idea was hotly disputed by her husband's *Dramatic Mirror*, which insisted that she "had adopted the method of 'underacting' before the great Italian actress appeared here." Unlike earlier American attempts at *A Doll's House*, the carefully prepared Fiske production approached Ibsen's text with studious

fidelity. Here and in her many subsequent Ibsen revivals, this redoubtable actress–director, a woman who had never finished high school,
championed a performance method based, above all, on an analytical
understanding of the dramaturgical design of a given work. "Ibsen's
plays have proved failures in some instances because stage managers
will not devote sufficient time to their study and preparation," she
liked to observe. "Ibsen shows us only the last hours. To portray them I
must know everything that has gone before. Ibsen makes that necessary, and provides the keys that unlock the past."[21]

The assimilation of Ibsen into the American repertory was, however,
not a process to be hurried. On her first extended road tour with *A
Doll's House* in 1895–6, Mrs. Fiske soon found that her efforts on behalf
of Ibsen's play were met by no small measure of confusion on the part
of the broad North American public she hoped to attract. In Pittsburgh,
the discussion scene, the final slam of the street door, and even the fall
of the curtain apparently made so little impression that at last the
stage-manager had to be sent out to assure the audience that the play
was over. Across the border in Toronto, the skeptical reporter for *The
Daily Mail and Empire* (22 February 1896) pointed out that James Neill,
Mrs. Fiske's road-company Helmer, depicted "such a pronounced
cad" that the real puzzle of "this absurdly over-drawn tale of 'domestic
infelicity'" became "how any woman, with the latent capacity for
unpleasant analytical discovery which Nora possessed, could ever
have married such a man."

To be fair, sophisticated Parisian audiences were no less befuddled
when the play at last reached them at the Théâtre Vaudeville on 20
April 1894, some two months after Mrs. Fiske's auspicious Ibsen debut
in New York. Gabrielle Réjane's performance as Nora gave the playwright his first, eagerly awaited boulevard-theatre success. Even the
caustic Sarcey, who found the play's outcome illogical and saw "only
expressions of dismay" on the faces of the audience at the end, was
nevertheless inclined to concede that the play was, in other respects,
Ibsen's best, "ingeniously constructed, full of pleasing details."[22] As
usual, all attention was centered on the character of Nora. Réjane,
already the toast of the French capital before this new triumph, was an
actress equally at home in comedy and social drama – no doubt the
reason why she was tempted by *A Doll's House*, which looks deceptive-
ly like both, though it is in fact neither. The astute manager Paul Porel,
anxious to lend his Vaudeville production an authentic Scandinavian
flavor, called in Herman Bang to direct it, and Bang's memoirs provide
us in turn with a vivid description of the event.

Although only indirect mention is made of Betty Hennings in his account of the Paris production, the vivacious Réjane's approach to the role of Nora clearly showed Bang the sharpest possible contrast to the performance he had followed so closely in Copenhagen, fifteen years before. Not the least of the differences lay in the piquant erotic fascination exerted by the French star, whose pliable features could, Bang says, "express everything except that which is modest." Fresh from one of her greatest successes as Madame Sans-Gêne, Réjane transferred, as it were, the robust spirit of Sardou's pert, saucy washerwoman to Ibsen's heroine – a spirit of personal rebelliousness that became one of the twin pillars of her distinctive attack. The end result was neither Sorma's bitter hostility toward Helmer nor Duse's elegiac tone of loss and regret. "For Réjane," Bang writes, "the play became a work about revolt":

In the atmosphere of a foreign world and a foreign play, she revolted against her husband, her fate, against love, and against herself. And here she could be victorious: Nora left Helmer and all his household, and she left unbroken and as the greater of the two. In this leave-taking scene, she went as someone who has finally thrown off her own shackles and freed herself.[23]

This revolt was prepared for and counterbalanced by the acute, sustained sense of fear that Réjane made the other supporting pillar of her interpretation, and which she fueled with all of her own enormous nervous energy. Duse had declined "to give the slightest start" at Krogstad's entrance, and the young Janet Achurch had shown the intruder only "youthfully unsympathetic contempt," certain that "his effort to make a serious business of the forgery was mere vulgarity."[24] Unlike these contemporaries, Réjane was struck with abject terror at the moneylender's first appearance. "This state of fear was established by her at once," Bang records, "and she allowed it to build into wild confusion, until it stiffened into inert numbness. In her hands, *A Doll's House* became, for an hour on end, a drama about fear."[25]

Sarcey protested that Nora appeared altogether too afraid, "terrorized out of all proportion to the reality of the situation," but this obstinate opponent's objection reveals less about Réjane's acting and more about the curiously wrong-headed conception of the play that he shared with more than a few of his (male) colleagues in the literary establishment:

And we all say to ourselves, in Paris at any rate: Why is Nora so upset about so small a thing? She has only to explain the matter to her husband . . . She cries, she throws herself in his arms, but she does not say to him the one thing she should say, which we are all waiting to hear: "I was wrong, but it was for you that I compromised myself, to save your life, and I did save it" . . . Helmer would be the last person to bear a grudge for her imprudence, since it was to save his life that this imprudent act has been committed.[26]

Others expressed their bias more freely. "A naive nature, a sophistic temperament, and a perverse heart are characteristic of Scandinavian women," Edmond de Goncourt recorded in his *Journal*, while Ernest Tissot (in *Le Drame norvégien*) agreed that "a kind of intellectual hysteria has crept into their heads, so poorly equipped for serious thinking."[27] Even the foolishness which Archer compiled from the British press in his "Mausoleum of Ibsen" (1894) pales by comparison with such Gallic *hauteur*.

The Russian theatre had its first, somewhat belated chance to see a major actress play Nora when Vera Kommisarjevskaya opened her new theatre in St. Petersburg with *A Doll's House* on 17 September 1904, by which date revolution, theatrical as well as political, was already at hand. Yet, representative though she was of the "grand" tradition of Duse and Réjane, Kommisarjevskaya's line of attack was anything but derivative or old-fashioned. As one of the important innovators of the pre-revolutionary theatre in Russia, she rejected the mere reproduction of everyday reality by the actor, calling it "uninteresting and unnecessary" and insisting that it "must disappear from the stage."[28] At forty, this keen admirer of Ibsen's plays knew her material well, and her Nora was a skillful fretwork of suggestive nuances and half-tones. She emulated Réjane's compulsive sense of fear in the role, but balanced this sense with an ecstatic expectancy that the miracle of miracles would surely occur. "She is totally consumed by demented fear of the impending consequences, by agonizing anxiety – yet at the same time she is filled with the joyous expectation that 'the most wonderful thing' may take place at any time – the proof of Torvald's boundless love for her." As such, this same observer continues, her frenzied tarantella became the pivotal point in her performance: "In it lay everything: her decision to die, her farewell to life and her beloved Torvald, trembling hope and inward struggle."[29]

The most clearly modern aspect of Kommisarjevskaya's characterization was perhaps the impressionistic manner in which she prepared the ground for Nora's so-called transformation. Beneath her carefree games with her three children and her own child-like trust in Torvald's affection ran an undercurrent of dissatisfaction and dislocation, hinting at the presence of a woman with as yet untapped inner resources, capable of making a decisive, uncompromising break with her past. The memoirs of Aleksandra Bruštejn, first released in 1956, paint a fascinating retrospective picture of the gradual process by which this actress sought to disclose her Nora's inner life:

Even in the first act, which almost to the end is without shadows for Nora, Kommisarjevskaya would shut herself off for a fraction of a second from her surroundings. In the midst of the laughter, the teasing, the games and noise with the children, her eyes turned inward on something agonizing, something oppressive. Then, with her familiar gesture, she drew her fingers across her forehead as if to brush away something unpleasant, something insistent – a fly, a cobweb – and Nora was once again happy and gay. But gradually the spectator began to understand: this woman is only tangentially happy, only tangentially gay. She lives two lives – one visible, the other hidden. In her visible life, the Nora of Kommisarjevskaya remained unchanged – the action takes only forty-eight hours – but in her hidden life she grows, acquires courage, and begins to grasp what she has never before understood.[30]

To make manifest the inner, spiritual life of the play and the character, Vsevolod Meyerhold would argue that one must remake the theatre, remorselessly eliminating all the realistic paraphernalia and Stanislavski-inspired verisimilitude with which Kommisarjevskaya's 1904 production of A Doll's House remained burdened. The actress's momentous decision to hire Meyerhold for her theatre in 1906 proved to be the contribution to the modern theatre for which she is chiefly remembered now. The first and best-known result of this brief collaboration was the young director's daringly experimental staging of Hedda Gabler, featuring Kommisarjevskaya in the title role. Barely a month afterward (18 December 1906), Meyerhold's radical revision of Kommisarjevskaya's earlier mise-en-scène for A Doll's House again startled the traditionalists. His chief concern in this production was not with the fortuitous social or psychological aspects of Nora's personal plight, but instead with the governing inner rhythm and spirit of the work itself. The aim of Meyerhold's Symbolical Theatre was to create a charged, allusive image of this spirit on the stage, rather than an allegedly exact and complete reproduction of life. "The urge to show everything, come what may, the fear of mystery, of leaving anything unsaid, turns the theatre into a mere illustration of the author's words," he declared in his first important manifesto from this period.[31]

Hence Kommisarjevskaya's realistic Norwegian interior, intended to create a believable stage environment in the spirit of the Moscow Art Theatre, was discarded and replaced by a stylized set stripped to the bare essentials. "In place of the lovely, soft furnishings that so credibly represented the doll-wife's warm nest, we are instead shown a cramped corridor passageway with a decrepit piano in one corner," wrote a disgruntled critic in Teatr i iskusstvo (Theatre and Art, 1906/52). An equally dilapidated three-legged table, two inconspicuous chairs, an arbitrarily suspended window flanked by ballooning, and cranberry-colored drapes that reached the full height of the stage completed the iconography of the doll's house. This, the same reviewer added tartly, "was evidently meant to represent a 'stylization' of the cozy atmosphere so often talked about in the play."

Others, however, were quicker to recognize that the iconoclast's innovation was reflected positively in the individual performances and "in fact liberated the actors from the false and debilitating conventions of the old theatre."[32] The basis of Meyerhold's leveraged strategy was his conviction that a bridge must be built between the actor and the spectator, whose engaged imagination is able and willing to supply that which is left unfinished or unsaid. Accordingly, for example, Kommisarjevskaya's tarantella – the crucial moment in Meyerhold's interpretation, toward and away from which Nora's life-dance moved – became, in the director's own words, "no more than a series of expressive poses during which the feet simply tapped out a nervous rhythm. If you watched only the feet, it looked more like running than dancing." How, he asks us rhetorically, would the spectator be affected if instead "a naturalistic actress trained by a dancing-master ceases to act and conscientiously shows every step of the Tarantella?" Far less profoundly, he would contend, than by a situation in which room is left "for the play of allusion," for "conscious understatement," and for "the power of suggestion" to do its work.[33]

At this late date in her career, Kommisarjevskaya was ultimately unprepared to embrace the views of this bold theatre reformer. The Ibsen productions in particular contributed to the breach that occurred in the wake of the long letter of stock-taking she wrote to Meyerhold in the summer of 1907.[34] "Every word in Ibsen's stage directions represents a clear light along the road to an understanding of his works," she objected. Meyerhold's production of Love's Comedy, in which she had played Svanhild, had, she agreed, "united the principles of the 'old' theatre with the principles of the marionette theatre" which she felt he stood for – but A Doll's House was an entirely different matter. Here, she insisted (exactly as the conservative Theatre and Art had insisted), "a very warm, cozy, and pleasant nest, isolated from the real world, must be created . . . We will change the color and texture of the materials. We will lay a new carpet (so the sound of steps is not heard). We will replace the chairs with something comfortable and low. From one side a red glow from the fireplace must be seen in the last act, so Linde and Krogstad are not obliged to play their scene by moonlight." From this passage one gains a sense of the chilling coldness Meyerhold (in deliberate contradiction of what the characters say) imparted to the Helmer household – as well as a strong impression of the letter-writer's inability to grasp the point of Meyerhold's anti-literalistic approach.

They soon parted ways, and Meyerhold moved on to other theatres in his ceaseless search for new theatrical solutions. In 1908, two years before her death, Kommisarjevskaya repeated her remarkable performance as Nora at Daly's Theatre in New York City, but the event made scarcely any impact on what Oliver Sayler called the "smug insularity" of American audiences at the time.[35] With Meyerhold's anti-naturalistic production of *A Doll's House*, however, the play was transported from the nineteenth century into the twentieth, from the fast-fading age of the actor-virtuoso into a new era of stylistic innovation dominated by the figure of the director.

NEW DIRECTIONS AND DIRECTORS

Charrington had directed and coached Achurch, of course; Bang had directed Réjane, Brahm had directed Sorma – and H. P. Holst had even "directed" Betty Hennings, if we care to stretch the point. For Craig, Reinhardt, Meyerhold, and the other major figures in the theatrical revolution that came to be known as the New Stagecraft, however, the director's function had a very different kind of significance. As early as 1906, Meyerhold had singled out Ibsen as a playwright whose works face a director with particularly serious pitfalls. The conventional director, he argues, tends to approach Ibsen's plays intent upon "enlivening" them and bringing out their meaning by indiscriminately embroidering on the life-likeness of every detail in them. Prominence is thereby given to even the most insignificant nuances and the most "secondary, parenthetic scenes," as Meyerhold calls them, with the inevitable result that the audience loses sight of the essentials and the leitmotif becomes obscured "because the director has placed it in a distracting frame." For, Meyerhold goes on to stress, "*the truth is that the sum of the meaning of the parenthetic scenes does not add up to the meaning of the whole play.*" Instead, a single decisive moment, emphatically presented, "decides the fate of the act in the mind of the audience, even though everything else slips past as though in a fog."[36] In other words, without a dynamic, virtually musical scoring of the dramatic text by the director-interpreter, the essence of Ibsen is lost in a plethora of detail, he would contend.

In 1922, at the height of his productivity and celebrity, Meyerhold again put his ideas about Ibsen to the test in a new, hastily improvised production of *A Doll's House* at the Nezlobin Theatre in Moscow. Rushed on to the stage in a matter of only five days, the extraordinary directorial impromptu epitomized "the undressing of the theatre" that came to be characteristic of this director's increasingly de-aestheticized style. Five of Meyerhold's pupils, among them Sergei Eisenstein, assembled a setting (if it could be called such) consisting of old flats propped back to front against the bare walls of the stage, some gridiron bars, and an odd assortment of old furniture, chests, and the like placed to create playing areas for the actors. The resultant visual chaos "gave the impression that everything was collapsing, everything was going to the devil, down and out," Eisenstein recalls. "Against this background the phrase of the self-satisfied bourgeois, Helmer: 'It's nice here, Nora, cozy,' could not but evoke a tempestuous reaction from the auditorium."[37] The constructivist stage arrangement thus literally bespoke – or so Meyerhold claimed – the disintegrating bourgeois milieu against which Nora rebels and which she ultimately leaves behind for "a life of work." In the nineteenth century, bowdlerized adaptations of A Doll's House had modified the "unpleasantness" of Nora's abandonment of her children in various ways. In Thora, the unpublished English-language script acted by Helena Modjeska in Louisville in 1883, there had been "a reunion, a running together, and a falling curtain on a happy family scene."[38] In the more tough-minded version prepared by Ibsen himself for Hedwig Niemann-Raabe's performances in Berlin and other German cities in 1880, Nora is forced by Helmer to the door of the children's bedroom; brutally informed by her husband that the children are now motherless "as you have been," she sinks helplessly to the floor beside the doorway as the curtain comes down. In Meyerhold's polemical Bolshevist "quotation" of Ibsen's text, an even more unexpected approach to the play's unsettling conclusion was adopted: when the Nora of the Nezlobin production deserted Torvald and his crumbling bourgeois world, she quite simply took the children with her!

If the controlled, presentational style of Meyerhold's actors, clad in their blue canvas working clothes, marks one end of a spectrum of performance choices, the opposite end of such a spectrum is represented by the wide-eyed, broad-gauge melodramatics of Alla Nazimova and Alan Hale in their 1922 screen version of A Doll's House – actually the fifth silent film of the play to be made in the U.S. Occupying a discreet middle ground between these polar opposites, the quietly "realistic" productions of this period (and long after) persisted in representing the play's suffocating bourgeois milieu of prejudice and hypocrisy as a rotogravure image of life, rather than a dramatic metaphor for the "despair, spiritual conflict, and defeat" Ibsen describes in the memorandum he entitled "Notes for a Modern Tragedy." In an interview given by Janet Achurch to the Pall Mall

Gazette before leaving on her Australian tour in 1889, this actress seems to have perceived Nora as a living contemporary rather than as a dramatic character, speaking of her life with Helmer as an "experiment of living" that they would no doubt try again sometime, and extolling the play as a salutary warning that should make women "much less reckless about marrying."[39] Still presented *au pied de la lettre* a generation later, it seems hardly a wonder that the play should strike a reviewer in 1921 as "a mere curiosity" in the theatre, so outdated that "you can feel nothing but a detached interest in it as a great piece of drama that was once something like life" (*Daily Telegraph*, 11 July 1921). Five seasons later, even the otherwise highly regarded performance by Madge Titheradge at the Playhouse caused the *Times* (10 January 1926) to dismiss the play itself as nothing more than "a melodrama written by a man of genius in his spare time."

In an effort to make Ibsen's modern tragedy seem more "like life," productions of *A Doll's House* in the twenties and thirties had begun to resort to modern dress – creating in the process a self-contradictory hybrid that inevitably defeated its own purpose. When Muriel Pratt, the star of the 1921 revival at the Everyman Theatre, played Nora "in her own bobbed hair and one of those knitted frocks that people never wore till lately," the *Observer* (12 July 1921) found the experiment "very disconcerting, for never would a modern woman submit to Helmer's orintological endearments. Thus, never for a moment does Miss Pratt become Nora; she merely impersonates her." At Dramaten in 1925, when she was nearly fifty, even the great Harriet Bosse created a Nora who was something of a flapper. At Oslo's New Theatre in 1929, however, Agnes Mowinckel's estimable revival attempted to modify the new, modern-dress strategy by incorporating "furniture and costumes from the past fifty years, presumably to avoid a 'historical' production and yet at the same time establish an atmosphere which emphasized the fact that the play does not take place in our own day." However interesting the idea, Kristian Elster nevertheless found the result "a little confusing" – not least because "every little scene was so over-embroidered" that the play's action became lost (as Meyerhold had foreseen) in the unselective and time-consuming elaboration of circumstantial details and misplaced emphases.[40]

By 1936, faced with a new, impressively cast Copenhagen production of *A Doll's House* set in "a handsome modern room in which the characters walked about like everyday modern people, each with impeccably natural behavior ... resembling perfectly ordinary individuals who had just come in from the street," Frederik Schyberg declared "once and for all: Ibsen's plays – and most of all naturally his

11   Sven Bergwall (Helmer) confronts Harriet Bosse (Nora) in a modernized
rendering of *A Doll's House* at the Royal Dramatic Theatre in Stockholm in
1925.

'problem plays' – can no longer be performed in modern dress."
Schyberg's arguments seem to present a paradoxical contrast to his
influential, staunchly anti-traditionalist reassessment of *Peer Gynt*. If *A
Doll's House* is to be rescued from perceived obsolescence, he insists, "it
must be presented as a picture from the period (and an image of the
period) – and it is so well constructed, so strong in its theatrical
temperament, that it would surely then work with redoubled force,
because the 'historical' premises have been provided for and the audience is not duped – and it has been here." Otherwise, when the
characters pretend to be our contemporaries, the clash between their
nineteenth-century manners and attitudes and their twentieth-
century costumes erects a barrier to our sympathetic understanding of
them (a barrier of which Meyerhold, of course, would heartily
approve). In the "modernized" 1936 production at Folketeatret, Else
Skouboe's sparkling and witty Nora none the less seemed to Schyberg
"a modern young woman wrestling in full seriousness with problems
and ideas that have been talked out by everyone else almost two
generations ago. In this manner *A Doll's House* became antiquated
theatre, whereas the solution had been to make it historical theatre."[41]

In London, just days before the Danish production at Folketeatret, a
new revival demonstrated the continued dominance here of "the
dingy parlours hung with penitential gloom" that James Agate so
deplored in English Ibsen performances. For this production at the
Criterion, praised mainly for Lydia Lopokova's convincing delineation
of a Nora already conscious of her own nagging unhappiness from the
outset, Motley designed a particularly ponderous reproduction of the
accepted Ibsen drawing-room. Endowed though it was with "an amazing fidelity to period," the hideous room's "stuffiness" overpowered
the characters on the stage.[42] Three years later, a fresh attempt
mounted by Marius Goring at the Duke of York's was no more fortunate in its efforts to update the play's physical milieu. Although the
dingy parlor was now given the full benefit of the interior decorator's
skill, Agate still had only scorn for "the amazing architecture of Torvald's summer palace" – a new-made bank manager's dream of elegance, which appeared "to be on the ground floor of Park Lane's latest
and most luxurious block of flats."[43]

Both these opposed stylistic alternatives were, in fact, equally at
odds with the "historical" approach advocated by Schyberg – an
approach that should permit the audience to view the work through
the prism of the age in which it was written, by incorporating a critical
perception of its "period" environment rather than erecting a
museum-like replica of some quaintly cluttered Victorian parlor. In

Halvdan Christensen's acclaimed revival at Nationaltheatret in Oslo (likewise in 1936), Schyberg found, quite unexpectedly, what he had been looking for. "The production is a victory for *A Doll's House*, but the victory has broader implications for the production of all of Ibsen's best plays," the Danish critic wrote. "Paradoxical as it may sound, when they are performed in historical costumes – and first then – they are lifted above all dependancy on period."[44]

Christensen (who as a young actor had been Helmer to the legendary Johanne Dybwad's Nora almost three decades earlier) both drew upon and commented on tradition by framing the action in a "felicitous and witty physical arrangement from the eighties – the palm in the window, the green upholstered mahogany furniture, the pompus white tile stove standing on the floor, and the hallway with its huge panes of glass looking out on one of those hopelessly 'elegant' staircases fróm the eighties." Within this recognizable yet subtly ironic pictòrial frame, Christensen's *mise-en-scène* orchestrated "every word and every gesture" to support his conceptual image of the play as "*the marriage trial* between two human beings and the outcome that trial can have when one of the two has usurped a position of dominance over the other." Unlike the "one-woman show" which the play had often become in the past, this production stressed a balanced ensemble of interlocking forces, thereby sustaining "a dramatic tension that discharged electricity through all three acts of the play, a dramatic tension that sprang like one spark upon the next, from scene to scene and from character to character," until at last "the play seemed a red-hot oven that sent its scalding heat pouring out over the auditorium."[45]

Regardless of how strong and cohesive the ensemble work in a given production may be, however, the stageworthiness of this utterly centripetal play hinges relentlessly on the figure of Nora herself, upon whom all the interlocking forces of the drama converge. Tore Segelcke, the mid-point in Christensen's ensemble at Nationaltheatret, emerged as one of the preeminent Noras of the new generation that followed Duse and her famous contemporaries. Hers was a thoroughly, fiercely modern portrayal of a distraught, self-dispossessed human being whose "eerie gaiety" in the first act gave unmistakable warning of the angry rebelliousness and bitter disappointment that were to follow. Her tarantella became "the outburst of a temperament rendered unbalanced and rebellious by her sense of aloneness in a sexual charade she had, down deep, always regarded as degrading." From the very beginning, Kristian Elster continues in his vivid account of Segelcke's Nora, her "gaiety" had an uneasy, overwrought quality about it:

The lark that twittered and the squirrel that scampered seemed filled with tension and fear – not fear of discovery as such, for there is something splendidly courageous about Fru Segelcke's Nora; she is to the depths of her soul a revolutionary. But she fears the wonderful thing that is to happen, but which mustn't happen for anything in the world.

In Kommisarjevskaya's performances, for example, this miracle of miracles was for Nora a source of joyous expectation; in Segelcke's reading, however, it became an obsessive illusion which "she has created for herself so she could live," and which she recognized for what it is:

For in reality she has seen through Helmer and herself and her doll-marriage long ago, and she clings in desperation to this dream of the wonderful thing. She has thought it for a long time, but now she says it: "For then I realized you weren't the man I had imagined." This is Nora, the woman who will not go on living her life on illusions and with a man she despises.[46]

Like her equally famous portrayal of Abbie in O'Neill's *Desire Under the Elms*, Segelcke's youthful Nora endowed the role with a robust, sensuous, but painfully vulnerable humanity. (When she reappeared in the play opposite a much younger Helmer twelve years later, the vulnerability became even more poignant.) The final reckoning with Helmer did not come as a proclamation of women's rights or even of a woman's rights; it was instead, Elster writes, simply "a woman's words to the man who has disappointed her expectations." She "speaks all these strange words with difficulty, searching for them, with full if slow deliberation," adds Schyberg's review, which describes her as "a splintered human being in spiritual panic who must leave house and home to regain control of herself and piece together the bits and shreds of her being in a new form, which she and we must then hope will be herself." It is Agne Beijer, however, who has left us the most sensitive description of this performance, which the great theatre historian saw on tour at Dramaten in 1939:

The basis of Tore Segelcke's Nora was her childish credulity. And, after the great betrayal when the miracle she expects does not happen, it was this childish credulity which causes her to grasp for a new illusion – belief in her own ability, single-handedly and in the face of difficulties of an entirely different order, to make something of life. In the final scene, when Tore Segelcke sits there searching for words and comes up with the famous slogans about her duty toward herself and all the rest of it that we can practically recite by heart, it is by no means an all-embracing program manifesto she embodies. Rather, she is a desperate human being who grasps at a straw, but who is

12   Nora's leave-taking as played by Liv Ullmann at Det Norske Teatret,
Oslo, in 1974.

enough of a child to believe that a human being can be saved by a straw, exactly as she was enough of a child before to believe that any judge would have to acquit her of forgery once he heard that she had done it to save her husband's life.

But this child-like quality of Fru Segelcke's was not merely the key to a psychological puzzle, it was also, above all, a natural mode of behavior, a touch of the gay and poignant teenage girlishness that still remains in the grown woman, the charm of which defied resistance. In the face of this charm, all the arguments Strindberg has armed us with about the dishonesty of Ibsen's reasoning collapse.[47]

The relationship between the interpretations of Tore Segelcke and Liv Ullmann, probably the two foremost Norwegian Noras of recent times, is quite striking. In her touring production with Det Norske Teatret in 1974, Ullmann's version of the role projected a sense of unfelt gaiety and painful self-awareness that might well call up associations with the Segelcke "tradition." Yet the change of emphasis was distinct and typical of a broader shift in outlook. Continually "on the edge of the abyss," Ullmann's Nora "*acts* her roles as the carefree wife and mother, as the coquette, the girlfriend, and the banker's fashionable wife," observed Inger Heiberg in *Stavanger Aftenblad* (1 April 1974). "But she knows exactly what is going on, never managing for even an instant to lie to herself or to us. The terror grows within her like a cancer, and never for one moment does she believe that her Helmer is capable of anything remotely 'wonderful.'" The implied question posed by Ullmann's approach was not why Nora leaves or what will eventually become of her, but rather how she could have endured this empty charade so long. In this bleak rendering of Nora's leave-taking, there was not even the ray of hopefulness suggested by Segelcke's performance. "No life in which she can develop awaits her, for she is already fully developed in the first scene," continued the Stavanger reviewer. "The insane asylum awaits her just as it had awaited Laura Kieler" – the woman often cited as Ibsen's model for the character of Nora. In her final encounter with Helmer there was no searching or hesitation, yet neither was there any evidence of the affirmative "discussion scene" that Shaw had seen as the crux of the play's modernity. "For when the confrontation casts her to the floor, she does not abruptly awake to see her husband as he really is," observed another critic. Instead, what she did seem to see was "the ridiculous and contemptible, the futile and degrading" in their mutual deception. "It is with the utmost exertion of will that she orders herself 'to find out whether society is right, or I am.' She fights a final battle to rid herself of the wedding band, struggles for the last time to free herself from her

13 A vivid impression of Jürgen Rose's set for the neo-naturalistic revival of *A Doll's House* directed by Rudolf Noelte at the Renaissance-Theater in Berlin in 1976. Helmer (Werner Kreindl), seated with his papers in the first act, seems at the greatest possible distance from Nora (Cordula Trantow) and her concerns.

husband's embrace ... There is not the slightest doubt or uncertainty about her leaving, let alone any hint of 'defeat.' But neither is there the slightest hope of a possible continuation or resumption of these Ibsenian 'scenes from a marriage.' "[48] This last allusion was in its way prophetic: exactly seven years later, Ingmar Bergman's startling reinterpretation of the play would crystallize and clarify the essential tendency already present in Ullmann's performance – which, in turn, drew its strength from the century-long acting tradition that viewed the play as a drama of outcome, undividedly focused on Nora's existential struggle for survival.

THE VICTORIAN PARLOR DISMANTLED

As even a casual theatre-goer will realize, the use of a more or less lightly stylized but substantially "museological" Victorian parlor set has remained the rule for revivals of A Doll's House, even in our own time. The tangible specificity of the "tastefully but not expensively furnished living-room" described in the stage directions has been moderated at times, but rarely abandoned altogether. In, for instance, Patrick Garland's scrupulously low-key, matter-of-fact London production at the Criterion in 1973, with Claire Bloom and Colin Blakely in the principal roles, the softly lighted parlor designed by John Bury sought to avoid what Plays and Players described as "the usual claustrophobic gloom of Nordic nights" by providing a more attractive living space "awash with wintry lights and lamps and rather giddy preparation."[49] A quite different but analogous example of cautiously modified realism was Arne Walentin's setting for the Ullmann performance at Det Norske Teatret the following year. Here, Walentin's design was a far cry from the clean, non-representational lines of his revolutionary Peer Gynt. It provided the Helmers with a rather drab period parlor, enclosed by rose-colored, flower-patterned walls evidently intended to suggest a Willy Lomanesque dimension of dream, illusion, and escapism. Yet even such exceedingly modest touches of covert symbolism seem radical when compared to, say, the massive hyper-reality of the authentic interior erected to house Rudolf Noelte's impressive revival at the Renaissance-Theater in Berlin in 1976. Jürgen Rose's stage design for this production reproduced a reality of material objects that faithfully reflected Noelte's own staunch belief in the importance of a recognizable environment in the performance of Ibsen's prose plays.

Some would contend, meanwhile, that it is just such an allegiance to material reality – indisputably rooted though it may be in Ibsen's own conception of theatre – that confines and ultimately reduces a work whose vision extends far beyond the realistic or the social plane. "The disservice that the drawing-room, teacups, wallpaper productions do to Ibsen is that the drama becomes invisible. It gets lost in the teacups and the 'pass the butter' and so on," argues Michael Zelenak, founder of the American Ibsen Theatre.[50] This semi-professional summer repertory company launched its first season in 1983 with a bold stylization of *A Doll's House* that assertively rejected both the drawing-room stage and the politely restrained "underplaying" that traditionally goes with it (not least in the North American theatre). At least two decades before this venturesome group started showing its Pittsburgh audiences a "new" Ibsen, however, European directors and designers had begun in earnest to challenge the conventional approach whose outward sign was the museum-like reproduction of a quaintly cluttered Victorian parlor. With his first production of *Hedda Gabler* at Dramaten in 1964, Ingmar Bergman literally changed the perception of Ibsen's prose plays in the theatre, by showing how effectively the dusty impedimenta of accumulated tradition could be swept aside. In a similarly revolutionary spirit, the German director Peter Zadek took the hammer to assorted icons in his widely praised reinterpretation of *A Doll's House*, presented three seasons later at the intimate Bremer Kammerspiele.

In some respects, the Bremen production recalled the tersely selective, suggestive style advocated by Meyerhold at the beginning of the century. Zadek and his designer Guy Sheppard created a stage space that was hardly a room or even a "setting" at all – a door on either side, a veranda window as background, an old-fashioned sofa at the diagonal mid-point of the stage, and virtually nothing more. As a result, observed *Bremer Nachrichten* (24 February 1967), "the play is removed from Ibsen's cozy . . . middle-class parlor. The characters are put on display. What is left when they have been stripped of their coziness is what the director shows us. A remorselessly harsh surgical operation, aimed at everything that creates atmosphere – Christmas tree, piano, children – and exists only for decoration." Zadek's version laid bare the inner essence of a work that is "not about women's liberation . . . but about the relationships of human beings to one another," commented Reimar Hollmann in *Süddeutsche Zeitung* (28 February). "What happens on the stage is emphasized; all else, like the trappings of a naturalistic novel, has been remorselessly cut away" – leaving, this critic continued, "the naive psychology and the frequently banal verbal exchanges ruthlessly exposed."

Like Meyerhold, Zadek adopted a critical attitude toward the play that openly questioned its underlying social assumptions. For this director, the key to A Doll's House was not Nora's "transformation" but the awakening of her social consciousness, marked by her realization in the last scene that society can and must be changed. Drawing on a distinctly Brechtian style for this experiment, he not only repudiated the conventions of realistic illusion and atmospherics but also re-arranged the text itself in epic manner, as a succession of clearly profiled individual scenes marked off from one another by blackouts that emphasized a sense of discontinuity and montage. "Zadek alters the flow of the action, presenting instead black-framed pictures of an action which compel the spectator to step back so he can think objectively," wrote *Bremer Nachrichten*. Hence "the course of events seems propelled not by external conditions but by the various characters as they encounter one another." The pivotal force in Zadek's ensemble was the comparatively dispassionate, self-controlled Nora of Edith Clever, a superb classical actress who, it will be remembered, was shortly to play a comparably tough-minded Aase in both the Hübner and the Stein productions of *Peer Gynt*. Devoid of all false poignancy or sentimentality, Clever's Nora was, in the words of the Bremen critic, "strong from the beginning: she just hadn't realized how strong she really was."

Of other contemporary productions that have sought to shift the audience's attention from Nora's inner struggle to the social and economic conditions that govern her and her situation, perhaps Rainer Werner Fassbinder's *Nora Helmer*, a video version made in 1973 and widely seen on European television, best represents this tendency taken to its extreme. "Everything in this play, including Nora, stands in need of liberation," Fassbinder said in an interview at the time. "Nora is not someone who has suddenly found the light of revelation. At the end she is just as crack-brained as before, and the struggle between Nora and Helmer is, so far as I can see, a struggle ... to win certain points, which I find very cheap but also very realistic. That Nora is supposed to be a champion of women's rights is something I've never been able to find in Ibsen."[51] In this heavily edited cinematic de(con)struction of *A Doll's House*, the heroine – played by the Fass-binder star Margit Carstensen – became a materialistic society woman cynically intent on the acquisition of power and the selfish preservation of her social and marital position. Here again, any sense of period was deliberately shattered. Wearing long, loose-flowing hair *à la* Lauren Bacall in a Hollywood movie from the forties (and dressed for Stenborg's party in a "naughty" peek-a-boo *peignoir*), Carstensen de-picted a timelessly bourgeois Hausfrau, fully as responsible as her husband for their unhealthy marriage and for the power struggle it has become. The harshness of Fassbinder's outlook was underscored by the deliberate omission of potentially ameliorating elements in the text. The Helmer children were nowhere to be seen; Krogstad's references to his own children and their plight were similarly deleted; and even the reconciliation scene between Mrs. Linde and the repentant moneylender was cut from the shooting script.

In Fassbinder's version, the root of the Helmer problem was ultimately the fact that both Nora *and* Torvald were dolls – unwitting puppets manipulated by the strictures and sanctions of their (read: our) repressive bourgeois society. In Carstensen's strong, heavily ironic performance, Nora – who hardly meant a word she said in the "discussion" scene – became another of those Fassbinder women who, in the film-maker's own words, "use their suppression as an effective means of terrorism." As such, she had no reason to leave at the end, for she had emerged from the struggle as the undisputed victor. As she stopped in the doorway and waited, watching her utterly drained and humiliated husband, she was manifestly the stronger. What is more, her victory had been foretold. At the beginning of the film, as the credits rolled, Helmer's hand had been seen resting heavily on Nora's shoulder; but on top of his hand lay Nora's own, displaying long, red-lacquered nails.

In the spirit of Zadek's *shockstil* but without the extreme sarcasm of Fassbinder, Hans Neuenfels' remarkable production of *A Doll's House* (staged at the Stuttgart-Württemberg State Theatre in 1972 and repeated in Frankfurt a year later) likewise took for granted a shared condemnation of the play, its characters, and the outmoded bourgeois system of values they represent. Above all, however, this impressively acted performance is likely to be remembered for having provided Nora with the most unusual exit of her long stage life. Neuenfels succeeded in suggesting a strange confluence of past and present – a sense that Nora and her husband were already living in their new home, a successful banker's grand, green-and-white palace dominated by a single towering window shrouded in heavy, funereal drapes. Viewed in a kind of Strindbergian double-perspective, the play moved through a succession of anxiety-driven, almost melodramatically posed pictures that recollected and reconsidered time past. "Something that has already taken place is repeated," wrote Günther Rühle in *Frankfurter Allgemeine Zeitung* (19 January 1973): "a mind that was weighed down by anxiety is seen through the prism of what it appears to have been freed of." The Helmer world was here a realm of irrationality and strife, where, Rühle went on, "only the hope of a miracle is left, since

14 Nora's extraordinary departure through the window at the end of Hans
Neuenfels' production of *A Doll's House* at the Stuttgart-Württemberg State
Theatre in 1972. Helmer (Peter Roggisch) is left in a mixture of despair and
disbelief. Setting designed by Klaus Gelhaar.

reason no longer accomplishes anything." Locked in their domestic
hell, nothing was really left of Nora and Helmer but the absurdly
puppet-like poses they struck – the Hausfrau languidly reclining on the
sofa, the wife-tamer and trainer with his apprehensive glances – and
even their children were brought in like a row of pretty figurines, "the
boys in blue velvet, with vacant, beautiful doll-eyes staring into empty
space, unreachable, inscrutable, frightened, and abandoned."[52]

Hence the unusual ending: clearly nothing short of "a miracle"
could enable Nora to extricate herself from this caricature of a marriage. Striking a resolute farewell pose which she had tried out in the
second act and using a ladder borrowed from the nurse, Elisabeth
Trissenaar slowly climbed to freedom through the large middle window in the background. Then, as Peter Roggisch's Helmer sat abandoned in the sofa, in the same position Nora had occupied earlier, and
contemplated the mystery of "the most wonderful thing," social comment merged with black comedy. Behind him in the background, the
new, fearless, decisive Nora could be seen peering in through the
window. This serio-comic Little Matchgirl image left an unmistakable
impression of one further irony – the inevitability of this Nora's return
to the security of a life of social conventionality and the occasional
macaroon.

The sharpest possible contrast to such newer radical "quotations" of
the play as these is represented by Ingmar Bergman's innovative
production of A Doll's House at the Residenztheater in Munich (30 April
1981), in which tradition was overturned for purposes that had
nothing whatever to do with ideological criticism of the play or subver-
sion of its underlying intent. Performed by one of West Germany's
finest acting companies, Bergman's terse, starkly simplified stage version explored, with unbroken and painful intensity, the spiritual and
psychological levels that lie beneath Ibsen's realistic superstructure.[53]
Earlier productions at the Residenz, notably by Jürgen Fehling (1950)
and Helmut Henrichs (1969), had taken the play in the direction of that
same modestly stylized realism that has characterized so many contemporary Ibsen revivals. Bergman's bold theatrical paraphrase was,
however, as much a rejection of this alternative as it was a clear and
final repudiation of the teacups and wallpaper of the Victorian parlor.

Nora, the title of his version, suggests its undivided focus on the
central character and her existential struggle to free herself, by breaking out of the stifling world of masks and roles in which she finds
herself a prisoner. Nothing in this production was allowed to distract
from the controlling conception of the play as a drama of destiny and
entrapment, in which Nora is conscious from the outset of her frustra-

tion and her longing to escape from a narrow, constrictive existence that is gradually suffocating her. The director and his designer, Gunilla Palmstierna-Weiss, evolved a strongly expressive visual image of this sense of oppressiveness and closure. The entire stage space was a limbo cut off from any contact with the world of reality – a void encompassed by an immense, non-representational box that was uniformly lined with a dark red, velvet-like fabric. Within this vast, confined space, a smaller structure was created by high dark walls that suggested the panelled interior of a court-room. The absence of doors or windows intensified the atmosphere of solemnity and constrictive solidity evoked by this maximum-security coffin-prison. "Neither air nor light nor sound from the outside world penetrated this closed, hermetically sealed realm of fixed social values and conventions," observed *Rheinischer Merkur* (8 May 1981).

At the geometrical center of the stage, a low quadrilateral platform stood like an island in the midst of this forbidding framework of wall-screens. A succession of fragmentary settings, each consisting of a bare minimum of indispensable furniture and significant objects, delineated the distinct developmental movements into which Bergman's *Nora* was divided. At first, a heavy, darkly upholstered sofa and chair took up the center of the platform; the background was dominated by an elaborately trimmed Christmas tree, mountains of presents heaped beneath it. Scattered across the front of the small stage-platform were more wrapped and unwrapped presents and toys: a helmet, a sword, a decorative brass doll's bed, and, most striking of all, two large dolls with pale and oddly human porcelain faces. Together, these objects made a silent but eloquent comment on the Helmer world as a playpen, a doll's house of eternal childhood. Then, as the alien forces that shatter this fragile world of game-playing and make-believe gradually took over, the playpen was discarded and the sole indicator of the arena of conflict became a large, round dining-table and four stiffly old-fashioned chairs grouped around it. For the final bitter and disillusioned settling of accounts at the end of the play, however, the focal physical object was not, as it is in Ibsen, the dining-table but a more intimate item of domestic furniture – a large brass bed that was an unmistakable replica of the miniature doll's bed seen among the toys at the beginning. (Bergman's unexpected solution to this scene has, in fact, at least one interesting precedent in Peter Ashmore's 1953 production at the Lyric, Hammersmith, which featured the popular Scandinavian stars Mogens Wieth and Mai Zetterling in the main roles. Here, to the shock of some of the London critics, the crucial final scene had been played in a bedroom setting that, by implication, stressed the sexual intimacy that had held Nora and Torvald together during their eight years of marriage.)

Bergman's method of direction inevitably exerts a pressure from the stage toward the auditorium that eliminates all distance. In his *Nora*, the radical dematerialization of the physical setting was accompanied by a choreographic strategy that served, in an even more startlingly direct way, to thrust the action forward and thereby engage the spectator's active and conscious participation in it. In this production the actors never left the audience's sight. Each in turn, the four characters who precipitate Nora's desperate struggle for survival simply stepped forward, as though bidden, to confront her, and then returned again to one of the six old-fashioned dining-room chairs that were deployed, with severe symmetry, along two walls of the "court-room." Seated there, they were once again actors, awaiting their cues in a drama in which the very concept of role-playing and masquerade is, Bergman has emphasized, the central metaphor. Yet, at the same time, these impassive watchers were still characters, chained together with Nora in the claustrophobic hell of Ibsen's domestic wasteland, visible in the subdued, softly diffused light like half-real figures in a dream landscape. Their very presence signified that a predetermined and ineluctable process was taking its course – a process during which Nora would eventually have to summon and come to terms with each of "her" characters in turn. (As the attempt to restage the Bergman version at the Stratford [Ontario] Shakespeare Festival in 1987 demonstrated, however, this device of the watching characters can, if misunderstood and hence clumsily handled, create a distraction that dissipates concentration instead of intensifying it.)

In the Residenz production, without a trace of unwanted expressionistic distortion or gimmickry, Nora was made the controlling consciousness in the play. Alone, in the midst of a setting that emphasized its own theatrical nature, she acted out a dream life, from which she was struggling to awaken. The associational, mutational arrangement of Bergman's version produced what Strindberg calls "the inconsequent but transparently logical shape of a dream." The play was no longer governed or even remotely influenced by strict, literal considerations of time and place. Rather, the fifteen brief scenes into which Bergman divided *A Doll's House* were emotional units linked together by contrasting moods and juxtaposed emotions. Although the basic plot of Ibsen's play naturally remained unchanged, its meticulously constructed logic of cause and effect – which, in Bergman's view, serves only to dissipate its potential imaginative impact on a contemporary audience by "closing doors, leaving no other alternatives" –

15   This Helmer (Mogens Wieth) talks away in exuberant relief to a Nora (Mai Zetterling) who has quite clearly already "taken off her fancy dress": for Peter Ashmore's London revival of *A Doll's House* in 1953, Reece Pemberton provided a multiple set that opened up the entire living area of the Helmer household – including the master bedroom.

was displaced by an intuitive logic of feeling, sustained by means of contrasts and associations. Characters came and went freely, in neutral space, with no need for parlormaids or ringing doorbells or carefully established "motivations" to aid (or impede) them.

Beneath a façade of charming, child-like submissiveness that Rita Russek's Nora so readily and engagingly adopted at will, a sense of incipient rage and frustration was evident from the very outset. Always the consummate and resourceful actress, this Nora was none the less unable to conceal a deep, angry impatience with life's pattern – a gnawing, even a romantic longing to transcend this narrow, confining existence of hers. ("To be carefree," is how she defines her longing at first: "Without a care, not having a care in the world.") From the beginning of their childish games it was clear that both she *and* Helmer were trapped within the fixed limits of roles that had been assigned to them. The fact that only Nora was consciously, if dimly, aware of the masquerade defined the perceptional gulf between them. Hence, the forces of disruption that break loose over her and shatter her ostensible domestic security were, in Bergman's interpretation, more than merely external forces; they arose just as certainly from within her, from her own consciousness of isolation and spiritual alienation. Once established, this mood of disillusionment and spiritual malaise continued to grow and spread until it colored every feature of the dramatic action.

Its first tangible manifestation was Mrs. Linde's sudden, startling intrusion into Nora's world. Heavily veiled and dressed entirely in black, she appeared like some spectral omen of disaster. As played by Annemarie Wernicke, this pale, dissipated figure from Nora's past bore little resemblance to the innocuous, quietly pathetic friend and stock confidante we know from countless productions of *A Doll's House*. Bergman's unsentimental reading produced a different and far harsher image of a woman filled with futility and resentment after her long years of deadening self-sacrifice, corroded in her very being by a bitterness that has consumed her warmth and her humanity. Her insistent determination to pry into Nora's past and force from her a confession of the complete "truth" translated her passive expository function into an active mode.

It was Krogstad, however, who proved to be the most startling and provocative surprise in this production. In Gerd Anthoff's performance, the hole-and-corner lawyer who tries to exploit Nora's forgery became a far more complicated and contradictory character than the mere moral degenerate described by Doctor Rank – not to mention the heavy-handed theatre villain perpetuated by a century of performances. Each of his "entrances" signaled a change of mood that was prepared for with emphatic slowness. A few moments before he was to step forward to take part in the action, this pale, black-clad figure could be seen rising from his chair and hovering silently beside the stage-platform, or even slowly circling behind it in a kind of theatrical slow-motion. His hands buried in the pockets of a heavy overcoat that enveloped him like a straitjacket, his menacing presence clearly bespoke the tormentor who is in turn the sufferer, dangerous and even brutal because he was himself trapped, isolated in a hostile world where he had discovered that "absolutely all roads were closed." His character thus embodied the palpable atmosphere of coldness and darkness – the sense of "freezing, coal-black water" – that was never very far beneath the surface in Bergman's interpretation of Ibsen's text. As such, his struggle to retain "a modest position in the bank," conducted by him with almost apologetic but dogged brutality, became a fierce and utterly desperate existential struggle for survival. In their first meeting, Nora's reaction to this bitter, melancholy anti-villain was one of cold contempt. In their second and crucial encounter, however, the mood changed and the tension between them became tinged by a curious irony. In this oddly compassionate scene, Krogstad seemed to have come not merely to coerce Nora but also to commiserate with her as a fellow-sufferer – someone locked together with him in a hell (or a nightmare) where everything moves in circles and events are doomed to be repeated over and over again. Condemned to suffer for a crime no different from Nora's, he now watched the fixed pattern repeat itself. In a series of spasmodic (and circular) movements, he even tried awkwardly to reach out to her, in order to persuade her of the ultimate futility and meaninglessness of the desperate action that "is the first thing most of us think of."

Krogstad's thwarted, self-contradictory action was a deformed image of the countless attempts made by all the play's characters to reach out to one another, without success. The aftermath of his confrontation with Nora, the famous tarantella, became the one last effort of this kind on *her* part to reach Helmer, to communicate her anguish to this amiable but hopelessly handicapped emotional illiterate who understands nothing of her pain. In Bergman's staging of this moment, the tarantella was not really a dance at all – at least not the frantic and increasingly more confused and pathetic dance that generations of Noras have performed, to the tuneful accompaniment of Doctor Rank at the upright, in order to distract her husband's attention from the fateful letterbox. Instead, Rita Russek's defiant, whirling tarantella, danced on top of the table to the relentless pounding of her tambourine, was not a coy maneuver designed to divert Helmer's attention, but a hieroglyph of desperation intended to attract it. This passionate choreographic outburst, watched thoughtfully by Rank and with incomprehension by Helmer, was virtually a mute, conscious cry for help in a situation that Nora herself now knew to be beyond help. Her dance was brief; the clattering tambourine she let fall to the floor signalled its finality, as the last game in a played-out masquerade.

If Nora's life with Torvald is a well-meant but utterly hollow fiction, constructed of roles to be played and poses to be adopted, her relationship with Rank is, Bergman's production shows us, the sole breathing-space in which a spirit of understanding and happiness, as opposed to assumed gaiety, prevails. Their scenes together were brief moments of rest that punctuated the rising tension of the drama and thrust it into heightened relief. Horst Sachtleben's characterization made it clear that only Rank's manifest love for Nora held any genuine meaning – although it was only a fleetingly perceived dream-image of love, as wistful and nostalgic as the old music-box melody ("Träumerei," from Robert Schumann's Scenes from Childhood) that attached itself to his figure throughout the performance. Rank's profound compassion for Nora was built on his love and his sympathetic understanding of her, and it in turn evoked a reciprocal warmth and compassion on her part that figured as prominently as her strength and her rebelliousness in the complex portrait of Nora that Bergman drew.

In the crucial scene in which Nora and Rank are alone with each other, Bergman resolutely pared away every detail of naturalistic clutter – Nora's dilatory and rather inane chatter about the pernicious effects of truffles, oysters and champagne, the distracting references to Mrs. Linde's presence in the next room, the interruptions of the maid – and in the process the "realistic" but emotionally diffused impression of characters talking at cross purposes disappeared as well. As Sachtleben's Rank knelt to her, his hand to his heart in a wryly theatrical gesture of supplication, the real purpose of his visit was perfectly transparent: his need to find a way to leave her with some memory or some expression of his love that would survive him. And Nora's purpose, as she in turn knelt before his chair and later stood behind him to cradle his head against her bosom, was equally plain: to comfort him by somehow assuaging the anguish and despair that now overcame him in the face of death. Nothing in this unit of action was permitted by the director to matter more than its emotional texture – least of all its function as a plot reversal in which Nora, having conceived the idea of asking Rank for money with which to pay off her debt, is prevented by his unexpected declaration of love from doing so.

Many critics of this play, and legions of directors along with them, have struggled with the almost unredeemable vulgarity that Nora displays when she prepares to solicit Rank's aid by flirtatiously dangling a pair of "flesh-colored" silk stockings before his eyes. ("So far as I understand it," wrote Strindberg with unconcealed disgust in his preface to *Married*, "Nora offers herself for sale – to be paid for in cash.") In Bergman's hands, meanwhile, this moment of perilously quaint Victorian eroticism underwent an exciting transformation. Slowly, in a virtually hypnotic manner, Nora helped Rank to push back the horror of death. As he began to relax, he leaned his head against her; slowly she covered his eyes with her hands. Then, with dream-like slowness, she drew a silk stocking (*not* flesh-colored!) across his closed lids, as though somehow conjuring up a consoling vision of loveliness for him – a dream of Nora dancing only for him ("and for Torvald, too, of course – that goes without saying"). Thus transformed, the moment became a warm, living icon of compassion asked for and bestowed, in the midst of the cheerless and rapidly darkening world of the play.

After Rank had appeared for the last time, following the costume ball at the Stenborgs, no symbolic calling-cards marked with black crosses were needed in this production to convey the fact – obvious by now to all but Helmer – that this character's departure from the play marked the end of all "amusing disguises," not only for Rank but also for Nora. A crucial irony in Bergman's interpretation is contained in his observation that this play is fully as much "the tragedy of Helmer" as it is a drama about Nora's development. As played by Robert Atzorn, this charmingly sincere and boyishly self-centered Helmer remained oblivious not only to Rank's suffering but also to the mood of icy disillusionment in which Nora now prepared to face the reckoning that was nearly upon them. Even the shock of Krogstad's revelations passed quickly over him. Once he had torn up the incriminating documents and had taken yet another glass of champagne to reassure himself that he would not "sink miserably to the bottom and be ruined" after all, he "forgave" his wife and resumed his determined efforts to make love to her.

This is, of course, the point in Ibsen's play at which, Shaw declares, the heroine "very unexpectedly stops her emotional acting" and demands instead that they sit down at the table for a discussion. In Bergman's *Nora*, no such "unexpected" point occurs (he would argue that it does not occur in Ibsen either). His Nora had begun long ago to be conscious of the futility of the roles they play at. Her wish is for an emotional "accounting," not an intellectual discussion around a table,

16   The final settling of accounts in Ingmar Bergman's *Nora*, as performed at
the Residenztheater, Munich, in 1981. Rita Russek is Nora, Robert Atzorn is
the suddenly awakened Helmer.

and any feeling of "unexpectedness" generated by her demand is
confined entirely to Helmer. Naked and asleep in their decorative
brass doll's bed, his sexual desire having presumably been satisfied,
Atzorn's Helmer awakened in the final scene to find himself face to
face with a woman in a black travelling dress, a packed overnight bag
in her hand. The utter vulnerability of his nakedness, accentuated by a
single, piercing shaft of light that turned his figure and the bedclothes
into a blaze of white, was confronted by what Bergman calls Nora's
"complete ruthlessness and brutality."[54] As he listened uncomprehen-
dingly and the other characters watched silently from the shadowy
darkness behind his bed, she reviewed the wreckage that he and her
father had made of her life. The climax of physical violence with which
she met his uncertain attempt to reassert the ritual of domination
("Oh, you think and talk like a naive child") subsided at last into the

deep sorrow that shattered her aggressiveness. But the locked pattern was now conclusively broken, as in a bad dream from which one finally awakens. Without a sound, as if by magic, a hidden aperture in the apparently solid wall swung open, and Nora stepped through it to freedom – an escape-artist who left the captors of her dream behind.

"Finis Malorum" is the final remark in Bergman's published script. Yet his interpretation of *A Doll's House* leaves no room for any easy, cathartic conclusions about the play (Nora achieves redemptive self-realization) or even for comfortably "open" ones (perhaps, given the grace of human understanding, "the most wonderful thing of all" is ultimately attainable). In his production the victory Nora achieves was rent by grief and an intense feeling of loss. The anguished conclusion of her bitter indictment of Helmer – "I've got to do it by myself. And that's why I'm leaving you" – was the most wrenching and painful statement this Nora had to make. Torvald Helmer, on the other hand, the "loser" in this confrontation, is perhaps – as others since Strindberg have also recognized – in part the victim of his entrapment in the socially imposed role of being the man, the husband. "And he collapses under it," Bergman has suggested. But this Helmer was even more obviously crippled and trapped by a deep inner malaise – a kind of ignorance of others and himself that a Bergman character like Johan in *Scenes from a Marriage* would later come to define, with bitter self-irony, as emotional illiteracy.

Above all, the uncompromising emotional honesty of Bergman's stage interpretation of *A Doll's House* lifted it – as its best productions have consistently tried to do – out of the narrow arena of problem-play relevance (or irrelevance) and redirected attention to what Ibsen himself has identified as his true subject. "For me it has been a question of human rights," he reminded the Norwegian Society for Women's Rights in 1898. "My task has been the portrayal of human beings."

4

Naturalism and after: *Ghosts*

Ghosts, this remorseless individualist's uncompromising repudiation of the forces of puritanism and death-bringing conventionality, both demanded and helped to foster a new style of acting. "The effect of the play depends a great deal on making the spectator feel as if he were actually sitting, listening, and looking at events happening in real life," Ibsen wrote to the Swedish actor–director August Lindberg shortly before the latter launched his ambitious touring production of the drama in August 1883.[1] The playwright's innovative dramatic method, which transformed the apparently natural speech and everyday surroundings of the realistic style to create a new kind of dramatic poetry, was not an end in itself, however, but rather the means by which he sought to compel the audience's attention and challenge it to contemplate a failed universe of collapsing moral and spiritual values, in which we perceived "all mankind wandering blindly on the wrong track."[2]

The social and intellectual establishment seems to have been quick to sense the threat to its own security. Erik Bøgh, the conservative literary adviser to the Danish Royal Theatre – which could otherwise claim credit for the world premieres of the two previous "modern" plays, *The Pillars of Society* and *A Doll's House* – rejected the new work Ibsen had submitted in November of 1881 because it depicted "a repulsive psychological phenomenon which, by undermining the morality of our social order, threatens its foundations."[3] The other major theatres in Scandinavia soon followed suit. "We find it impossible to believe that any theatre, or at least any theatre of rank and importance, would wish to perform this drama," proclaimed *Dagbladet*, a Copenhagen daily.[4] After Ludvig Josephson, then head of Nya teatern in Stockholm, had pronounced Ibsen's play "one of the filthiest things ever written in Scandinavia" and had flatly refused to allow a production of it, Lindberg decided to seize the initiative. He rehearsed the capable stock company he had recently acquired from Terese Ellforss, and then took to the road with a highly creditable production of *Ghosts* that eventually toured both the provinces and the capitals of all three Scandinavian countries.

After opening in the small coastal town of Hälsingborg on 22 August 1883, Lindberg's troupe carried its bold enterprise to Folketeatret in the Danish capital, where most critics now had only high praise, particularly for the carefully coordinated ensemble-playing of Lindberg's company and for his own introspective interpretation of Osvald, which they likened to his widely admired portrayal of Hamlet. The dignified, rather mannered acting of Hedvig Winterhjelm (of whose Mrs. Alving Ibsen in fact later expressed approval) struck reviewers as "a bit preachy in certain places," but Lindberg's fine performance set the tone for a generation of naturalistic Osvalds to come. Above all, it was this actor's physical and facial expressiveness in the part that impressed his contemporaries most forcibly. William Archer, who saw the touring production in Christiania in 1893, has left a revealing account of the "slow, deliberate, dreamy" quality of Lindberg's Hamlet-like Osvald, "the manner of a man to whom the world has become unreal." Strindberg's argument (developed at length in the Preface to *Miss Julie*) that the subtler reactions of modern psychological drama depend primarily on the expressiveness of the actor's eyes and upper face finds, in fact, no better practical illustration than Archer's vivid account:

short, curling black hair, and a small black moustache, a very pale face, and those blinking, uneven, sort of light-shy eyes one so often sees in broken-down debauchees, one or other of the eyebrows having a tendency to rise now and then, without any apparent cause, and seemingly involuntarily ... Lindberg had actually invented and worked out in its smallest details the *manner* of the man, which, though it harmonized entirely with Ibsen's intentions, was by no means to be found ready-made in them.[5]

A comparable description by Georg Nordensvan, another first-hand observer, emphasizes just how clearly Lindberg's characterization revealed an intricate, carefully integrated pattern of shifting reactions and changing attitudes to the reality around him: "The different phases all found their proper expression, the 'worm-eaten' hopelessness, together with the rekindled desire for life, the nervous tension succeeded by apathy, the coldness of death, outbursts of child-like misery and of the selfishness of the invalid – at certain moments intense sensitivity and touching tenderness, always simply expressed, with no exaggeration of the pathological."[6]

Although a few theatres in Scandinavia began to open their doors to
Ghosts in the wake of Lindberg's initiative, audiences elsewhere were
still unable to see the play in the 1880s except under the special
circumstances of a tour or a private showing of the kind arranged by
such theatrical innovators as Duke Georg of Saxe-Meiningen. Even
before Lindberg's opening, however, an intrepid band of amateurs,
led by the once-popular Danish actress Helga von Bluhme, had distinguished itself by presenting the world premiere of the play, acted
for the first time in the original language, on 20 May 1882 at the Aurora
Turner Hall in Chicago and subsequently seen by audiences of Scandinavian immigrants throughout the Middle West. It was not until
1887, meanwhile, that the prominent German actor Friedrich Mitterwurzer toured several major mid-western cities with the first stage
version of *Ghosts* in English, which he renamed *Phantoms, or The Sins of
the Fathers*. Posters billed the play as "Forbidden in Germany,"
although by then Fritz Wallner had succeeded in presenting his influential matinee performance of it at the Residenztheatre in Berlin (9
January 1887), directed by Anton Anno and attended by Ibsen himself.
(The sensational event had even been cautiously reported in the American press: "It will be long before the last word has been spoken,"
declared one wary notice, "for we have to do with an important
creation and a man of genius and both can afford to wait for the time of
clearer and calmer judgment."[7]) Nothing, however, had quite prepared American audiences for the modernity of Mitterwurzer, whose
subtle, understated style in the role of Osvald must have appeared as
unusual to them as the play itself. A former member of Dingelstedt's
renowned Burgtheatre ensemble, he favored a restless, supple, facially
expressive attack that made him an ideal interpreter of Ibsen and the
new psychological drama.[8] Clemens Petersen, who saw the Mitterwurzer production in Chicago, wrote the elder Bjørnson that it was
excellently acted, although the playhouse was "disagreeably empty."
Hastening to pursue his customary theme, this bitter Ibsen opponent
added the fervent hope that the playwright would turn out "a new
Gengangere or *Rosmersholm* or some such" every year, "for then I will
live to see this bubble burst."[9] Petersen's abuse is mild, however,
compared to the "shriek of execration" (Archer's phrase) that greeted
the play's first performances in England.

The critical controversy and even hostility that frequently attended
the many and various private and itinerant productions of *Ghosts*
during the 1880s erupted into a veritable firestorm of denunciations
and scenes of moral outrage when the play at last reached the stages of
the three world capitals – Paris, London and New York – in the

nineties. André Antoine's production at the Théâtre Libre on 30 May 1890, the first performance of an Ibsen play in France, left Parisian audiences shocked and bewildered. A little less than a year later, J. T. Grein's single production of the work at his Independent Theatre (13 March 1891), stunned the entire English-speaking world. Also, once *Ghosts* had been acted for the first time in English in New York, initially at a matinee performance at the Berkeley Lyceum on 5 January 1894 and again at A. M. Palmer's Garden Theatre later that same month, it touched off the full-scale "pawing and bawling" that accompanied the American assimilation of what H. L. Mencken facetiously called "the Ibsen legend" – "that fabulous picture of a fabulous monster, half Nietzsche and half Dr. Frank Crane, drenching the world with scandalous platitudes from a watch-tower in the chilblained North."[10]

As we know, Antoine's *Ghosts* was above all an important plank in the platform of theatrical (rather than moral or even literary) reform upon which the Théâtre Libre was founded. The new movement called for nothing less than the complete rebirth of the theatre, replacing stagnation and imposed patterns with something vital and alive, "remaking the stage until it is continuous with the auditorium, giving a shiver of life to the painted trees, letting in through the backcloth the great, free air of reality."[11] Consonant with Zola's demand for an objective, scientific exploration of reality in the theatre – the representation on the stage of "a fragment of existence" or, as the critic–playwright Jean Jullien called it, "a slice of life" – Antoine insisted that, to accomplish this aim, the director must "not only fit the action in its proper framework but also determine its true character and create its atmosphere." His true-to-life settings (created first, "without worrying at all about the events that were to occur on the stage") were designed to concretize the vital role played by environment in the dynamics of existence for, he insists, "it is the environment that determines the movements of the characters, not the movements of the characters that determines the environment." For Antoine, light – "the life of the theatre, the good fairy of the *décor*, the soul of the staging" – contributed in a very special way to the creation of a convincing atmosphere: "Light acts physically on the audience: its magic accentuates, underlines, and marvelously accompanies the inner meaning of a dramatist's work." (Small wonder, then, that this director was so strongly attracted to *Ghosts*, which partakes so obviously of this same attitude toward the metaphoric effect of light on the stage.) Above all, however, the naturalistic aesthetic hinged on the development of a new style of acting, in which, as Zola himself put it, the actors should now "not *play*, but rather *live*, before the audience." The cardinal principle governing this style is contained in Antoine's observation that "every time the actor is revealed beneath the character, the dramatic continuity is broken."[12] In general, the naturalistic emphasis on the deterministic role played by each significant, verisimilar detail implied the absolute necessity of achieving the integration of all the various elements of play production – setting, lighting, costumes, and acting – into a meaningful, unified whole. In accomplishing this integration, the figure of the director emerged during the last decades of Ibsen's career as a power hitherto unequalled in the theatre.

In the particular case of *Ghosts*, however, Antoine's initiative was so overshadowed by public bewilderment and critical indignation that it becomes exceedingly difficult in retrospect to disentangle general incomprehension on one side of the footlights from misinterpretation and technical insufficiency on the other side. Ibsen's allusive, retrospective method of bringing the events of the past slowly but irrevocably to bear upon the present proved, in the Théâtre Libre production, to be the source of greatest confusion. Sarcey declared the play better suited to reading than to performance: "All the action is contained in the conversations, in philosophical questions debated and discussed by people who do not bother to explain them clearly." Most reviewers grappled with long synopses of the play and the antecedent action. The writer Henry Céard, who had read the play for Antoine's troupe, had even offered to provide a prologue that would have explained the tangled events of the Alving past to the audience. Sarcey's long review in *Le Temps* (2 June 1890) makes it abundantly clear, however, that a major part of the difficulty lay in the performance itself – specifically in the adoption by Antoine and his company of a pugnaciously "natural," uninflectedly conversational style of acting that proved inadequate to the demands placed on an actor by Ibsen's layered, intricately orchestrated text. "Never will I admit that players who do not make themselves audible to the public are good actors," declared this critic, who complained that he and those seated around him lost "something like one-half of the play" for this reason:

Antoine, who has no voice to start with, speaks under his breath with his back turned. It pleases him to go to the remotest part of the stage and there with his partner to engage in long conversations in an undertone. It would seem that this is meant to give a more natural effect, as if it were more natural to show one's back than one's face or to mutter instead of speaking loudly and steadily. Mlle. Luce Colas [Regine] stammers constantly: could this also be because this is more natural? The words of M. Janvier [Engstrand] disappear into his old beard, and Mlle. Barny herself [Mrs Alving], save in a few passages where volume is absolutely necessary, stifles her speech as if she were in a sick chamber.

No great harm is done when the action is largely revealed by the actors' movements and mime. But in this case we have what is called in the language of the theatre "*un dialogue posé*": the characters analyze each other, and the drama lies entirely in the succession of thoughts and feelings they express.[13]

These observations take us beyond the simple fact of Sarcey's well-known antipathy to Ibsen and to Antoine's methods, and suggest a more fundamental discrepancy between flatly "natural" stage speech and the more difficult art of prose-poetry practiced by Ibsen in his "modern" plays.

Even George Moore – whose vivid eyewitness account of the Théâtre Libre production is highly complimentary (being a call for the establishment of a similarly independent theatre in Britain) – admits he experienced difficulty in hearing Antoine's actors, and his notes on their performances sometimes cast considerable doubt on the overall balance and effectiveness of the ensemble. Arquillière's cassock-clad Pastor Manders (who seemed to Sarcey "not to have understood one word of his role") struck Moore as "a dreary old bore" whose "intolerable sermonising" ruined the first two acts for him.[14] Lost to the novelist completely, it seems, was "the entire discourse of the workman with the wooden leg"! The voluptuous Regine of Luce Colas, taking her leave of the stricken Osvald in the last act, went out "pushing her way violently through the swing doors," evidently impelled, Moore seems to think, by a realization "that the fatal taint inherited from their common father has descended on her" (184).

For Antoine's Osvald, however, the enthusiastic Irish theatre patron had only admiration, and his notes on the actor's approach to the role call to mind the typically naturalistic embroidery of physical details and contrasting reactions that had already characterized Lindberg's performance. "The nervous irritation of the sick man was faultlessly rendered," Moore records (183). At times, losing his temper at his mother's interruptions, Osvald's speech became "querulous already with incipient disease." At other moments, smoking and puffing at his pipe, he spoke "with an air of familiar contentment." Then, in the final moments of his sanity, before darkness came upon him, he and his mother sat side by side talking: "The mother calls upon him to cherish his father's memory, and the boy answers not in tragic phrases, but in the words so simple and so true, that listening, the heart turns to ice" (184–5).

As this account suggests, Antoine's *Ghosts* was, to the virtual exclusion of other facets of the play, seen as a deterministic tragedy of mother and son, caught together in what Moore calls "the remorseless web that life had spun." The novelist's description of their last moments together testifies eloquently to Antoine's (and Ibsen's) ability to create on the stage a detailed, charged picture of external reality that also revealed the inner emotional truth of the situation:

> Startled by some incoherency in his speech, she calls in terror to him. The scream rescues him for a moment out of the night that is deepening in his brain, that is approaching blackness, and for a few moments more he speaks reasonably.
>
> The sun has risen, the world is bright with the dawn. Mrs. Alving draws the curtains, letting the sunlight into the room. But Osvalt [sic] still sits with his back to the light, now mumbling in toneless voice, "The sun, the sun." Mrs. Alving stares at him in speechless terror, her hands twisted in her hair. And he still mumbles, "The sun, the sun." (185)

Osvald *vermoulu* – the clinically explicit psychological and physiological portrait of the young Alving as sketched by Lindberg and Antoine – became an abiding tradition that culminated in, for example, the widely acclaimed performances of Ermete Zacconi, the first actor–director to stage *Ghosts* in Italy. Zacconi's "representation of the progressive moral and corporeal decay of Osvald contained details so true and so excruciating," felt playwright Roberto Bracco, "that the spectators felt unable to bear them, and did not realize that they bore them, because his art nailed them to their seats."[15] Especially during the play's earlier stage history, Osvald's (unmentionable) physical disease and resultant mental anguish were seen as the undisputed focus of the drama – hence the (misguided) Victorian outrage. Yet, as the Norwegian writer-director Gunnar Heiberg was led to observe after seeing *Ghosts* again at the Théâtre-Antoine at the end of the century: "Both Antoine and Lindberg, like no small number of other actors, mastered Osvald. The role is one of those which someone either can play or else cannot play. And once having played it, it is not so difficult. Even mediocre actors would be able to get something effective out of it."[16] Instead, Heiberg (himself responsible for the influential world premieres of both *The Wild Duck* and *Rosmersholm* at Bergen's National Stage) found himself searching in vain for a completely satisfactory interpreter of the play's real protagonist – Helene Alving – and the process of her tragic self-realization. Hedvig Winterhjelm had seemed to Heiberg stagey and rhetorical; Sophie Reimers, who acted a "stately and dignified" Mrs. Alving in the first, belated Norwegian production of the play in 1890, likewise struck him as no match for the compelling Osvald of Halfdan Christensen; and in Paris he found the role played with no more than "sensitivity and intelligence":

But that imposing personality who sits alone in her big manor-house in the west country, alone and in the rain, reading and thinking, searching for freedom, because now she has placed society at a distance and so is able to observe it and judge it, with the gravity of her sorrow behind her and with hopes for a grave sort of happiness – her I have never seen on the stage.

And then comes the day when she must prove she really did mean what she thought, that it was freedom she had achieved, that she would be capable of translating her love into action.[17]

Marie Schanzer, the actress who played Mrs. Alving in the historic Sunday matinee production with which Otto Brahm opened his Freie Bühne in Berlin (29 September 1889), did not differ markedly from the pattern Heiberg describes. ("Here was no spiritually strong woman who, through bitterest experience, has attained a firm understanding of life," wrote the critic for *Frankfurter Zeitung*. "Here instead was a mocking, obstinate lady.")[18] Alice (Mrs Theodore) Wright, on the other hand, both initiated and embodied the English tradition of a much more forceful and psychologically dominant Mrs. Alving as the focus of the drama and its "star" – a greatly variable and uneven tradition, to be sure, extending from the impatient vehemence of Janet Achurch in the part ("a mountain of fierce egotism, of warped, twisted, self-assertiveness") through the "almost aggressively depressing" Helene Alving created twice by Beatrix Lehmann (in 1943 and 1951) and the "strong, sad dignity" of Flora Robson (Old Vic, 1958) to the newer "murmured naturalism" of Irene Worth's low-key approach in the 1974 Jonathan Miller revival.[19]

The Mrs. Alving of Alice Wright (a prominent amateur of her day) had been described by a recent commentator as "an intellectual but womanly woman, domestic and practical, something like Ellen Terry's Lady Macbeth."[20] On that momentous March evening in 1891 when J. T. Grein launched his Independent Theatre, however, her achievement was virtually lost in the torrent of abuse heaped on the play by the London critics and their editors. It is for the famous anthology of "gibberings" collected by William Archer in the *Pall Mall Gazette* that the event is remembered, not for Wright's performance. Nevertheless, even Clement Scott, who might be expected to view the play as "a wretched, deplorable, loathsome history," had some praise for this actress's "breadth, womanliness, and tenderness" in a characterization that Shaw would later call (a little ironically, it is true) "an achievement quite beyond the culture of any other actress of her generation."[21] Far more revealing than these critical generalizations, meanwhile, is an eyewitness account of this eclectic interpretation, in which the most notable crux was Wright's righteous determination to show Osvald as doomed "to fester on alive" at the end. The result was a closing scene that represents an interesting contrast to the corresponding moment in Antoine's production, as we have already seen it recounted by George Moore:

Dawn comes – she loops back the curtain. Oswald asks with a blank face for the sun.

"What do you say?" she asks unsuspectingly with her tender voice.

"The sun – the sun."

She comes to him – terror grips her – first physical terror – then the mental terror before the situation. She finds the morphia pills, screams, hesitates – but her last words are No, no.

The sun – the sun.

And she leaves him in his haunted night, she will not lay the ghosts.[22]

Ultimately, however, these early performances of Ghosts in London and in Paris at the beginning of the 1890s remain so enmeshed in the critical confusion and recriminations surrounding the play itself that an objective assessment of them in purely artistic terms is hardly possible now. The sheer force of Puritan indignation unleashed by the introduction of the play to New York audiences renders such an assessment even less feasible. No one, of course, had paid much attention to Mitterwurzer on tour. Then, exactly two weeks after Grein's tumultuous premiere in London, New Yorkers were given their first glimpse of Ghosts, produced in German as Die Gespenster by Gustav Amberg, whose popular foreign-language playhouse on Irving Place had been in the vanguard of the Ibsen movement in the New World. However, this experiment attracted far less notice than its counterparts in Europe – unluckily for Amberg, whose estimable theatre collapsed in bankruptcy at the end of the season. As has already been mentioned, the real pawing and bawling broke out only after Ibsen's drama had been acted for the first time in English in Manhattan, at the beginning of 1894. Ida Jeffreys Goodfriend ("who seldom, if ever, reached anything permanent in our theaters," in the opinion of G. C. D. Odell) was Mrs. Alving, but Osvald was played by no less a figure than the morbidly picturesque Courtenay Thorpe (at least forty-five at the time and possibly much older, according to Agate). Thorpe's technically brilliant, harrowingly pathological portrait quickly became a popular sensation, later repeated by him in England opposite both Wright and Achurch. (When Shaw saw his performance in 1897, he joked that so ruthlessly terrifying an Osvald, "who shewed no mercy, might have been burnt alive in the orphanage without a throb of compassion.")[23]

Here again, however, any real sense of the quality of the performances (or lack of it) was conclusively obscured by the ensuing moral commotion – less familiar but certainly no less colorful than the London madness recorded by Archer. "The spectacle of a 'worm-eaten' son proceeding through paresis to idiocy, and loudly declaring his animal passion for the pretty servant-girl who is also his half-sister, can excite no other feelings than those of melancholoy and disgust," proclaimed *The Critic* (13 January 1894). "True to nature it undoubtedly is, but the small talk of everyday life is not what people go to the theater to hear. The real is one thing, the realistic is another." William Dean Howells might acclaim the production as "a great theatrical event," but William Winter, whose thunderous denunciation in the *Tribune* (26 January 1894) is justifiably renowned for the pig-headed extravagance of its vituperation, professed nothing but contempt for "the nauseous offal of Mr. Ibsen's dissecting table," destined to attract only, "those uneasy persons, of no sex in particular, who hang limp upon the fringes of nastiness and think that everything is bold and strong ('virile,' they commonly call it) which happens to be shameless and impudent." *Ghosts*, he sneered, "is the sort of play that requires ammonia. The smell of it leaves onions far astern."[24] The furious Winter's rages set the acid tone for the play's reception in most of the other New York dailies as well. (In Boston, the Governor scornfully refused a box at the Tremont Theatre, and at an adjacent church the Reverend Isaac J. Lansing preached vociferously against the "atrociously immoral production ... so atrocious that even to denounce it in public is almost degrading.")

Misguided moral outrage is, again in this case, rather difficult to distinguish from the confusion that might have been caused by an insecure and uneven performance. As was also true of Antoine's production of *Ghosts*, however, one senses the lack of a consistently evocative, analytical, psychologically penetrating style of acting capable of articulating Ibsen's layered text with clarity and authority. At any rate, for the first fully satisfying production of this particular play Manhattan theatre-goers would have to wait until 1903, when Mary Shaw's "thrillingly effective" performance as the suffering Mrs. Alving, supported by George Fawcett's capable stock company, was welcomed as "the most acceptable individual, as well as ensemble interpretation of *Ghosts* that New York has ever seen."[25]

FROM KONGENS NYTORV TO THE M.A.T.

By 1903, of course, a great deal had changed, both within the theatre and in the world outside it. Ibsen, no longer able to write at seventy-

17   A Byron photograph from the first act of the controversial New York production of *Ghosts* ("Ibsen's Famous Drama of Heredity") in 1903, starring Mary Shaw as Mrs. Alving and Frederick Lewis (in the doorway) as Osvald. A curious touch of irony is added by the picture of Captain Alving prominently displayed on the mantelpiece behind Pastor Manders (Maurice Wilkinson).

five, was now very near the silence (as Joyce had put it in that remarkable birthday letter of his two years earlier). The scandals that had
surrounded *Ghosts* were a thing of the past, at least in Scandinavia. At
that time, to its discredit, the Danish Royal Theatre had been the first
theatre in the world to refuse to produce the play. At last, to its credit,
the playhouse on Kongens Nytorv staged a belated but pivotal production (29 January 1903) that presented the play in what seemed an
entirely fresh light, undistorted by the extraneous moral polemic that
had previously surrounded it. Svend Leopold, the critic for *Teatret*,
summed up the occasion without undue exaggeration when he wrote:
"The performance of this play proves once more that Ibsen is given his
most outstanding interpretation here in Copenhagen. No stage in
Europe performs the Norwegian poet as perfectly as the Danish
national theatre. Every time a truly *great* evening occurs in this theatre,
it is invariably with one of the Norwegian plays."[26]

Directed by Johannes Nielsen, the Royal Theatre's *Ghosts* (actually
the third major production of the play in Copenhagen) bore the unmistakable stamp of William Bloch, Nielsen's mentor and also his
unacknowledged collaborator in this case. Beginning with Bloch's
epoch-making interpretation of *An Enemy of the People* in 1883, the ideas
and techniques of stage naturalism had been firmly implanted by this
director in Scandinavia, well before they had taken root elsewhere. In
an impressive succession of Ibsen productions that included *The Wild
Duck* (1885), *The Lady from the Sea* (1889), a miscarried *Hedda Gabler*
(1891), and a brilliant rendering of *The Master Builder* (1893), Bloch
responded with creative vigor to the challenge of a dramatic style that,
as the playwright put it, took "real life, and exclusively that, as the
basis and point of departure."[27] Yet the emphasis that Bloch placed on
concrete, significant details in his Ibsen productions was never an end
in itself but always a means – later to be adopted by other naturalistic
directors from Antoine to Brahm, Stanislavski, and Nielsen himself –
of achieving an evocative inner authenticity. "The theatre should be
not a mirror of life," Bloch maintained throughout his career, "but a
reflection of the hidden life of the soul, acting not a direct imitation,
illustrating 'reality,' but the indirect revelation of the ever-changing
facets of the soul."[28] In his aesthetics (as, indeed, in Ibsen's), the
attention to the outer dimension of unmistakably truthful detail served
a far more important purpose than that of merely chronicling reality or
creating an apparently life-like impression. This attention, grounded
in what Strindberg came to call the "greater" naturalism, was a strata-
gem for deepening the audience's perception of the essential spirit
and meaning of the play, by revealing an inner world within the

18 Photograph (from Act III) of Johannes Nielsen's painstakingly naturalistic production of *Ghosts* at the Danish Royal Theatre, Copenhagen, also in 1903.

seemingly precise context of everyday life. "The inanimate, material objects and the so-called life-like touches were his means of illuminating and breathing life into the setting, the situation, the stage action – of creating the necessary atmosphere around the only true reality in art, that of the soul," writes one observer about Scandinavia's foremost exponent of stage naturalism in the age of Ibsen.[29]

Especially in the detailed promptbook which Nielsen prepared for the 1903 *Ghosts*, one recognizes the abiding influence of Bloch's theatrical method and philosophy in a production which, in turn, remained in the repertory substantially unchanged until 1942. This promptbook contains not only set descriptions, floor plans, and intricately charted patterns of movement, but also very circumstantial instructions concerning stage business and line interpretation – all designed to amplify, but not change, the integral *mise-en-scène* woven into the play by Ibsen himself.[30] Conceived in this spirit, Nielsen's faithful but considerably elaborated rendering of Mrs. Alving's "spacious garden room" at Rosenvold became, with its solid walls and ceiling, its lighted lamps and chandelier, and its heavy furnishings, an uncompromisingly life-like comment on the lives and actions (past as much as present) of its inhabitants. In this respect, the indoor settings we encounter in all of Ibsen's later plays reflect a sympathy for the naturalistic effect of milieu on the characters; as such, these Ibsen rooms share a sense of constriction that often seems to give them a dramatic quality independent of the characters. Proceeding from a similar conviction, Bloch offered a succinct comment on this idea of endowing a given stage space with a specific mood and atmosphere of its own: "When I walk into the auditorium at night, after the curtain has gone up, the air, the atmosphere up on the stage should make me feel the same as any guest walking into a strange parlor: the kind of house it is, the kind of people there, and what goes on between them, before I even step inside."[31]

On the other hand, just as concentration and elimination were Ibsen's principles in developing character and dialogue, so these same principles were applied by him to the ostensibly "realistic" but scrupulously selective settings and related stage effects in his plays. To a certain degree, however, this economy of detail was over-ridden by the naturalistic director's avowed commitment to amplification and embellishment (Bloch liked to use the phrase "carrying on the creative process"). As a result, the setting in which *Ghosts* was played at the Royal Theatre typifies an approach that reached a climax of sorts in another benchmark performance of the play during this period, staged by Stanislavski and Nemirovitch-Danchenko two years later at the Moscow Art Theatre. Stanislavski's work diary for this production, which opened at the M.A.T. on 31 March 1905, provides a running account of the great Russian director's earnest, even frantic search for an appropriate stage environment that would project the specific atmosphere he sought, a "Norwegianized" image of "an old family house, filled with the sins of generations," in which "every corner reeks with the atmosphere of vice."[32] To achieve the desired effect, Stanislavski assembled an extraordinary collection of practicable architectural elements that were tried and continually rearranged as rehearsals progressed, including a bay window with a vista of fjord and glacier (from which "one gets a sense of cold, eternal destiny"), a lighted fireplace, a staircase and alcove, upper passageways with arches and balustrades, walls crowded with portraits of ancestors and covered with velvet or silk panels ("old materials, beautiful, faded"), and even cornices and a ceiling "decorated in Norwegian style, with reindeer, primitive figures, etc." (Small wonder that the Moscow critics were chiefly impressed by the "virtually ethnographic" quality of the result: "Anyone who wants to get an impression of a typical family home in the far North – with all its curiosities, down to the arrangement of the rooms and their furnishings – must see *Ghosts* at the Art Theatre: every detail bears the clear stamp of a careful study of everyday Norwegian life.")[33]

Although far more directly governed by Ibsen's stage directions than the rather overpowering M.A.T. decor seems to have been, the Royal Theatre setting exhibits a number of strikingly similar touches, as a glance at the floor plan and corresponding scene photograph will show. The portentous family portraits so dear to Stanislavski's heart (for which Ivan Moskvin, who played Osvald, had to be photographed in make-up to look like his father) were clearly in evidence here as well, hanging in the same kind of intimate corner nook that the Russian director also demanded as an acting area for the final scene. Located beyond the curtained archway at the back, the narrow, glassed-in "winter garden" described by Ibsen was seen here as a "veranda – greenhouse with flower stands, high plants (palms etc.)," and its large glass wall looked out on a "Norwegian landscape horizon" dimly visible "behind a gray-blue rain scrim." At the end of the second act, the night sky outside the glass was lit up by the glow from the orphanage fire, while later still, after the self-seeking Regine has left Osvald and his mother to their final, harrowing encounter, the audience watched as the cold (white-green) light of the first morning twilight slowly gave way to the brighter yellow, white and red illumination cast on the distant landscape by the rising sun.

The creation of a solid and convincing physical environment such as this, in which the characters of the drama were seen to live a life of their own, was the indispensable basis on which directors like Bloch and Nielsen proceeded to build a complete performance. "Whereas before it only implied a logical arrangement of positions and settings, *mise-en-scène* has now developed into an art that requires an intensive study of the individual roles, a minute working out of all details," Bloch had declared as early as 1884.[34] Each detail contributed its share to an organic totality which he regarded as the ultimate goal of the director – a psychologically motivated integration of the play's complex character relationships into what he termed "the inspired life of the ensemble." Within the "musical harmony" of this coordinated pattern, every role, no matter how small, was methodically developed; every action and every movement on the stage was assigned a precise meaning. As a result, the multiplicity of particulars and responses taken from the circumstances of daily life lent a Bloch performance an added dimension of intensified dramatic mood and atmosphere that is readily discernible in the production of *Ghosts* prepared by Nielsen under his guidance. The wealth of specific details and nuances contained in the surviving promptbook (in which a number of the notes seem to be in Bloch's hand, though it is hard to be certain) make this document an unusually concrete illustration of the character of the theatrical mode for which Ibsen's "realistic" plays were originally intended.

As we know, the opening scene of *Ghosts* is a textbook example of Ibsen's dramaturgy, in which the charged encounter of the two participants in the scene, the crafty, scheming Engstrand and the almost equally cynical Regine, conceals the exposition so that it becomes virtually imperceptible. In Nielsen's exactingly planned *mise-en-scène*, this episode yielded an emotional coherence and shape that set the tone for the entire production. Stanislavski, too, was greatly preoccupied by this crucial opening moment, and the solution he devised for his M.A.T. production is typical of his emphasis on physical activity and its associated motivation as a means of bonding character to environment and creating a sense of the flow of life:

In Ibsen's text the carpenter (Regine's father) enters the living room without motivation and stands there doing nothing while engaged in a lengthy conversation. But this is the theatre. There must be changes! So I invented this: From the start of the act he is busy fixing the lock on the door leading into the garden. Then a steamer passes. The carpenter begins to hammer. At the noise, Regine hurries in. The scene continues with him doing his job while she tidies up the room.[35]

By contrast, Nielsen's directorial concept imparted a different kind of balance and tension to this scene, in which Engstrand, dressed in work clothes and a wet carpenter's apron, was a grimly comic intruder bent on only one thing: his scheme and Regine's induction into it. As the curtain rose, the audience heard an unseen quarrel in progress. Quickly the participants in the row came into view, Engstrand (Elith Reumert) pushing his way forward into the room. A retreating Regine (played with "robust animal health and a broad, voracious smile" by an older veteran, Elga Sinding)[36] clutched a large garden syringe which she held "raised against him."

The text of this scene moves swiftly through a mosaic of topics – the rain, "the young master asleep upstairs," Jacob's fondness for the bottle, the orphanage project, the gullible Pastor Manders – but its real subject is Engstrand's own plan to coax Regine back to town with him. In an instant, with his use of the word "father," their relationship becomes clear – clearer still as their discussion turns to Johanne, Regine's mother, and her "esteem" for the late Captain (by then Chamberlain) Alving. In Nielsen's concept, Engstrand played his cards with serio-comic shrewdness and hypocrisy. As his "daughter" complained ("with genuine indignation") of his brutal treatment of her mother, "feigned martyrdom" colored his reply ("That's right, I'm to blame for everything"), delivered with a sigh and a slap on his game leg as he advanced further into the room. Regine's sneering, Frenchified disparagement of the offensive leg ("Pied de mouton") was met at first with "diplomatic agreement" ("You've learned a lot out here, I'll admit that"), before Engstrand abruptly shifted to a new tone in his very next remark ("and that'll come in handy now, Regine"): "discreet – sly – hinting – close to R., in a low voice."

After a pause (Ibsen's), Regine asked ("cynical egotism in her question, arms crossed, looking at E."): "And what was it you wanted me for in town?" Cautiously at first, Reumert's Engstrand began to outline his plan for "starting out in something new." Her rebuke of his swearing – "intense but hushed, looking up at the ceiling (Osvald!)" – was thus motivated not by any dislike of blasphemy but solely by her desire to avoid being overheard. Then, as she listened "with cold-blooded calculation," her foster-father unfolded his scheme for his so-called sailors' home, "intense energy in the presentation of his plan." She nodded "with cynical irony" as she asked her demonstrably rhetorical question, "And I'm supposed to – ?" As Engstrand began to explain "lewdly" ("Just come along to town with me and you'll get dresses enough"), she shifted position uneasily and laughed. Quickly, however, the laugh turned to a sneer ("But *I* don't want to live with *you*"), as she tried with "a haughty shove to push E. to the background."

The latter's broad hint that some nice officer – "maybe even a captain" – would take up with her was a tactical error. Her first reaction, as she stood "with arms crossed, tapping her foot," was a "contemptuous" rejection of the very idea of marrying a seaman. Contempt turned to fury, however, when she realized the point of his innuendo: "R. angrily seizes the flower syringe from the sewing table and raises it at him," notes the promptbook, while the cringing Engstrand beat a hasty retreat toward the background ("Now, now, you wouldn't strike me"). Brandishing her horticultural weapon aloft, she pursued her noxious parent toward the glass veranda. As she urged him to be quiet, he replied "brutally," "Funny how much you worry about that young Mr. Alving." Once again she tried to silence him, "listening toward the ceiling above," but his following reply ("Aha! You don't mean to tell me it's him – ?") made her renew her assault, "again striking out with the garden syringe and driving him out into the veranda."

Once there, Regine spotted Manders coming toward the house, abruptly changed course, and hustled Engstrand out into the front hall. His parting salute, delivered as he popped back into the living-room, acquired an almost comic edge: "I am your father, you know, whatever you say. I can prove it from the parish register." Then he disappeared, leaving Regine to make a hasty repair of her appearance before a mirror on the piano, seize a flower-pot, and strike a suitably domestic pose for the edification of the impressionable Pastor, who entered a moment later, collar turned up, shaking rain from his umbrella and his hat.

The naturalistic emphasis on a skillfully varied and particularized mosaic of character motivations and responses which this scene illustrates remained the guiding principle throughout Nielsen's entire *mise-en-scène*. In it, as in earlier productions of *Ghosts* elsewhere, the interpretation of Osvald's character focused particularly on the credible depiction of the incipient disease which is gradually eroding his mind – an illness whose mounting pressure becomes evident in his sudden changes of mood, his querulous and nervously impatient reactions, and his anguished weariness and weakness at the end of the play. As acted by Nicolai Neiiendam, who had also played the part at Dagmar Theatre five years before, the distribution of Osvald's developing illness took on a virtually symphonic character; in the director's script, musical terms are actually used to describe the progression of rapidly shifting attitudes. ("Mood – sad; tone – quiet; tempo – andante sostenuto," reads one such notation, accompanying Osvald's first-act line about his father's accomplishment of "so much that was good and useful, although he died so young.") For Stanislavski and

Moskvin, the spine of Osvald's character was his "inner drama": the fact that he knows from the outset about his illness and its consequences. By contrast, Nielsen's *mise-en-scène* and Neiiendam's performance laid greater stress on the *process* of collapse, the gradual deterioration of Osvald's passionate longing for the joy of life. The final phase in the young man's desperate struggle to live became, in this actor's hands, like "a fire that is about to die out and is extinguished."[37] In the long closing scene after the cynical Regine's departure, Osvald's final descent into madness was delineated by a virtual kaleidoscope of swiftly changing moods and reactions, recorded in scrupulous and revealing detail in the promptbook:

"Regine would have done it for the asking."	Spontaneous outburst. Rises, crosses . . . to the bookcase, forehead against its edge.
"Is it very late, Mother?"	Even tone. Back of neck against the bookcase, looking toward the window, slack posture.
"No, it was a good thing you managed to rid me of all those ideas. Once I'm over this one thing – "	Slowly. Nervous twitching in the face – headache coming on – an attack threatens (hand to back of neck) – with an effort of will.
"And meantime the sun will rise. *And then you'll know it all.*"	Hand pressed against his forehead. Tone quite cheerful and even.
"The *disease* that is my INHERITANCE – is seated here."	The disease breaks out – staring eyes – madness and terror.
{"Don't scream. I can't bear that." "Yes, Mother, it sits in here, lurking."	Outburst, grasps his head. Quiet again.
"I have had *one* attack down there."	As before, demonstrating with enormous (quiet) intensity.
"It's so unspeakably repulsive, you see."	Racing tempo – fever – terror – madness – fury.
" . . . Just like becoming a helpless infant again. Having to be fed, having to be – . Oh – words cannot describe it."	Hand to his forehead. Osv. presses his face against his knees.
"It might not necessarily be fatal right away, the doctor said."	Standing leaned against the table – period of exhaustion – warning of lethargy to come.

"You'll have to live through it. If only I had Regine here now . . . *she* would have helped me, of that I'm certain."	Brutally. A *short* advance toward Mrs. A. Osv. in full tempo – nervous, driving speed – tone remorseless.
"Regine would have done it. She was so splendidly carefree."	Crescendo.
'So now it must be you who comes to the rescue, Mother."	Throws off her embrace, shouting.
"You promise – ?"	Takes her hand.
"Yes, let us hope so."	After the tension – heavy and exhausted.

This practical demonstration culled from the promptbook represents, of course, only one side of an intensely two-sided encounter in which Betty Hennings – whose Helene Alving was perhaps the most richly conceived of the thirteen Ibsen heroines she played during her long career – created "a splendid picture of an aristocratic, stoic woman ready to bear anything and dare anything for the sake of her child."[38] Her portrayal of a proud, elegant Mrs. Alving relied on an attack essentially similar to that already described, based on a succession of subtly modified, muted nuances that colored her "vivid, nervous mimic reactions, the constantly changing tones of her voice, all the infinitely varied, almost imperceptible revelations of the life of the soul."[39] Margarita Savitskaya, who played the role in the Moscow Art Theatre production, was strictly cautioned by Stanislavski to avoid a spuriously "tragic" tone. "Let her, on the contrary, play a carefree, playful, elegant Frenchwoman," her director insisted. "She should play light French comedy up to the end of the second act. Even in the beginning of the third act she must minimize the tragedy and not give it its head until the end."[40] Almost as if she had been given the same advice, Hennings gave a carefully controlled performance as a quick-witted, strong-willed woman with a keen perception of life's ironies. In particular, her scenes with Pastor Manders (Peter Jerndorff) cast a spell of unbroken, almost mesmeric credibility that, in the words of one critic, "made the audience listen, intently and breathlessly involved, as though it had come by accident to overhear the most intimate exchange between two human beings. Here was true illusion."[41] Their encounters ranged in tone from ironic banter and bitter mockery to the note of vague, suppressed regret that suffused their parting in the last act, where Manders' (otherwise notoriously obtuse) leave-taking ("Good-bye, Mrs. Alving. And may the spirit of law and order soon prevail in this home") acquired an entirely unexpected emotional dimension:

1st time M. says, "Goodbye, Mrs. A.," she turns and goes slowly toward him. Hand clasp [and repeat]: "Goodbye, Mrs. A. etc." Mood that of the last, sorrowful time two people meet.

As she, in turn, wished him goodbye, she spoke "very quietly, with a sad glance at Manders" and then, catching sight of Osvald, walked away. (In this respect, the Royal Theatre performance reminds one of the strength of Stanislavski's argument that "since Regine, as well as Osvald, is a ghost," then "the main burden of the play is carried" by these two characters and their mutual relationship.)

The closing moments of Hennings' performance emphasized simple maternal sorrow and eschewed the image of the exquisite, weeping madonna that Duse would draw, "moving from grief to grief in some grey saraband of woe" (Agate). As she went on trying ("softly and mildly") to console the son she had already lost ("Now the attack has passed"), she caught sight of the sun breaking forth, turned down the lamp on the table, and blew it out. Dawn came: "The room's light (green-white) – subdued – against the air's (white-red)," notes the promptbook cue. Sunlight flooded through the window in the corner nook where Osvald now sat motionless, slumped in an armchair, his muscles slack, his face without expression. At first his mother shrank back in fear as he continued to call for the sun; then she fell to her knees beside his chair, trying in vain to rouse him; quickly she sprang to her feet again. At this juncture, however, every actress and her director face a perplexing dilemma. A few have boldly prepared themselves to administer the fatal overdose; many (following in Alice Wright's footsteps) have made it equally plain that such a course of action is unthinkable; while most have probably adhered to Ibsen's prescription, leaving Mrs. Alving to stare in speechless torment at her child, her hands twisted in her hair. Betty Hennings and her directors chose a different solution entirely. Suddenly fumbling in Osvald's breast pocket, this Mrs. Alving discovered the pillbox containing the twelve morphine capsules ("Where has he put them? Here!"). Next, she opened the lid of the box ("No, no, no! – Yes!") Then, presumably in her agitation ("No, no!"), she spilled the capsules on to the floor, retreated to a chair by the round table, and collapsed across the tabletop, overcome by emotion. The inevitable result was only further ambiguity: "Was it an accident or was it intentional that the saving pillbox with the morphine tablets fell on the floor this evening, scattering the contents to all sides?" demanded the reviewer for *Dannebrog*. "The playwright has undoubtedly left open the question of whether the mother does give her child 'the sun,' i.e., death. But this evening one got the impression that Mrs. Alving would *not* fulfil her son's request. And that surely must be wrong." (To which objection Ibsen might conceivably have responded with the reply Archer says he made to him: " 'That I don't know. Everyone must work that out for himself. I should never dream of deciding such a difficult question' ... He said he thought the solution perhaps lay there: that the mother would always put off and put off 'coming to the rescue,' on the plea that where there is life there is hope." [42]

THE KAMMERSPIELE INITIATIVE

The highly successful Royal Theatre production of 1903 thus epitomized the style of "discreet" realism (that adjective is used several times in the promptbook) which continued to retain a firm hold on subsequent performances of *Ghosts*, both in Scandinavia and elsewhere. In contrast to an earlier poetic work such as *Peer Gynt*, which has continued to foster new and imaginative conceptual reinterpretations in the theatre, Ibsen's major prose plays have generally, by their very nature, tended to elicit less in the way of freer formal experiments based on symbolic design concepts, radically stylized costumes, expressionistic lighting effects, and the like. Reinforced as it is by the precisely detailed *mise-en-scène* which Ibsen has written into each of these plays, the mode of theatrical representation initially evolved by Bloch and his European contemporaries in the late nineteenth century has, with obvious modifications and adjustments of character interpretation, continued to influence revivals of them in the present century.

To continue a moment longer with the pertinent example of *Ghosts* at the Royal Theatre: for the play's revival there in 1942, in which Poul Reumert's legendary portrayal of Pastor Manders revolutionized the accepted stage interpretation of the role, both the setting itself and the style of staging associated with it seemed, to the astonished eyes of critic Frederik Schyberg, not to have changed one bit. Reumert's imposing, resolutely uncomic and unbabyish prelate remained, above all, "the only man Mrs. Alving has loved in her life," and the actor's inspired ensemble-playing with Bodil Ipsen cast both their roles in a new perspective, charged with "flashes of a past erotic relationship, denied, but never forgotten." Yet the contradiction of this effective renewal remained, for Schyberg, the almost spectral presence of the old traditions, embodied for him in "*the parlor*, which when the curtain rose looked unalterably the same as before!" – when, in the opinion of this staunch supporter of modernism, "the parlor was in the style in which theatre pieces once were played, during the years between 1890 and 1910, but are preferably no longer."[43]

Instead, in terms O'Neill might have used, Schyberg goes on in his review to describe his own vision of the appropriate environment for *Ghosts*, a room which "must speak of the strange destiny of the house of Alving. In this room human destinies have been blighted. The house is damp from the eternal rain and musty from the air in which human beings perish like flowers that wither from neglect." This critic's imaginative word-picture is, willy-nilly, an almost perfect description of the actual setting designed by Edvard Munch for Max Reinhardt's production of *Ghosts* in 1906. With a simple change of surname from Alving to Rosmer, the description would do equally well as a concise characterization of that hazy, mysterious room-with-a-view designed by Edward Gordon Craig for Eleonora Duse's production of *Rosmersholm* in that very same year. "Ibsen's marked detestation for Realism is nowhere more apparent than in the two plays *Rosmersholm* and *Ghosts*," Craig wrote in the program for Duse's performance in Florence. "The words are the words of actuality, but the drift of the words, something beyond this. There is the powerful impression of unseen forces closing in upon the place: we hear continually the long drawn-out note of the horn of death."[44]

As Craig's famous program declaration reminds us, the anti-naturalistic innovators who altered the direction and meaning of modernism in the theatre during the early years of the twentieth century were particularly drawn to the challenge of establishing an alternative to the naturalistic manner of staging Ibsen's so-called realistic plays. The genesis of this alternative was a desire for a much more acutely defined conceptual approach to the plays, shaped by the New Stagecraft's triple goal of simplification, stylization, and suggestion. One important aspect of the new modernism, inspired by its distaste for the alleged "drabness" of stage naturalism, was the renewed emphasis which it placed upon the role of the designer as an artist enjoying equal standing with the director. (One notices, for example, the absence of any mention whatever of a designer in many of the early productions of *Ghosts*.) Out of this new concern with the interpretative power of modern design and pictorial art in the theatre arose the historic invitation which Reinhardt extended to Munch, Scandinavia's foremost painter in the Ibsen era, to provide a series of design sketches for his production of *Ghosts*, which opened his intimate Kammerspiele in Berlin (8 November 1906) and formed the centerpiece for a compact cluster of other innovative Ibsen performances, including *Rosmersholm* (1905), *Hedda Gabler* (with Hermann Bahr, 1907), and a reprise of *Love's*

Comedy (1907), the play with which Reinhardt had begun his directing career seven years previously.

As a young actor in Otto Brahm's company, Reinhardt had achieved a measure of success in such "character" parts as Foldal, the would-be poet in *John Gabriel Borkman*, Old Ekdal in *The Wild Duck*, and especially Jacob Engstrand, a favorite role which he repeated in his own production. Brahm's *Ghosts* was clearly the source of inspiration and point of departure for Reinhardt's own experiment with the play. The influence of Albert Bassermann's seminal interpretation of Osvald was unmistakably felt in the Kammerspiele performance as well. The strongest link, however, is to the highly conceptual tendency evident in Brahm's approach, which caused his commentators to describe the play as a work "rooted in sorrow": "The dark path [Ibsen] traces runs along the walls of the graveyard, " Alfred Polgar was thus prompted to write in response to Brahm's interpretation. "Tall cemetery crosses – social custom and duty – hover, oppressive and life-denying, over everything."[45] Munch's extraordinarily evocative setting, which not only lent the Kammerspiele performance its distinctive visual tone and texture but also conclusively shaped the entire directorial image of the play, in effect carried this view of the work much further. By deliberately transferring it from the realm of reality (where it had remained firmly anchored in Brahm's production) to an imaginative level at which poetic and atmospheric values became far more emphatic than any of the earlier naturalistic productions had attempted to make them, the Munch–Reinhardt collaboration opened the eyes of contemporary critics and audiences to an entirely "new" Ibsen.

Instead of confronting the spectator with a physical environment consisting of a complex filigree of realistic details, in which no individual element was given particular emphasis, Munch's expressively simplified living-room setting for *Ghosts* stressed certain specific visual motifs, intended to heighten and deepen the dominant mood of the production. In this interpretation of the drama, the precise, logically ordered mosaic of reality – Ibsen's objectively rendered environment – was de-emphasized in order to intensify and render transparent certain predominant themes. Needless to say, Munch was no ordinary stage designer (though he had previously created the set of Lugné-Poë's production of *John Gabriel Borkman* in 1897), and his design work for *Ghosts* took the form of a number of sketches meant as purely intuitive visual responses to moods and situations found in the play. In these sketches, however, the contours of reality are not distorted in an expressionistic manner. Rather, reality is painted in a particularly revealing light and given a specific coloring in order to project an

19   One of Edvard Munch's most evocative sketches for Reinhardt's
Kammerspiele production of *Ghosts*, Berlin, 1906.

imaginative vision of the inner rhythms and tensions of the drama.
When we look at the living-room milieu Munch depicted, we do
indeed find numerous items one would call realistic: a table with
chairs, a chaise longue on a carpet, a coffee table beside it, a fireplace, a
grandfather clock, paintings on the wall, even a potted plant. The end
result of Munch's technique is, however, a distillation – something
akin to what the American painter Andrew Wyeth once described in an
interview as "painting reality with an edge, with a meaning. It's what's
behind it that's important." In just this sense, Munch's sketches for
Ghosts represent what could be called a regenerative decimation of
strict, old-fashioned realism, done – and here again Wyeth would also
agree – in the service of a world behind forms, beneath surfaces. In an
undated letter to Munch, Reinhardt writes of the crucial importance of
revealing that which "stands between and behind the words" in Ibsen.

Hugo von Hofmannsthal describes the evocative end product of
Munch's efforts as a room "of medium size, a sort of salon in the style
of 1850," but the combination of colors and the shape of the furnishings "breathed a spirit of oppressiveness, of grief and of the sense
of destiny that broods over this tragedy, just as a tragic overture
breathes the motif of the opera," he tells us.[46] Held in dark colors of
reddish brown, black, gray, and violet and dominated visually by a
large, black chair, this room virtually exuded a heavy atmosphere of
joylessness and constriction. The black armchair, a significant object in

all the interior sketches Munch made, seemed to Reinhardt to epito-
mize the quality of mood he sought. It "tells you all you want to
know," he assured designer Ernst Stern, who expressed practical
reservations. "The dark coloring reflects the whole atmosphere of the
drama. And then look at the walls: they're the color of diseased gums.
We must try to get that tone. It will put the actors in the right mood."[47]
Although a large window in the background looked out on a fjord,
Munch's stifling chamber seemed closed in like a prison by sharply
outlined, threatening mountain peaks that nearly obscured the view of
the sky, further heightening the feeling of predestined entrapment
that communicated itself, with almost Strindbergian intensity,
throughout the performance. "Every line, every mass of space, height,
width – all played their appointed parts in this relentless modern
drama of fate, and the figures moving in it, almost as if driven by some
unknown force, seemed to be placed there by fate itself," one critic
remarked. "They were like necessary spots in the design of the whole
scene, like an accent in a bar of music."[48]

Hence, both by approaching *Ghosts* with the avowed objective of
endowing the inner spirit of the play with life and visible form, rather
than attempting to recreate external "reality" on the stage, and by
interpreting it as a drama in which destiny, rather than character or
psychology, constitutes the tragic axis, the Munch–Reinhardt collaboration marked a definitive break with the earlier naturalistic style
of production. The profound, even overpowering effect which the
Kammerspiele performance had on its audiences depended on an
intense rapport between the stage and the spectators in Reinhardt's
intimate playhouse. Here, however, this rapport no longer relied on
"making the spectator feel as if he were actually sitting, listening, and
looking at events happening in real life," as Ibsen had instructed
Lindberg. The great evocative force of this theatrical experience derived not so much from the detailed interaction of characters as from
the revelation of a single coherent image of the inner tragic rhythm of
the drama – a conceptual image that made of it a tragedy of destiny, of
human beings inescapably trapped and doomed to suffer.

Each of the individual figures in the work was subordinate to this
larger pattern of significance. For Brahm, the goal of stage direction
had been "truth" and the attendant circumstances of actuality; for
Reinhardt, its uppermost purpose was the projection of a completely
conceived and coordinated theatrical vision. "Every sentence sounds
as if it had just been created; every situation has a face of its own, every
pause its importance, every figure stands at the right spot. Nothing
disturbs, nothing is there for its own sake only," declared Siegfried

Jacobsohn in his assessment of the "inexpressible beauty" of this production. "There are no longer the personalities of the actors; they are the persons in the poet's world brought to life."[49]

Underlying the young Alexander Moissi's portrayal of an elegiac, wraith-like Osvald was something of the same sense of inescapable anguish and perceived futility that Albert Bassermann brought to the role when he played it for Brahm at the turn of the century. ("Bassermann enacts the last hours of a condemned man," Polgar later recorded. "He does not play the despair of a struggle certain to end in defeat, but rather the despair of a human being who is unable to struggle – because all weapons have been knocked out of his hands, because he is unable to conceive of how to defend himself."[50]) This quality of weariness and helplessness, especially strong in Bassermann's mime, led in Moissi's predominantly lyrical reinterpretation to an emphasis on Osvald as the anguished spiritual sufferer, rather than the hapless victim of physical disease. Beside him, Agnes Sorma (Brahm's first Regine) gave her Mrs. Alving the stature of a monumental symbol of maternal grief and forlorn hope, a "mater dolorosa" (to borrow Jacobsohn's phrase) whose overwhelming sorrow bespoke the humanity in Ibsen's work, rather than its spirit of rebellion. "*Die Sorma* was no Helene Alving," wrote the distinguished Berlin critic Alfred Kerr. "She was simply Osvald's mother. Not a sturdy spirit, in whom lay the active energy of the individualist. A superior woman, to be sure: but superior only in terms of feeling, only in her sensitivity, not in terms of will-power."[51] The effect of her performance must have seemed to Reinhardt's audience a wholly unexpected change from the defiant, even heroic approach to the role adopted by Else Lehmann, Brahm's star, who fought a desperate struggle to keep up her courage as Mrs. Alving, steadfastly holding back, as Polgar says, "each stab of pain, each throb of emotion, in order to remain strong."

Not least, as Edvard Munch's sketches so graphically reveal, the interplay of light and shadow held crucial interpretative prominence in the Kammerspiele rendering of *Ghosts*, as indeed it does in the thematic design of the text itself. Responsive lighting changes, at once realistically motivated and symbolically expressive, emphasized and interpreted the drama's changing moods, serving to amplify and intensify the tragic pulse of its performance in the theatre. The muted tones which Ibsen's stage directions imply – the "gloomy fjord landscape veiled by steady rain" – underwent unobtrusive modifications, both in hue and texture, as the production progressed. Reinhardt's detailed memorandum to Munch concerning the lighting changes he envisioned is, in itself, a fascinating illustration of the eerie atmosphere he sought and achieved, in which light and shadow literally act out a drama of their own:

Act I: Murky gray rain weather, lighter outside than inside. Light mainly from the window on the left. Windows: wet, dark-stained. Humid, pallid rain atmosphere. Variations through the lighting. Forenoon.

Act II: Gathering twilight. Increasingly deep shadows. At first lighter, then darker and darker until it becomes black outside. Inside, toward the end, a standing lamp brightly illuminates a part of the room, particularly the table, leaving the corners of the room ghostly dark [*gespenstisch dunkel*]. At the end, a weak red reflection of fire beyond the windows. Afternoon – evening.

Act III: Night. Lamp. Later very slowly: pale glow of light increasing in strength toward the end, which together with the lighted lamp creates a strangely ominous half-light. At the very end, full, cold, pitiless sunlight from behind, so that the play ends with a grandiose symphonic finale. Night – early morning . . .[52]

In this evocative atmosphere the darkly clad figures in the drama appeared weirdly unreal, like their own ghosts. As the past into which the characters are helplessly locked is at last fully revealed, the sinister shadows that hover in Munch's designs and Reinhardt's notes sprang to life, ruthlessly pursuing and engulfing the human figures on the stage. "In the last, despairing moments of the play," Julius Bab tells us, while the darkness was gradually pierced by the penetrating, cold gray shafts of the dawn before sunrise, "as Mrs. Alving rushed behind her son, towards the lamp, shadows as high as houses cast on the walls accompanied her like pursuing demons."[53]

From Reinhardt's time to our own, directors have continued to seek out and present exceptional alternatives, of a more or less radically stylized character, to the naturalistic attitude that has tended to dominate in performances of Ibsen's major prose plays. In the case of *Ghosts*, its production at the Kammerspiele, which Reinhardt continued to revive throughout Europe until 1914, proved to have far-reaching consequences because it revealed a new Ibsen – or, more correctly, it demonstrated that the symbolic Ibsen of the later plays, the poetic Ibsen of the early works, and the angry author of *Ghosts* were, after all, one and the same man. Similarly, in totally different ways, the Ibsen designs created by Munch and Gordon Craig in 1906 crystallized the desire to create what Craig called "a place which harmonizes with the thoughts of the poet," rather than yet another authentic Victorian parlor. "Ibsen can be acted and staged so as to be made insignificant and mean," Craig went on to remind the audience in his program

20   Two contrasting views of *Ghosts* at the Munich Kammerspiele: above,
Mac Zimmermann's *Jugendstil* environment of angles, curtained alcoves, and
glass, designed for Fritz Kortner's production in 1953. Below, the starkly
simplified, mausoleum-like setting created by Jörg Zimmermann for the last
act of the Hans Reinhard Müller revival of the play in 1975.

article for *Rosmersholm* at the Teatro della Pergola: "Therefore we must ever remember our artistry and forget our propensity towards photography, we must for this new poet re-form a new Theatre."

Particularly in the post-war period, productions of *Ghosts* have been increasingly characterized – not least in the German theatre, so directly influenced by Reinhardt's methods and example – by a steadily growing dissatisfaction with the whole idea of erecting a photographic replica of reality on the stage. Two revivals of the play at the renowned Munich Kammerspiele illustrate contrasting alternatives. As late as 1953, the finely detailed, naturalistically textured production staged by Fritz Kortner at this theatre still made use of a setting that exhibited a full complement of what the reviewer for *A. Z.* (18 September 1953) slyly referred to as "the trophies of the 'good taste' of home life" in Ibsen's day: heavy portières, gas-lighted chandelier, period furniture, grand piano, glass-bead curtains, straw flowers in Moorish vases, and much else. While still operating within a recognizably realistic context, however, the setting for the Kortner production also sought in its own terms to emulate Munch's example, albeit in a non-expressionistic mode, by painting the reality of the place and the play in a revealing light. Thus, the cluttered *Jugendstil* environment created by Mac Zimmermann on this occasion was an uncomfortable room of oblique angles, curtained alcoves, and glass, upon which both the meaning and the physical presence of the conservatory, the shadowy dining-room beyond it, and the upper storey of the house could all be seen to impinge.

Then, on this same stage in 1975, the period clutter of the setting for Kortner's production was swept aside to reveal an open, flexible stage space which, in Hans Reinhard Müller's new *mise-en-scène*, was defined entirely by selected, symbolically weighted details keyed to what Reinhardt had referred to in the Munch designs as the psychology of color. As a result, observed Armin Eichholz in *Münchner Merkur* (8 October 1975), the play's environment now seemed "turned to stone" by a stark decor with "no conservatory, no doors, only smooth gray furniture and an ominously tall black stove, surrounded on all sides by the steady rain." "No more velvet. Salvarsan and penicillin were discovered long ago, but have not done away with the play's true theme: the life-lie," the director declared in a program article for the production: "The stage picture should be reminiscent of *Huis clos*, Sartre's closed world. No window, no doors in sight, no pictures. Only furniture which becomes more sparse from act to act. The stage picture moves forward, toward the spectator. At the end: only two steps, the fireplace, a chair. Stage and auditorium become one." As the stage itself grew progressively more confined and cave-like from act to act, designer Jörg Zimmermann's encroaching "mausoleum walls" seemed, to Eichholz as to other observers, the visible sign of the oppressiveness of "the utterly squandered past that is exposed, beat by beat," in Ibsen's "destiny quintet."

As this critic's comment suggests, the choice of production style in this case reflects a broader tendency to approach *Ghosts* as something more than a realistic social drama – not as allegory, surely, but rather as a trans-historical work possessing a dimension of universality it shares with its classical "model," *Oedipus Rex*. When Helmut Henrichs staged a somewhat uneven production of it at the Residenztheater in Munich in 1965, he had sought to view the text specifically in these terms, as "a chamber play in which a classical tragedy lies concealed," yet the "discreetly realistic" living-room *mise-en-scène* adopted by Henrichs was completely at odds with his stated intention. ("The alternative to this might have been a directorial concept that brought out the larger-than-life proportions of Ibsen's characters and conflicts in a more expressive way," Joachim Kaiser commented at the time.)[54] Four years after, for a glittering revival at the Thalia Theatre in Hamburg starring Paula Wessely for the first time as Mrs. Alving and Mathias Wieman in his customary role as Manders, director August Everding elected to use a more deliberately stylized decor by Jörg Zimmermann, who for this occasion designed a somber, cavernous interior (*Frankfurter Allgemeine Zeitung* called it a "living-hall") whose bluish-black columns drew attention to the play's classical dimension and its affinity to Greek tragedy. Here again, however, the German critics felt that the production failed to resolve "the hitherto comparatively tame debate over the problem of a performance style for Ibsen."[55]

There was, meanwhile, nothing tame or indecisive about the radically conceptualized, at times even expressionistic solution adopted by Luc Bondy in his revival of *Ghosts* at the Schauspielhaus in Hamburg in 1977. An austerely furnished, two-storey bomb-shelter of a set, created by Rolf Glittenburg, looked out on rain that never ceased to fall. Hanging overhead, a heavy cement-block ceiling "threatened to demolish Mrs. Alving's nice parlor" and dwarfed its human inhabitants and their surroundings. At the top of a staircase leading to the upper storey of this cheerless, neo-Gothic Rosenvold, a high, narrow doorway opened on a void "from which Mrs. Alving emerged several times, resembling an ancient, faded fresco – a figurine in the midst of this 'superstructure.'"[56] Understandably, perhaps, the inmates of this claustrophobic domestic hell tried repeatedly to escape into the open air, setting off into the downpour only to be driven back by the elements. Bondy's ensemble, so securely interlocked that the five figures in the drama seemed to Klaus Wagner (*FAZ*) "like light and shadowy accents in a group picture," stressed a style of grotesque tragi-comedy that bordered at times on (symbolic) farce. Thus, Mrs. Alving boxed her son's ears in exactly the same way Regine had boxed her father's; Manders and Engstrand tried without success to sit down in the same chair at once. Manders, played in this production by Hans Michael Rehberg, stood out particularly as "the semi-comic counterpart and double" of Mrs. Alving (Doris Schade), unwittingly putting on her spectacles instead of his own in precisely the way *she* puts on his worn-out moral clichés ("Surely a child ought to love its father") in her crucial scene with Osvald, before she comes to the guilty realization of her own irreparable mistake.

In English theatre, on the other hand, Pastor Manders (whom Harold Hobson once called "that mythological ogre of theological insanity") has as a rule been treated as a caricature and an embarrassment by directors and audiences convinced that any laughter he may elicit is *prima facie* evidence of the quaintness of a hopelessly antiquated classic, rather than part of a dramaturgical design that consciously mingles humor and horror. As a general principle, humor and melodrama have been perceived as the Scylla and Charybdis which any production of *Ghosts* on the English stage must at all costs avoid. In recent times, understated acting has become the approved method for steering a safe course, and it is in pursuit of this goal that experiments in non-realistic staging have been undertaken.

For the Alan Bridges revival at the Aldwych in 1967, for example, Jocelyn Herbert provided a relentlessly gray monochrome design, based on nineteenth-century motifs and surrounded by large panes of rain-wet window, that was intended to match and facilitate the muted tones and restrained, unhistrionic reactions of the performance. More than one reviewer found, however, that the polite contemporary reserve of Peggy Ashcroft and her fellow actors seemed out of key with the bruising emotional undercurrent of Ibsen's tragedy. "Determination to soft-pedal anything that might strike modern audiences as absurd or dated leads to minimizing all its big effects," declared *The Times* (15 June 1967). 'When the orphanage goes up in flames the cast stroll over to the window with no great excitement, and even Oswald's final madness is handled with well-bred restraint."

When Jonathan Miller took up the challenge of the play seven years later, his rigorously subdued performance at the Greenwich Theatre Festival (17 January 1974) succeeded where Bridges had partially failed, by making *Ghosts* into what J. C. Trewin called "a plain state-

21   From the first act of Gerhard Knoop's staunchly traditionalist staging of
Ghosts at Det Norske Teatret, Oslo, in 1964.

ment and none the less exciting for that."[57] The visual metaphor of
bleakness and constraint in the Jocelyn Herbert decor gave way to a
more explicit image of imprisonment – a huge string cage (reminiscent
of the silver hanging cords of Josef Svoboda's famous setting for the
National Theatre production of *The Three Sisters*), within which Miller's
designer, Patrick Robertson, confined the entire action of the play.
Working in this suitably allusive framework, the director and his cast
set about creating a performance from which any trace of the larger-
than-life proportions of Ibsen's characters and conflicts was systematically eliminated. As a result, Irene Worth won praise for portraying an
average, middle-class woman, rather than the "improbable patrician"
Mrs. Alving had been in the past (Harold Hobson in the *Sunday Times*).
The unexpectedly easygoing and sensual Manders depicted by Robert
Stephens likewise seemed to transform even the troublesome pastor
from a "booming diehard" to an "oblique charmer" (Irving Wardle in
The Times). Meanwhile, Miller's ending must have come as the greatest
surprise of all to theatre-goers who might have recalled the Old Vic
production of *Ghosts*, scarcely more than fifteen years earlier. In those
days, Osvald met his terrible end graphically, slouched gray and inert
in his seat with, eyewitnesses tell us, "only his tongue moving faintly

in his open mouth like a baby struggling to be born." At the climactic moment of sunrise in Miller's staunchly "anti-melodramatic" revision, however, Osvald simply fell quietly asleep in his chair.

In the program for the first production of *Ghosts* at Det Norske Teatret in 1964, Tormod Skagestad expressed his theatre's determination to render Ibsen's drama "relevant, alive, and contemporary for the generations living now." Performances in its own language have sought to "contemporize" *Ghosts* in a number of different ways. In, for instance, the shadowy, almost Piranesi-like dungeon-room created by Guy Krohg for a revival of the play at the Danish Royal Theatre in 1969, one finds a radical departure from the traditional naturalistic parlor that had held the stage there for so long. At Det Norske Teatret, meanwhile, the nature of the "renewal" was linguistic rather than scenographic; although Gerhard Knoop's *mise-en-scène* broke no new ground in theatrical terms, Skagestad's "adaptation" of the work to contemporary New Norse thrust *Ghosts* (once again) into the midst of a heated debate over language reform and classlessness in today's Norway. Often, in Scandinavia as elsewhere, directors have turned to depth psychology as another means of stretching and expanding the play's meaning for modern actors and audiences alike. John Price's probing production for Det Danske Teater (a touring company) in 1978 is a good example, stressing as it did the undercurrent of latent, frustrated, or repressed erotic relationships which the director perceived in the play. In that same year, Pål Løkkeberg's modern-dress *Ghosts*, first directed by him in 1972, returned to Nationaltheatret in Oslo as one of an impressive round of Ibsen revivals presented there to commemorate the playwright's sesquicentennial. In this production – actually prepared by Løkkeberg with the help of a clinical psychologist – Mrs. Alving's growing realization of the harm her moral cowardice has, in the first place, done to her *husband* ("I'm afraid I made life miserable for your poor father," she tells Osvald) became the crux of a penetrating psychological performance by Helen Brinchmann.

This sesquicentennial cycle of productions in Oslo (specifically *Ghosts*, *The Lady from the Sea*, and an intimate chamber production of *Little Eyolf*) acquired more than passing topical interest, in that they redirected attention, in principle and in practice, to the significance of coming to terms with the Ibsen tradition and absorbing it, rather than rejecting it out of hand, when attempting to shape a more "modern" and relevant approach to his plays in the theatre. "To demystify without destroying dramatic effect – that is the main thrust of the Norwegian style of Ibsen," declared Jens Kistrup in a review article entitled "The Modern Ibsen: A Playwright for All" (*Berlingske Tidende*,

22   The dungeon-like environment designed by Guy Krohg for a revival of the same play at the Danish Royal Theatre, Copenhagen, in 1969. Osvald (Peter Steen) begs his mother (Bodil Kjer) for the sun.

6 July 1978). In the specific case of *Ghosts*, this critic described the underlying secret of the style as "a double one. On the one hand, it can go very far in the direction of the (melo)dramatic – for instance, in the battle Osvald must wage with his mother for the right to live and to die. On the other hand, it is able to preserve the irony in the almost comedic secondary characters in whom Ibsen specialized." In a more general sense, these new Norwegian revivals revealed a thoroughly contemporary but not an artificially rootless or "timeless" Ibsen – for, as Kistrup argues, no matter how advanced his plays can be said to be, even he remains "the product of his own presuppositions":

And no matter how many torpedoes Ibsen may plant under the ark in *Ghosts* – society, marriage, the family, ideals, sexual and ethical codes, all of these are blown to bits! – this entire play is still placed within the framework of the naturalistic parlor which a whole century of theatre audiences have known as a symbol of security. That has been the playwright's chance: he was radical and revolutionary without rendering the theatre rootless. He never operates in a vacuum. He creates a tradition and yet is still part of a tradition.

5

Ibsen's "new method": *The Wild Duck*

"In the course of time a variety of crazy ideas are apt to collect in one's mind, and one needs an outlet for them," Ibsen wrote to Georg Brandes early in the summer of 1883. His head filled with plans for the play that was to become *The Wild Duck*, the dramatist compared the solitary, individualistic revolt of Doctor Stockmann in *An Enemy of the People* to his own compulsive need to forge on alone into new territory. "The majority, the mass, the mob will never catch up with [Stockmann], and he can never have the majority with him," Ibsen told the Danish critic. "At the point where I stood when I wrote each of my books there now stands a tolerably compact crowd; but I myself am no longer there. I am elsewhere; farther ahead, I hope."[1] Fifteen months later, when the new play was finally ready, Ibsen sent the fair copy to his publisher in Copenhagen, Frederik Hegel, with another letter that likewise shows his awareness that in *The Wild Duck* he had consciously and decisively altered his technique. "But the study and representation of these characters will not be an easy task; and therefore the book should be offered to the theatres as early as possible in the season," he instructed Hegel, who also acted as Ibsen's literary representative. "In some ways this new play occupies a position by itself among my dramatic works, in plan and method differing in several respects from my former ones. I shall say no more on this subject at present."[2]

Later critics have tended to discuss Ibsen's "new method" in *The Wild Duck* mainly from a literary point of view, in terms of such matters as its increased use of direct symbolism, its adoption of a central controlling image (the wild duck), and its new emphasis on human psychology and psychological motivation. Valid as all these considerations may be, however, it seems clear that Ibsen himself saw the change in his approach chiefly as a *theatrical* departure that would profoundly affect both the actor's approach and the nature of the spectator's perception. One finds convincing evidence of this concern with the theatrical dimension in the long, detailed letter Ibsen dispatched to Hans Schrøder, who as managing director of Christiania Theatre had accepted *The Wild Duck* for production there and had wired the playwright in Rome seeking advice (12 November 1884). Ibsen's prompt reply goes far beyond his customary exhortation that, "in both the ensemble acting and the staging, the play demands truth to nature and a touch of reality in every respect."[3] In this (frequently reprinted) letter, every aspect of performance, from the atmospheric character of the lighting to the significance of even the smallest roles in the ensemble (the two servants, Petersen and Jensen, and the guests at Werle's dinner party), is given due consideration.

Between the lines of Ibsen's letter one easily discerns his anxious awareness that the new play's acute theatrical irony (the subtle mingling of comedy and seriousness in word, action and visual image), the far greater complexity of its character inter-relationships, and its deliberate diffuseness of focus all contributed to a performance challenge that no modern play of his (or of any of his contemporaries) had yet presented. In particular, this work's multiplicity of focus and its dynamic combination and juxtaposition of moods and impressions makes a new kind of demand on the creative involvement of the theatre spectator, who is drawn into the creative process by being compelled to proceed along the very same path of associations and suggestions that the author traveled in composing his theatrical image. The audience thus not only witnesses the representation of the finished work, but is also made to participate in its emergence and assembly. "The image planned by author, director, and actor is concretized by them in separate representational elements, and is assembled – again and finally – in the spectator's perception."[4] This observation is borrowed from Sergei Eisenstein's classic discussion of the theory of montage, but with obvious modifications it serves to identify a fundamental structural dynamism at work in *The Wild Duck*. It is this principle which eventually evolved into the impressionistic theatrical pointillisme used by Chekhov – who knew Ibsen's play intimately and deplored its production at the Moscow Art Theatre as "a withered, weak, and uninteresting performance."[5]

Without the benefit of either stage performance or past experience with this mode of literature, the reading public (including even William Archer) at first received *The Wild Duck* with utter bewilderment. Nor, in fact, did its belated French and English premieres do much to alleviate the confusion. Antoine's ineffectually "symbolic" performance with the Théâtre Libre ensemble (28 April 1891) is probably best remembered now for Sarcey's mildly amusing caricature of the play's "single hermetically sealed secret" ("as mysterious as the great secret of the Freemasons that no one has ever known, not even the grand master of Freemasonry"): "Oh! that wild duck, absolutely nobody ever, no, nobody, neither you who have seen the play, nor Lindenlaub and Ephraim who translated it word for word, nor the author who wrote it, nor Shakespeare who inspired it, nor God or the Devil, no, no one will ever know what that wild duck is, neither what it's doing in the play, nor what it means."[6] Jules Lemaître, although more open to the effect created by Antoine's production, was likewise left with a confused impression of the play as "a pure comedy – at times even a farce – which finally turns toward tragedy ... Antoine and his comrades played it too dramatically, too slowly, too seriously, too majestically, thereby making it harder to understand for part of the audience."[7] The predominantly unsigned London notices of J. T. Grein's single subscription performance at the Royalty Theatre (4 May 1894) are, if possible, even less enlightening, concerned as they are with the "obscurity" of the play's symbolism, the "gloominess" of its outlook, or (in the case of one outraged critic for *Truth*) the excessiveness of the on-stage drinking which it requires and evidently condones! Archer's initial misgivings were swept aside by Grein's experiment, Winifred Fraser won praise for conveying simple, childlike innocence in her touching portrayal of Hedvig, but the harsh final verdict handed down by Clement Scott was widely shared: "If the *Wild Duck* were presented for a run tomorrow at a theatre where the paying public secures its seats in the ordinary fashion it would be laughed off the stage, for such eccentricities are not as yet tolerated or even recognized by a healthy and vigorous public opinion that keeps the atmosphere of the theatre free from absurdity and affectation."[8] (In New York, it was not until 1918 that a production of the play for "the paying public" was even attempted – and then only because Arthur Hopkins, its director, was able to give the role of Hedvig to Alla Nazimova, the vibrant and passionate "tiger cat in the leash of art" whose Ibsen heroines had been holding American audiences spellbound for more than a decade.)

In Scandinavia, meanwhile, a markedly different situation prevailed from the outset. Here, the challenge of Ibsen's new method in *The Wild Duck* was taken up without hesitation – and largely without the confusion and controversy that greeted it elsewhere – by a cluster of important directors that included August Lindberg in Sweden, Gunnar Heiberg and Bjørn Bjørnson in Norway, and William Bloch in Denmark. It is their productions, rather than the contentious performances given by Antoine and Grein, that afford a truer and better substantiated impression of a theatrical style in basic harmony with the playwright's stated intentions. Heiberg, whose finely detailed production at the National Stage in Bergen (9 January 1885) was the drama's world premiere, has left a sensitive impressionistic description of the play that affords a revealing contrast to the unsympathetic opinions of Sarcey and Scott:

The Wild Duck is not just a drama that abounds in engaging characters, not just a poem in a strange and lovely style. *Rosmersholm* and *Ghosts* are that, too – with a kind of cold marble repose about them. But in *The Wild Duck* there is neither coldness nor marble . . . Sometimes one feels that once one lived among these people, long ago. One longs for them with a sad longing, as if for something that once was and will never come again . . . It is as though *The Wild Duck* were built on painful memories, on strange experiences from one's own youth. And this gives the play a secret, intimate charm, a gentle atmosphere found in no other play of [Ibsen's].[9]

All four directors instinctively recognized the formidable challenge they had been faced with. "With Doctor Ibsen's newest play we have entered virgin territory where we have to make our way with pick and shovel," Lindberg wrote to the playwright before going into rehearsal for his production at the Royal Dramatic Theatre in Stockholm, which opened three weeks after Heiberg's: "The people in the play are completely new, and where would we get by relying on old theatrical clichés?"[10] In a letter to his father Bjørn Bjørnson, whose production at Christiania Theatre followed only two days after the world premiere, pinpointed a new and pressing consideration that confronted him and his fellow directors in rehearsing this particular play:

Day and night *The Wild Duck* was with me. It has clamored its way into my very being. I lay in the stillness of the night and heard the lines. And *heard* the pauses. The ones that had to lift the words. Those to come, or those which had already been spoken. They can loom larger after the pause that precedes them – or in the silence that follows them.[11]

William Bloch, the fourth member of the group, seems to have had little of a general nature to say about *The Wild Duck*, but his production of it at the Danish Royal Theatre in Copenhagen (22 February 1885) became the ultimate realization of the aims and principles of the modern movement to which all four directors belonged. The Bloch performance is also of particular interest because surviving production records, including a detailed promptbook with the director's notes and diagrams, allow us to "revisit" it in circumstantial detail, in order to gain a fuller understanding of the relationship of Ibsen's play to the theatre practice of his own time.

As mentioned earlier, Bloch's preceding production of *An Enemy of the People* at the Royal Theatre (4 March 1883) had been a turning-point, in the wake of which the new program of stage naturalism was convincingly established in Scandinavia. With its detailed ensemble direction and precisely coordinated staging, Bloch's *Enemy* pointed ahead to his work with the far more complex Ibsen drama that was to follow two years later. The effect created was one of unbroken, life-like credibility, attuned to that "truthfulness to nature" upon which, the dramatist had insisted, the effectiveness of this play's performance depended – "the illusion that everything is real, and that one is sitting and watching something that is actually taking place in real life."[12] Bloch's interpretation, a lucid crystallization of the new naturalistic concepts, built up a weave of tangible detail, nuance, and reaction that amplified but never distorted the thematic line of Ibsen's text. "The care with which Bloch had brought out even the minutest detail, had polished the smallest facets created a theatrical phenomenon whose parallel had not been seen in any Scandinavian theatre," wrote Sven Lange. "The performance shone like a glittering and brilliant diamond behind the footlights."[13]

The intense and dynamic interplay of character and environment that was to characterize all of Bloch's Ibsen reached remarkable proportions in his *Enemy* in the raucous fourth-act public meeting where Doctor Stockmann is brought face to face with the "compact majority," a gallery of types in which "life, movement, and individuality extended to every group and every figure."[14] Rather than giving Emil Poulsen's pugnacious and determined Stockmann a faceless mob to contend with, Bloch took his cue directly from Ibsen's earnest suggestion to "give the minor parts in the fourth act as far as possible to capable actors; the more figures you can have in the crowd that are really individualized and true to nature, the better."[15] In this spirit, Bloch added no fewer than fifty-three distinct individuals to Ibsen's cast of characters, each one identified by his occupation and, by implication, his age (there were only four women in the crowd, apart from Petra and her mother). One is a blacksmith, another a typographer, a third a wholesale merchant, others are sea captains, masons, clerks, and so on. Each was given a carefully integrated role to play as the public meeting progressed – not for gratuitous effect but in order to establish the tangibility of the atmosphere and the society in which Stockmann finds himself branded an outcast, thereby intensifying the drama around his figure.[16] (So inseparable from the spirit of this play did Bloch's concept seem that his meticulous *mise-en-scène* enjoyed a long afterlife, both at home and abroad. Herman Bang used it to bring some order into Lugné-Poë's hopelessly unruly premiere at the Théâtre de l'Œuvre in 1893; Poul Nielsen resurrected it intact at the Royal Theatre in 1915; and it once more formed the basis for the famous Comédie Française revival that starred Maurice de Féraudy as an aged Stockmann in 1921.)

Built on these same principles, Bloch's subsequent production of *The Wild Duck* bears even more eloquent testimony to the power of a style of Ibsen interpretation that would continue to maintain its influence on the theatre for the next half century or more. "The effect of [Ibsen's] art is doubly potent when brought to life on the stage," declared *Dags-Telegrafen* (24 February 1885), and most reviewers of this justly celebrated performance agreed. Bloch's method, which stressed the credible fabric of Ibsen's play through close attention to concretely observed details and reactions taken from daily life, was a direct response to the demand for those "touches of reality" which Ibsen himself emphasized in his letter to Schrøder. As such, however, this approach sought neither to overlook nor subvert the mesh of powerfully symbolic and poetic resonances underlying the "realistic" surface of *The Wild Duck*. As a director, Bloch was keenly responsive to Ibsen's subtle subtextual dramaturgy, and his concern with the surface dimension of recognizably credible detail was invariably his means – the only means he knew – of heightening the audience's perception of the play's inner poetic dimension. David Belasco, Bloch's exact contemporary, once put it this way: "If dramatic art is anything at all, and if it is worth being perpetuated, the reason is that it is, above everything else – far above the mere purpose of supplying pleasurable entertainment – an interpretative art, which portrays the soul of life." To achieve this end, however, Belasco, like Bloch, was convinced of the need to confront his audiences with truth: "the mirror which reflects nature to them in the theatre must be neither concave nor convex. Its illusion must be true, and only to the extent that it is true will it necessarily stir their imagination."[17] (Belasco did not understand Ibsen, but Ibsen would have readily taken the American director's point.)

The creation of a charged stage environment that would participate in and accentuate the rhythm of the dramatic action was a paramount objective for both Bloch and Bjørn Bjørnson in their various Ibsen productions during the 1880s and 1890s. In *The Wild Duck*, subtle changes in lighting – calculated, as Ibsen himself had suggested to Schrøder, "to correspond to the basic mood that characterizes each of the five acts" – were skillfully orchestrated in Bloch's *mise-en-scène*, progressing from the indoor evening lighting of the first two acts, through the daylight of the early afternoon (Hjalmar retouching photographs in Act Three) and the reddish twilight and oncoming darkness (Hjalmar's departure in Act Four), to the cold, gray light of morning in which the final tragic movement of the drama is played out. Still in the age of gas lighting at this time, the Royal Theatre utilized dimmer shields and so-called colored "mediums" to achieve these soft, atmospheric color effects and modulations. In Bloch's promptbook, one can trace his efforts to impart, at every juncture in the performance, the texture and immediacy of life itself to these changing moods, in a manner intended to support and clarify the thematic line of Ibsen's text.[18]

Haakon Werle's richly and comfortably furnished study in Act One, with its spacious and elegant sitting room adjoining it, and Hjalmar Ekdal's manifestly simpler studio, with its strangely evocative inner loft, were not mere static backgrounds for the action. Each served an organic dramatic function. Werle's room, for example, was treated by Bloch as something more than just an appropriately furnished realistic interior (rug on the floor, various tables, upholstered chairs, a sofa, a fireplace, and a large desk cluttered with documents, newspapers, journals, account books, almanacs, writing materials, and so forth) designed to convey the comfortable and expensive atmosphere which is indicated by Ibsen's (somewhat less particularized) stage directions. In addition to all this, small but significant details – the guns and hunting equipment with which the walls were decorated in Bloch's production, the safe he substituted for the more cultivated bookcase in Ibsen's stage directions – provided their own implicit, visually provocative comment on the owner of the house. Concrete details such as these were not incorporated by the director simply for their picturesque, decorative value, nor were they the result of an essentially romantic taste for local color and ethnographic accuracy, such as was to permeate the Dagmar Theatre *Peer Gynt* one year later. In Bloch's method, stage-setting served a much more central and integral dramatic function. It was utilized to enrich and intensify the particular mood and atmosphere of the play, to function as a visual image of its thematic architecture. As such, the scenic environment became animated and charged with an independent expressive potential of its own.

In addition, Bloch used an evocative mosaic of details to open up further vistas that lay just beyond the audience's range of vision. The impingement of aspects of the environment that lie on the periphery of what is actually shown on the stage is, as we know, a device which is used to great effect in nearly all of Ibsen's later prose plays. In *The Wild Duck*, the mood created by the setting was suggestively expanded by Bloch to take in other rooms not directly visible – at the beginning of the play, the office into which Old Ekdal is admitted and from which he later emerges, a seedy and improbable interloper in the ostensibly festive gathering, is one such room; the adjoining salon in which the dinner is being held is another. From this offstage dining-room, the stage directions tell us, "the hum of conversation and the laughter of many voices can be heard. A knife is tapped against a glass; silence; a toast is proposed; cries of 'Bravo!'; then the hum of conversation starts again." Characteristically, Bloch was not content merely to furnish this largely unseen room as completely as the study itself. He also sought to concretize this detail of action even further by writing out the actual after-dinner speech which precedes the toast. This speech, transcribed verbatim in his promptbook, was not intended to be entirely audible, thereby disrupting Ibsen's opening dialogue. Instead, it was meant to be just barely noticeable in the background, as an atmospheric embellishment (or, as Stanislavski would later call it, a plastic value) accentuating the light post-prandial mood that contrasts so vividly with the darker note introduced immediately afterwards in the action of the play proper.

The bohemian atmosphere of Hjalmar Ekdal's attic studio aroused great interest wherever the play was first seen on stage. Even the terrible Sarcey was obliged to admit that at least this aspect of the Théâtre Libre production "was in fact ingeniously designed." ("We paid for it with an intermission of an hour and five minutes," he added peevishly.) "As difficult as it is characteristic, the studio decor with its mystical attic in the background belongs unconditionally to the best one has had occasion to see at Christiania Theatre," Henrik Jæger wrote of Bjørnson's production.[19] Lindberg's production, which opened at Dramaten nearly a month before Bloch's, had actually caused considerable commotion with its microscopically truthful depiction of the Ekdal environment. His actors moved in convincing naturalistic fashion among the furnishings, handling props that possessed the solidity and authenticity of observed reality. The doorframes were solid, the doors boasted real door-knobs, and there was even a greatly discussed night-commode, complete with chamber-pot and wash-basin, which provided a telling visual comment of its own on the humble circumstances of the ruined Ekdals. Along similar if less controversial lines, Bloch's *mise-en-scène* exploited to the fullest the life-like qualities and nuances of this milieu in order to develop and enhance the dramatic mood it suggested. The poor photographer's studio, the Copenhagen critics agreed, was "a splendid setting full of atmosphere in the different lights in which it appears . . . and a striking frame, spacious but desolate, around the life of the Ekdal family."[20]

23 Valdemar Gyllich's chiaroscuro design for the interior loft in William Bloch's production of *The Wild Duck* at the Danish Royal Theatre, Copenhagen, in 1885.

While the rather conventional interior for the first act could be readily put together (as was the custom) from scenery available in the stockroom, the unusual Ekdal environment was a wholly different matter. To capture its special flavor, Bloch asked Valdemar Gyllich, a scene-painter solidly in the coloristic tradition of the eighties, to provide a design which even today is redolent of this artist's strong feeling for the dramatic interaction of light and shadow. In terms of the actual arrangement of the stage, meanwhile, Bloch's floor plan corresponds closely to the setting seen in Bjørnson's production – and in countless other productions of the play for generations to come. In one sense Ibsen's stage directions do describe a venerable theatrical cliché – the artist's "humble but cozy" garret familiar from scores of nineteenth-century artist dramas and operas. The point here, of course, is that the sense of cliché is deliberate: Hjalmar, the indolent photographer, fancies himself an artist, his sensitive "artisticality" is his life-lie, and so what more fitting and romantic place to dwell than in a garret, complete with its pleasantly untidy clutter and its large studio window (doubtless with a good north light). Except for the snow on the window in the last act, we might as well be in Paris. Bloch tried to follow Ibsen's lead closely and expanded on his instructions deftly. On the "living" side of the room, beneath the window, stood a sofa, a table, and chairs, while on the "professional" side the audience saw a tiled stove (atop which perched a stuffed eagle!) and several objects one might expect to find in a modest photographer's flat: a tripod, a gilded, brocaded armchair and small marble-top table to pose beside, and a fancy mirror above a mahogany corbel. (At the opening of the fourth act, when Gina has finished taking portraits of the irksome young couple, the gilded chair and marble table were set up in front of a foldaway landscape screen in the middle of the studio.) At the back, to the left of the double sliding doors, stood a bookcase crammed with even more domestic clutter than Ibsen had conceived: "on its shelves photographic plates, books, pamphlets, jars, boxes, small bottles, a glue pot, a flute, a hammer, pliers, household items, a suitcase with Hjalmar's lounging jacket."[21] For the last two acts the prop list adds another significant item to the jumble on the shelves: a pistol.

In Bloch's production the main source of fascination, however, was the large, irregularly shaped interior loft that lay beyond the sliding doors in the rear wall. This was the real object of Gyllich's evocative chiaroscuro design – a striking physical embodiment of the drama's shadowy atmosphere of fantasy, lies, and self-deception, at once real and weirdly unreal in its appearance. The floor plan for the production delineates an obliquely angled and very spacious area for the loft, taking up as much of the total stage area as the Ekdal studio itself. Filled by Bloch with an intriguing assortment of disparate objects – packing-cases, a pair of geographical globes, hampers, a table, an old dresser piled with large books, photographs of large groups of anonymous people, a dead pine tree – the mysterious loft, seen only in fleeting glimpses during the course of the play, exuded its own particular atmosphere of a dead and haphazardly constructed past. Then, among all these mouldering and inanimate objects in the attic Bloch placed a small handful of live birds (four hens and six pigeons, to be exact), in order to convey a suggestion of the living creatures that have their abode there and play their unwitting but essential part in the escapist fantasies of Ibsen's dreamers. The effect was quite perceptible and, the reviewer for *Dagbladet* (24 February 1885) reported, "the audience grew accustomed quicker than one might expect to the evolutions of the participating pigeons and hens in the background." (Bjørnson, too, was quite taken by the idea of avian sounds in the attic, but he made a very different choice. Johannes Brun, who acted Old Ekdal and was also an accomplished mimic of all animal noises, was evidently persuaded to endow the wild duck with an audible offstage vocal presence.)[22]

Invariably, the "abstract, symbolic, allegorical" dimension of Ibsen's drama which in general greatly preoccupied the Scandinavian critics was, they emphasize, decisively and consistently translated by these naturalistic directors into concrete terms of living reality. Gunnar Heiberg's work was widely admired because, as one contemporary observer put it, "he senses the mood of the play, the spirit in which it was created, and conceives of it as theatre – not as literature."[23] In a similar way in the Bloch rendering of *The Wild Duck*, "when the art of the actors created a rounded totality and when the pointed arrows of the dialogue turned into living speech on the lips of the characters, the symbolism . . . retreated into the background," remarked the reviewer for *Morgenbladet* (24 February 1885). Hence, for example, the interpolation of real birds and their indistinct peripheral sounds helped to build a tangibly perceived atmosphere that rendered this specific domestic milieu believable and comprehensible – not only to the audience, it must be added, but also to the actors, who were thereby enabled to "live" their roles with stronger psychological conviction.

Such touches were never introduced by Bloch simply as interesting but isolated flourishes in a picturesque *tableau vivant*, however, for the sum of these details had to add up to an integrated organic whole. Every movement on Bloch's stage, every role in the play, from the principal characters to the busily occupied servants and individualized guests at the dinner party in the opening scene, was given a transparent, precisely grounded motivation. In particular, Bloch persistently argued, the life of a dramatic character does not abruptly commence at the moment he makes his entrance on the stage. The actor must respond to the unreal life of the theatre as though it were real; each and every movement in the performance must be saturated with the truthfulness and conviction of reality. Yet, since the theatre reflects only a corner of the larger fabric of living reality, every line of dialogue must, as in life, mirror the past. "If the character portrayed is to appear to the audience in the theatre not as an abstraction, living only a hollow life within the narrow circumference of the given conditions of the play, but a living creature, possessing within himself infinite possibilities," then Bloch would insist that "the thoughts and feelings he reveals to us must be shown as they take root in his mind. Every utterance must be given a life of its own. It must be conceived, be born, live, and die."[24]

In forging an ensemble, Bloch deliberately laid stress on a multiplicity of facets and reactions, a variety of emotions, rather than seeking to establish a single interpretational throughline or attitude. Throughout his production of *The Wild Duck*, attention was concentrated on a continually varied but relaxed and fluid pattern of action, movement, and character inter-relationships – a pattern quite consistent, in other words, with the multifarious, even impressionistic character of Ibsen's dramatic design. Not surprisingly, some observers seemed perplexed by the effect created. "The Ekdal family and its friends function like a small orchestra in which each instrument is tuned in its own key," declared one observer. "To put it concisely: the characters fall away from one another, like a kaleidoscope in which the glass pieces refuse to form a picture; one or another of the glass pieces may, taken by itself, appear very lovely or amusing – but this does not satisfy the viewer looking into the kaleidoscope."[25] Evidently without realizing it, this writer has described that diffuseness of focus and juxtaposition of impressions and images upon which the very effect of Ibsen's play depends and to which, as a director, Bloch seems to have responded with unusual sensitivity.

Bloch's promptbook, filled with circumstantial instructions about stage business that usually built upon and amplified Ibsen's stage directions, conveys an exceptionally clear impression of the dynamic and kinetic character of his theatrical style. The judicious interpolation of physical actions, in Stanislavski's sense of utilizing stage objects for the purpose of endowing a scene with the conviction of reality, bonded Ibsen's characters to their environment. Gina and Hedvig, for instance, busied themselves throughout with domestic activities – tidying the house, sewing (shirts), serving (real) food, reading, and of course retouching photographs. The coordinated rhythmic flow of such activities served to integrate the individual figures into a fabric of human relationships, thereby making the common pattern that underlies their related actions – a wounded struggle to survive – more coherent and more evident. The irony Bloch produced by counterpointing the meaning of words and the meaning of actions is seen in the promptbook, for example, in the tense confrontation that occurs between Gina and Hjalmar in the fourth act, after Hjalmar has returned from his "strenuous walk" with Gregers, his head filled with vague notions about "the demands of an ideal." Determined to take over everything himself, including the household accounts, he demands to know why Gina has not told him the truth about the payments for Old Ekdal's copying work:

GINA. I couldn't. You were so happy because you thought he got everything from you.
HJALMAR. (*Walks to the window*) And instead he got it from Werle.
GINA. Oh well, there's plenty more where that came from.
HJALMAR. Light the lamp for me! (*He draws the curtain.*)
   (*Pause, during which* GINA *walks to the mantelpiece stage right, where she gets matches. Then back to the table stage left to light the lamp. She does not look at* HJALMAR, *while he stares intently at her.*)
GINA. (*Lighting the lamp*) Besides, we don't even know if it *is* Werle – it might just as easily be Graaberg –
HJALMAR. What's all this pretense about Graaberg?
GINA. I don't know. I only thought –
HJALMAR. Hm!
GINA. (*Trims the wick*) I wasn't the one who got Grandpa the copying to do. Berta did, after she came to the house.
HJALMAR. Your voice is shaking.
GINA. (*Puts the shade on*) Is it?
HJALMAR. And your hands are trembling. Am I wrong?
GINA. (*Looks directly at him, standing by the table*) Come straight out with it, Hjalmar. What has he been saying about me?
HJALMAR. (*Turned half away from her*) Is it true – can it be true – that you had some kind of relationship with Werle while you were working in his house?
GINA. (*Comes forward*) It's not true. Not then, anyhow . . .[26]

Unlike Lindberg, who used a number of new or comparatively unknown actors in an effort to banish mannerisms and stereotypes from his production of *The Wild Duck* in Stockholm, Bloch cast the play with some of the foremost performers of the day, several of them veterans of earlier Ibsen campaigns at the Royal Theatre. Betty Hennings, the world's first Nora in *A Doll's House* and subsequently one of Ibsen's favorite actresses, was thirty-five when she played Hedvig, but her rich characterization radiated a touchingly child-like trust and devotion to her father, made vividly physical in "her industriousness, her affection for [Hjalmar], and her total despair at the prospect of losing him."[27] Hjalmar Ekdal, mournfully playing on his flute, was conceived by Emil Poulsen as the virtual antithesis of his Torvald Helmer – a blend of essential naivety and lightly melancholy charm and warmth. A bit pretentious, a bit self-centered, "his utterly flabby and unmasculine walk and posture, his repeated preference for looking at himself in the mirror and striking poses to impress his surroundings" made Poulsen's characterization a graphic, even flamboyant image of "the phoniness, the falsity and the hot air in Hjalmar's character."[28] (Too graphic and flamboyant for Ibsen, it seems, who, determined that "Hjalmar must not be played with any trace of parody," reportedly took issue with Poulsen's performance on this ground.[29]) The dominant impression created was perhaps more metatheatrical than naturalistic: an intelligent actor playing the role of the photographer who plays the role of artist–actor. "His Ekdal believed in himself," Edvard Brandes wrote of Poulsen's complex, faceted portrayal. "He was utterly wretched in fine company, truly stingy, happily at home in the attic, and unspeakably tousled when put on the spot. The continual variation between false pathos and the commonest everyday talk flowed naturally from his lips, and he held the character within this chosen framework with an iron hand."[30] (The tone of witty irony and self-satire inherent in Poulsen's interpretation caused a somewhat later Norwegian observer to contrast his performance with the "truer," more serious portrayal given by Arnoldus Reimers in Bjørnson's production, where Hjalmar seemed a character who "is in the first place a bright, agile intellect blunted and made stupid by self-conceit and the uncritical admiration of others – stupid in what for Ibsen is the most abominable sense, stupid in the way one becomes by toying with life, by exploiting everything, including the good found in the people he meets, for the narrowest egoistical purposes.")[31]

Gregers Werle – "an idea in jacket and trousers," in the opinion of *Morgenbladet* – is in fact a character whose ambiguous nature and function made scant sense to the play's early audiences. Acted in Bloch's production by Peter Jerndorff, a seasoned performer who had appeared in every previous Ibsen play staged at the Royal Theatre, this misguided but dangerously sincere zealot appeared only as an hysterical eccentric: "a hot-headed epileptic, a hollow-eyed, deathly pale, loud-mouthed but otherwise naive conscience awakener" who disappeared soundlessly from the drama.[32] On the other hand, the highpoint of this production and the pivotal force in Bloch's ensemble was unquestionably Olaf Poulsen's legendary portrayal of Old Ekdal – a role which, in the hands of the greatest comic character actor of his generation, succeeded magically in fusing intensely human proportions and formidable symbolic weight. "The symbolic refrain 'the forest avenges' resounded with almost mystical power from his broken voice," declared *Morgenbladet*, and fellow critics agreed. His first stealthy intrusion among Werle's dinner guests, hunched and shyly delighted, his comings and goings with (real) hot water for that toddy which is his defence against the terror of reality, and his energetic hunting and rabbit-shooting in the attic all made Olaf Poulsen's characterization of Old Ekdal seem, to Edvard Brandes and others, a perfect blending of "the tragic and the comic in this strange figure." Shaking and decrepit though he was from age, poverty, and drink, there nevertheless remained "a certain indefinite and undefinable aura of a past, dimly recollected military spirit under his whole faded and shabby personality" (*Dagens Nyheder*). Played by this brilliant actor, the ruined figure of Old Ekdal thus became the craggy, grotesque focus of this picture of drifting, foundering humanity, "the most perfect conceivable archetype of a man who has in every respect suffered shipwreck in life."

In spite of the forceful impact of the individual acting presentations in this production, however, the essential strength of William Bloch's directorial approach to Ibsen's drama resided, ultimately, not in its separate details but in its vigorous totality. Rather than isolate a single motif or choose a single mood for emphasis, Bloch deliberately accentuated the density of Ibsen's dramatic texture, the complexity of the pattern of interwoven and mutually sustaining themes and character relationships. The suggestive power and expressiveness of his interpretation of *The Wild Duck* derived from the *accumulated* effect of a multiplicity of fine points; a mosaic of nuances in the setting, the lighting, and the psychological shadings of character interpretations blended into the interaction of the ensemble. The subtle fusion of all these ingredients lent this textbook example of stage naturalism its distinctive character and life, and bestowed upon it an added dimension of evocative, intensified dramatic atmosphere.

"HERE RULE THE NIGHT AND THE DREAMS"

The finely detailed, solidly illusionistic style of Bloch and his contemporaries established a performance tradition which, in this case, seemed for a great many years almost incontrovertible. Unlike such works as *Ghosts* or *Rosmersholm* or *Hedda Gabler*, which Reinhardt, Craig, and Meyerhold so decisively reinterpreted during that same revolutionary autumn following Ibsen's death in 1906, *The Wild Duck* remained surprisingly, almost stubbornly, impervious to the innovations of the anti-naturalistic movement that swept across the face of Europe during the early years of this century. Even the look-alike quality of the production photographs preserved for this play seems striking in retrospect. Part of the explanation for this conceptual homogeneity is undoubtedly the exceptionally precise, prescriptive way in which Ibsen himself has "directed" his play on paper. Perhaps another part of the answer lies in the fact that the "macrorealism" of, say, the shipwrecks in *Peer Gynt* or the impinging mill-race in *Rosmersholm* is far more readily adaptable to stylization than the "microrealism" of the animated dinner party and very tangible luncheon so essential in *The Wild Duck*.

For more than half a century, in any case, the filigree of realistic details and business at the heart of Bloch's original production lived on in the two performances of *The Wild Duck* staged by Nicolai Neiiendam, at the Danish Royal Theatre in 1921 and at the smaller Frederiksberg Theatre in 1942. ("We saw again with pleasure William Bloch's old, exemplary *mise-en-scène*, in which the characters are positioned so carefully, with almost calculated subtlety at the crucial moments," observed Frederik Schyberg on the latter occasion.[33]) When Nationaltheatret in Oslo again revived the play in 1949, Halvdan Christensen's "intricately detailed, intimately realistic" production once more exemplified the vigorous older tradition that had prevailed unabated in Norway. Agne Beijer described Christensen's quietly intense approach in this performance as one which "unobtrusively and objectively placed the milieu for the action in the decade to which it belongs, and which let real, everyday people remain real, everyday people, with dialogue that remains everyday speech, without undue emphasis on profound pauses and vague symbolic images."[34] This same production was repeated unchanged at Nationaltheatert as late as 1955, when it was revived by Gerda Ring in Christensen's naturalistic *mise-en-scène* and with most of his original cast. In this same year in Stockholm, moreover, even the innovative Alf Sjöberg's immensely successful rendering of *The Wild Duck* at Dramaten adhered faithfully to this accepted representational pattern, with its period settings, costumes and accessories. In the physical arrangement of scenes like the gentlemen's luncheon in Act Three, Sjöberg's staging also followed time-honored conventions. "One is grateful to him," concluded *Svenska*

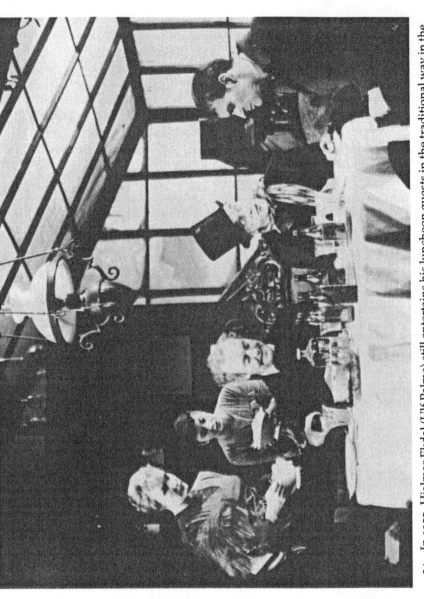

24 In 1955, Hjalmar Ekdal (Ulf Palme) still entertains his luncheon guests in the traditional way in the third act of Alf Sjöberg's revival of *The Wild Duck* at the Royal Dramatic Theatre, Stockholm. Molvik (Gunnar Hällström) sips his akvavit while Gina (Eva Dahlbeck) and Hedvig (Margit Carlqvist) fuss over their Hjalmar, and Relling (Anders Henrikson, in the Abe Lincoln hat) exchanges a sharp word with Gregers Werle (Olof Bergström). Setting designed by Georg Magnusson.

Dagbladet (13 March 1955), "because he has in no sense played clever tricks with [the production], but has been content with a subtly realistic *mise-en-scène* in faithful 1880s decor."

By the 1950s, however, a changed attitude toward the play in performance had nevertheless begun to take form, notably in terms of more complexly psychological interpretations of character. In Christensen's production, for instance, the ill-fated Hedvig was now seen in an unconventional light, as an ugly, precocious little teenager whose physical awkwardness and mental anxiety suggested a clear bond between her and the tormented, even tragic Gregers Werle portrayed by Olufr Havrevold. In the Sjöberg performance at Dramaten, Olof Bergström's alienated and compulsive Gregers represented an even bolder departure from the stereotyped view of this character as either an unsympathetic prig or else a psychopath brimming with fanaticism. In Bergström's reading, he was instead a man consumed by a neurotic attachment to his mother, in whom moral righteousness became the expression of the covert hatred he harbored for his father. His antithesis was the Hjalmar Ekdal created by Ulf Palme – an oblivious egoist who, as the director's manuscript notes express it, "uses every means just to carry on, to survive, to overcome." Palme – the perfect Jamie in the world premiere of *Long Day's Journey into Night* at Dramaten the following year – was the embodiment of a potentially tragic figure who remains "comic" only because he fails to recognize his own situation and hence never achieves tragic consciousness. As a result, the play was for Sjöberg "a comedy about life that goes on – with the comic hero who sails along, borne by the wind and by belief in himself, avoiding every shoal."[35]

In England at mid-century, meanwhile, the chief and insuperable obstacle to a satisfactory production of *The Wild Duck* remained Hjalmar, who had been portrayed as a buffoon ever since Granville Barker first showed off his "Shavian" Hjalmar at the Court Theatre in 1905. ("If Hedwig at the end had emerged from the sliding doors of the garret and made an irrefutable little speech, asserting her intention to get a comfortable settlement out of Werle, and explaining that her father did not really care two straws whose child she was, it would not have been very incongruous with the spirit in which some of the scenes were played," Desmond MacCarthy had recorded on that occasion.)[36] "He is glorious fun," James Agate exclaimed with delight when he reviewed the absurd antics of Milton Rosmer in the part in 1925: "The whole of the action is centred in the preposterous carryings-on of the farcical photographer."[37] Although Robert Eddison won distinction for himself simply by attempting a serious, unfarcical Hjalmar at the

Bristol Old Vic in 1953, the contagious urge to play the part for laughs seems to have remained peculiarly indigenous to what Wardle once called "the mutton-chop whisker Ibsen" of the English theatre. Thus, when Emlyn Williams took his turn at "the farcical photographer" in 1955, Kenneth Tynan found himself in a Stockmannesque minority of one in denouncing the parody: "Of course, Hjalmar Ekdal is a man of straw, but this is a point that Ibsen himself can be trusted to make; the actor need not be at such pains to show that he too sees through the character."[38] It might well be said – and many critics and directors did say so at the time – that London audiences had their first opportunity to see *The Wild Duck* in a fresh new light when Ingmar Bergman's seminal reworking of the play came to the Aldwych in Swedish in 1973, as part of Peter Daubeny's tenth and final World Theatre season.

In Bergman's revival, which began its lengthy run at Dramaten on 17 March 1972, the detailed naturalistic environments that had dominated productions of it in the past were replaced by condensed, deliberately fragmentary sets composed of a few tangible, carefully selected objects on an otherwise empty stage. The novel scenographic style of Marik Vos' "decors" bore a certain resemblance to the technique Bergman had introduced in his equally revolutionary *Hedda Gabler* eight years earlier. Simple, stylized wall-screens were again used to define the contours of the two interiors required in the play, each of which was in this case confined to a relatively shallow area at the front of the stage, serving thereby to accentuate the close-up impression of the figure compositions on which Bergman's approach depended. Beyond these low, shallow settings one saw only the enveloping blackness of a void that was occasionally pierced, in the Ekdal acts, by abstract projections of roof-beams. Within the setting itself, the atmospheric interplay of light and shadow reinforced the effect of oneiric semi-reality that prevailed, even in Haakon Werle's "expensive and comfortably furnished" study.

In Bloch's production, as we have seen, this study was treated as a real and substantial environment designed to make its own comment on the life of its inhabitants. For Bergman, on the other hand, its "reality" was created solely by the living presence of the actors, once they stepped on to the low platform which it occupied. A relatively cold, green-tinted room of angles and corners, it was defined only by a back screen and an aristocratic fireplace with poker and tongs that stood on one side, with no wall behind it. Four upholstered chairs and an ornate writing-table were the only pieces of furniture. A pair of high, ornamental candelabra, standing in either corner just outside the actual playing area, hinted at the elegance and opulence called for in

Ibsen's stage directions. Hanging on the wall above the businessman's desk, a richly framed portrait of a woman, presumably his late wife, was conspicuous. Earlier naturalistic productions, including Halvdan Christensen's, had regularly crowded the walls of Werle's study with "costly" artwork in order to strengthen the sense of milieu. Quite obviously, the blurred, solitary portrait in Bergman's version was meant to serve a very different purpose – not, as one bedeviled commentator thought, as "the symbol of Gregers' Oedipal complex," but rather as an image as ambiguous and multifaceted as the woman it presumably represented – about whom the various characters in the play express such different views, and whose presence broods over the action as strongly as Beate's in *Rosmersholm* or Captain Alving's in *Ghosts*. The portrait thus bespoke the irrevocable presence of the past in the play, the awareness that old sins cast long shadows and that, in the end, "the forest will have its revenge."

The forest had a kind of palpable presence in Hjalmar Ekdal's humble, more cluttered studio, where the most prominent pictorial element was a large screen depicting an old-fashioned woodland scene. In a concrete sense, it was the same cheap portrait photographer's prop that Gina has been seen putting aside in countless naturalistic productions; in another, more imaginative sense, however, it was a suggestive reminder, virtually a vision of the great forest of long ago, about which Old Ekdal warns us so often. Where the pair of stately candelabra had stood in Werle's study, dried-out old spruce trees could now be glimpsed (the "four or five withered Christmas trees" that are, as Doctor Relling remarks, the same to the old hunter as "the great, fresh forests of Høydal"). Even the rectangular screen used to delineate one corner of the studio carried, in its faintly flowered and leafy wallpaper, a tantalizing hint of this motif of the encroaching dream forest. Depicted in this way, the Ekdal world conveyed the impression of a "waking reality" suspended in a void, "an island in the sea of flight from reality."[39]

Other sharply defined contrasts to the more patrician Werle establishment were suggested by Bergman with deft economy, especially through the strategic placement of the sparse furnishings. The position occupied by the elegant fireplace in the previous setting was now taken by an ugly old iron stove. At the opposite side of the stage from it, in the area formerly occupied by Werle's commanding desk, a dilapidated sofa and table arrangement served both as a work place for the none-too-energetic Hjalmar and also as the center of domestic warmth where the indispensable meals in the play could be served. Here in this warmly illuminated area the Ekdals gathered – frequently watched

25 "In the attic": the abode of the wild duck as it was seen in Ingmar Bergman's production at the Royal Dramatic Theatre, Stockholm, in 1972. Stage design by Marik Vos.

26   Another untraditional view of the Ekdal studio and the loft: Paul René
Gauguin's design for the Norwegian director Pål Løkkeberg's production at
the Danish Royal Theatre in 1965.

closely by Gregers, "the outsider who intrudes in order to influence
the life of the family" and who hence often sat "as far removed as
possible from the dining-room table, the natural gathering place of the
family, with his back towards the audience so that he shared his
watching attitude with them."[40]

Beyond a doubt the director's most unexpected and most provocative innovation was his redefinition of the nature and location of the
attic, the abode of the maimed wild duck and the realm of illusion and
diversion for three generations of Ekdals. In a bold reversal of the
play's perspective, his production placed Ibsen's fateful and fleetingly
perceived "interior loft" squarely before the audience's view and virtually in its lap, with the interesting result that characters entering it
did not thereby disappear from view but were instead revealed and
brought closer to the spectator, both physically and metaphorically.
Bergman "has with a resolute touch burst the bounds of the perspective box by placing the imaginary loft almost where the spectators are
sitting," recorded Henrik Sjögren in *Kvällsposten* (18 March 1972).
"Accordingly they can observe every one of the characters who turns
toward the wild duck [whose 'basket' was the prompter's box]."

Bergman was not the first director to conceive of the Ekdal attic in
dematerialized terms, as a place of the imagination rather than a

physical reality. Nor, in fact, was he the first to bring the attic forward. Almost seven years earlier, for example, the Norwegian director Pål Løkkeberg had staged a revival at the Danish Royal Theatre (5 September 1965) in which, in contrast to the completely tangible domestic reality of the studio itself, the "attic" was envisioned as a shadowy, wholly imaginary area that surrounded the Ekdals – and the audience – on all sides. On a large "map" of the play's topography, the painter and designer Paul René Gauguin has sketched out the principal theoretical assumptions and impressions upon which he and Løkkeberg based their unusual spatial conception. "The attic is around us, within us, beneath us, *also* in the auditorium," reads one notation on this diagram: "No doors. *The location* shifts from rear stage to forestage with a lighting change. When *we* are in the attic, the acting area is 'reversed' (or the room 'rotates' in a topographical sense)."[41] Hence, characters leaving to go *out* to the "attic" worked a stylized "mechanism" and walked upstage; but scenes taking place *in* the attic were turned round on a imaginary revolving stage, as it were, to be acted before the audience. In this and other respects, Gauguin's forcefully expressive design juxtaposes reality and unreality in a manner that has, ultimately, little in common with the rigorous simplicity of the Bergman production. Using heavily textured materials – wood, velvet, and burlap netting – Gauguin counterpointed the realistic specificity of Gina's "warm" domain ("poor but cozy, many small objects") and Old Ekdal's smaller area beside the stove with a sense of darkness and unlimited space ("the forest and the depths of the sea") beyond the stylized, freely suspended window.

The imaginary attic in Bergman's production, which was entered through a side door in the stage-right wall of the studio, was likewise located in the no-man's-land between the audience and the stage. Here, however, the similarity to the earlier production ends. Bergman's reinterpretation depended not on a complicated scheme of scenic metaphysics but on a simple and direct appeal to the spectator's imaginative involvement. Only the facial expressions of the actors and projections of roof-beams on the stage floor and on the black background above them served to indicate where they were and what visions they saw in this boundless kingdom of the imagination. "Without stage properties and with only the aid of the lighting and the art of the actors, Bergman creates, before the eyes of the audience, the fantasy world that Hjalmar and Old Ekdal have built up around themselves," wrote Leif Zern in *Dagens Nyheter* (18 March 1972). "Here rule the night and the dreams, in scenes of such intensity and poetry that I have never witnessed their like."

As this comment and countless others like it suggest, Bergman's transposition – which, once accomplished, seemed to uninformed and initiated viewers alike both completely consistent and disarmingly self-evident – produced a startlingly vivid sense of immediacy in the theatre. "More than in any other production of Ibsen's play that one recalls," wrote one critic of the touring production, the attic became "an image of that secret fantasy life that these escapists and losers have not been strong enough or courageous enough to realize for themselves. The small living-room of Hjalmar Ekdal becomes a doll's house of eternal childhood above which, in the scenes with the wild duck, the roof-beams soar like the lofty vaults of a cathedral, while from afar one hears the surge of the wind."[42] The withered Christmas trees, obscured by the conventional placement of the attic at the rear, were now, for the first time, brought forward to form a profoundly express-ive component of the Ekdal milieu. As a result the thematic bond between studio and forest was made manifest; time present and time past flowed together in a fluid and indissoluble concurrency. "The symbolic essence of the play thus becomes central and more securely welded to the clockwork mechanism of the dramatic action than I have ever experienced it before," Sjögren concluded.

Even this apparently cinematic technique of juxtaposing the main action of the play with exposed glimpses of "offstage" characters and simultaneous peripheral scenes implied but not written out in Ibsen's text – a technique which Bergman himself insists is "the oldest theatre device that ever existed" and has "not a whit to do with film" – finds an antecedent in, for example, Bloch's evocative, metaphoric use of total stage space. In Bergman's hands, however, the reality of such scenes is created *solely* through the medium of the actor's art. As such, his *Wild Duck* epitomizes a cardinal principle of his theatre poetics – the resolute subordination at all times of the technical dynamics of staging (which seem to have preoccupied Ibsen so much in the plays of this middle period) to the primacy of the actor's creative presence. "Once you agree that the only important things are the words, the actors, and the audience, then it isn't the setting that matters," he has said of his work with *The Wild Duck*. "The actors must materialize, before the eyes of the audience, the magic of the attic. And they cannot do that at a distance; with their eyes, their way of walking and standing and moving, they create it in front of you. So you can see it. That is the magic of the theatre."[43]

During the great Dramaten years of the early 1970s, even relatively minor roles in a production like *The Wild Duck* were filled (exactly in the spirit of Ibsen's letter to Schrøder) by leading members of the familiar

Bergman "company" with whom he had worked over the years, both in plays and motion pictures. Berta Sørby ("She must be beautiful and witty, *not* vulgar," the dramatist himself had urged) was played by Harriet Andersson as a gracious, self-confident woman devoid of any trace of commonness, though a reviewer for one of the socialist papers did see her, "clad in brilliant reddish purple for both of her big entrances," as an image of "social democracy entering into a marriage of convenience with the makers of money."[44] The imposing Anders Ek gave "a subdued, secretive portrait" of Haakon Werle himself, with "the strength of the wild animal about him."[45] Holger Löwenadler was Old Ekdal, "a grandiose ruin of someone who was once a human being," characterized by what Leif Zern described as "this strange blend of old warrior and dreamer." Even Erland Josephson was called upon to impersonate one of the stuffy guests at Werle's dinner party.

At the core of this impressive ensemble was the quartet of characters around whom the action of the play revolves – a quartet carefully balanced by Bergman to reveal a subtly shaded lattice of tensions and contrasts, rooted in Ibsen's own character descriptions and articulated by the director in terms of a distinct rhythm of movements, gestures, facial expressions, and vocal intonations. By means of this rhythm Bergman succeeded in distilling and revealing the inner essence of each of the characters with cameralike definition of focus:

> The images of human beings in a particular social situation which Ibsen shows us possess an almost supernatural clarity and sharpness. The figures reveal themselves in every subtle detail of words and movements, and they do so with formidable logic until they stand there etched into our consciousness, lit through to the bare skeleton.
>
> And naturally this sharp clarity oversteps the bounds of realism. Nothing in this imperfect world is ever so clear. Driven to its fullest consequence, realism becomes unreal: the X-ray vision suddenly exposes not living and vaguely contradictory human beings, but rather psychological constructs in a laser-sharp, two-dimensional projection.   (Bæckström, *GHT*)

Hjalmar Ekdal (Ernst-Hugo Järegård) and Hedvig (Lena Nyman) seemed, to many observers, less like father and daughter and much more "like two children of the same age, a loving brother and sister." "Incestuous" was the spurious adjective attached by one or two critics with an inflexibly Freudian cast of mind, but a powerful sense of domestic warmth and tenderness, rather than any suggestion of incest, was the real thematic point at issue here. Their eager embraces and natural displays of affection in the earlier, lighter scenes deepened the sense of Hedvig's naive, almost animalistic dependency on her father. "The warmth in the Ekdal home stems from her hunger for life," commented Zern, who regarded Hedvig and her final meaning-less self-sacrifice as the true axis on which Bergman's "miraculous" *mise-en-scène* revolved. An almost imperceptible limp gave an added sense of her symbiotic identification with the crippled wild duck, and thus Hjalmar's impulsive, physically brutal rejection of her embrace in the fourth act took on an even greater significance and poignancy. Järegård's uncomplicated Hjalmar was a blithe egoist who fed on the applause and encouragement of his surroundings, a born actor "who played bad theatre with his life and enjoyed doing so," remarked Sjögren in his review. "A little man, a clown without a core, so eccentric that he falls far outside the norm," this Hjalmar was, to Sjögren, a figure with none of "the great artistic power and the enormous imaginative wingspan" of the character as created by Ulf Palme in Alf Sjöberg's earliest production. Järegård's open cherubic face, his curly hair, and his soft velvet attire all bespoke the charming and much-prized child whose adoring wife and daughter literally even helped him to put on his slippers. In this context the earthy, maternal Gina of Margaretha Krook was called on to play "mother" to both these children, and their simple, helpless dependency on her predicted their defencelessness against Gregers Werle, the outsider whose intrusion destroys their childish fantasy world forever.

For most of the reviewers it was Gregers, the fourth member of the quartet, who seemed unquestionably the mid-point of the production and the central character in the play. Max von Sydow's reading depicted not a villain but rather "an idealist whose good intentions one cannot doubt for a moment," wrote Åke Janzon in *Svenska Dagbladet* (18 March). "What is both sympathetic and subtle about von Sydow's interpretation is that, for all his professed conviction, his Gregers makes a deeper impression as a seeker of truth than as a speaker of truth." A very tall man who assumed a stooped, cramped posture, his short nervous laugh and his habit of crossing his arms over his chest to hide his hands under his armpits ("as though he were trying to do himself into a straitjacket," thought one observer) suggested, to many of the critics, deep inner anxiety and insecurity. "He complains more than he accuses," remarked *Sydsvenska Dagbladet* (18 March), and in the two extremely effective encounters with his father – to whom he bore a physical resemblance and of whom he seemed in mortal terror – "his attacks [were] as shaky and powerless as his gestures and posture; he seems to be ready to run away at any time." Although Gregers and Hjalmar were diametrical opposites in physical appearance, they seemed to share a lack of self-assurance and self-knowledge: "they suffer from the same disease, even though the symptoms are different," Zern argued. "Gregers, too, goes outside himself to find the solution to his problems. Precisely like Hjalmar – and like Peer Gynt, for that matter – he assumes a role that does not express his true self." This untraditional Gregers was naturally interpreted in many different ways by the critics, as suffering from a severe Oedipus complex, as carrying on a sublimated father-rebellion, or even as representing the failed political revolutionary in the class struggle. Yet Bergman's aim was not to impose a psychological or an ideological over-simplification on Ibsen's play but rather to amplify, in concrete theatrical terms, the matrix of dynamic emotional relationships upon which the play builds. In these terms, the effect of this new and more complex characterization of Gregers was to intensify and enrich the dramatic impact of his confrontations with Haakon Werle, his relationship to Hjalmar, and, above all, the three crucial conversations he holds with Hedvig on the subject of the wild duck.

The process by which Hedvig comes to take her life and the nature of Gregers' involvement in that process became the prism through which all the other events in the drama were refracted and assimilated. In their first, dream-like scene together, as the plain, shy, snub-nosed little girl told Gregers about the "different world" of the loft, with its strange collection of old paint-boxes, old picture-books, and old clocks that no longer run, she acquired a radiance "as if sunlight and soft shadows moved across the childish face, dreaming about that which will never come to pass" (Zern). The second of their conversations – skillfully transferred by Bergman to the shadowy precincts of the "attic" itself, where the actors could now face the audience directly – strengthened the sense of mutual understanding and even comradeship that existed between these two dreamers. As Gregers implanted the suggestion of offering up the wild duck to appease Hjalmar ("Suppose, for his sake, you unselfishly sacrificed the thing dearest to you in the whole world?"), his movements to draw Hedvig close to him and her response carried implications of a mesmeric, even an erotic seduction of her will. An incisive cut to eliminate the potential anti-climax of Gina's return at the close of the scene caused the fourth act to end on the line with which Hedvig seemed to signal her compliance: "I'll do it tomorrow morning" (with the explicit reference to "the wild duck" deleted).[46] In the third and conclusive step of the process, the psychological seduction was completed as Gregers recalled her to her blunted purpose – without recourse to the hortative exclamations in the text and using only a pause and one simple statement: "But I still believe in you, Hedvig."

Perhaps the darkest and most chilling aspect of Bergman's interpretation of *The Wild Duck* was the fact that never for an instant was the audience in doubt about the deliberate and premeditated character of Hedvig's suicide. On the one hand, small but telling cuts – in particular the deletion of the short scene in which Old Ekdal lectures the child about how to shoot ducks properly – tended to strengthen the impression that the wild duck never *had* actually been Hedvig's intended target. Moreover, the chance that she might have shot herself by mistake – surely the least desirable of the many ambiguities in Ibsen's drama and one which must inevitably be resolved by the actress, at least in her own mind, in performance – now no longer existed as a logical possibility. As Hjalmar, already warming to his new role and calling histrionically for his notes and the draft of his "memoirs," ordered Hedvig from his presence, she slipped out quietly, pistol in hand, only to reappear moments later on the shadowy forestage. As the projection of the roof-beams rose above her head, she came forward, took aim for a moment at the unseen duck's "basket," hesitated, and then crouched in an unobtrusive heap as the others continued their unwitting, self-centered conversation in the background. The audience thus experienced these last terrifying moments through Hedvig's consciousness, saw them through her eyes. "We see her listening to the conversation that makes her shoot herself," observed one critic. "And the voluntary sacrifice of her death thereby became, to an even greater degree, a judgment upon the intractable childishness of the adults."[47] In Ibsen's text, Hjalmar indulges in a stream of overwrought, potentially absurd fulminations (about Hedvig's "conspiracy" with her mother and Mrs. Sørby, about her "betrayal" of "the poor photographer") which even William Bloch had deleted from his playing script. Alf Sjöberg's version had likewise made deep cuts in this section. Following this tradition Bergman's rendering, utterly devoid of sentimentality, concentrated with even more rigorous simplicity on the essential, profoundly human issue of Hjalmar's doubt:

GREGERS. Hedvig would never leave you. Never.
HJALMAR. She's been shrewd enough to keep on the good side of me, that's all.
GREGERS. You can't believe that, Hjalmar.
HJALMAR. That's the terrible part of it. I don't know what to believe. And I never will know.
(A pistol shot is heard.)
GREGERS. (*Exultant*) Hjalmar! Do you know what that was?
HJALMAR. Papa's shooting in the attic.
(GINA rushes in.)
GREGERS. No, you don't know. But I do. That was your proof.[48]

Following the shot, the suspense generated in Ibsen's play by the ensuing confusion over who had actually fired at what deepened into irony, for the audience of this production knew what the characters themselves did not yet realize. Then, as Relling and the parents gathered around the crumpled form on the darkened forestage, Bergman added a bold visual stroke that heightened the oppressive sense of finality and ultimate futility created by Hedvig's suicide. Juxtaposed with the shadowy group in the foreground was the startling image of Old Ekdal, seated before the photographer's forest backdrop in his old lieutenant's uniform, still intoning his favorite refrain: "The forest will have its revenge – but I'm not afraid at any rate." Perhaps only Gregers was truly afraid, for he recognized the terrible finality of the judgment that had been passed on all of them – and as he left the Ekdal home, he held in his hand the revolver that Hedvig had used on herself.

The precisely orchestrated, rhythmical coordination of visual and aural impressions that rendered the closing moments of Bergman's production of *The Wild Duck* so moving reflects the uniquely "musical" way in which he went about translating the play's atonal "score" into the syntax of the theatre. His dematerialized, strenuously actor-oriented approach did not, it is true, make quite the emotional sense to some that it did to others. "A very good production, but mostly in the acting," the American director Harold Clurman called it in an apparently serious reply to an interviewer's question: "The sets weren't much ... they cost about $15. You wouldn't accept them here."[49] Particularly in Europe, however, this influential, much-imitated production has had a considerable, sometimes even an explosive impact on the hitherto accepted view of this play in performance.

Probably the most radical exponent of Bergman's device of exposing the attic sequences to view and thereby bringing them closer to the audience has been Peter Zadek, whose production of *The Wild Duck* at the Schauspielhaus in Hamburg in 1975 was actually compared by some critics to its Swedish predecessor. Here, however, the device served a critical rather than an emotional purpose. Like the slapstick parody of the play presented by Manfred Karge and Matthias Langhoff in East Berlin two years earlier, Zadek's highly polemical *Wild Duck* sought, by laying bare the machinery of the theatre and shattering scenic illusion at every juncture, to reveal the bankruptcy of the play's moral viewpoints, epitomized by what Klaus Wagner terms the "bizarre idyll" of the Ekdals' "private zoo" (*Frankfurter Allgemeine Zeitung*, 7 April 1975). In Zadek's version, which utilized a stage completely open to the bare fire-walls of the theatre, Hjalmar's studio was deployed by designer Götz Loepelmann on two levels. By climbing a staircase to the second storey, the Ekdals reached their "private hunting preserve": an attic, fully visible to the audience and spanning the width of the stage, which literally overhung their modest, recognizably bourgeois living-quarters.

In general, in a spirit more reminiscent of Brecht or Peter Stein than Bergman, this long, deliberately slow-paced "quotation" of Ibsen's play adopted a wide range of stratagems intended to arouse the spectator's critical awareness, with the ultimate objective that "the audience semi-circle would be linked to the stage in an unbroken electrical circuit" (Wagner). During Werle's first-act party, for example, the house lights were only partially dimmed and could be seen reflected in the shimmering semi-darkness of the playing area, while the game of blind man's buff played by the businessman's guests "challenged the audience to participate." At other times projectors were occasionally trained on the spectators in an accusatory manner. Gregers Werle (Hans Michael Rehberg) virtually stepped out of his role at times to address the audience directly. The end result was a bitter social satire that continually teetered on the brink of travesty. Even the cynical Doctor Relling, as played by Heinz Schubert, was a parody of a raisonneur who took his seat in the audience after the intermission and conducted his angry exchanges with this unmoved, adolescently fanatical Gregers ("The Exorcist in the Attic," one critic called him) across half the auditorium. To underscore the negation of any trace of catharsis, Zadek let his unusual *vox populi* mount the stage again at the end of the play to lead the applause (and boos) and work the curtain for the first call.

(A rather similar production, both in terms of its Marxist point of view and its theatrical concept, was presented by the expatriate Rumanian director Lucian Pintilie at the Arena Stage in Washington, DC in 1986. This unusual interpretation was hailed by *Time* as the "rediscovery" in Ibsen's play of a vein of social criticism and class consciousness. Pintilie's variation – unlike the sarcastic Zadek performance in this respect – seemed determined to take Ibsen's work seriously as a social document "about the corrosive effects of wealth and envy": "Thus the privation of the ruined Ekdal family and the shame they feel at taking handouts from their former business partners, the Werles, permeate every emotional connection in the play."[50] In terms of its staging, meanwhile, this production followed Zadek's example in a number of ways. Werle's party took place in shadow, behind an elegant mirrored wall that in fact concealed Hjalmar's impoverished garret. Here, the Ekdals again made their laborious way up a staircase from the living floor of the studio to an attic above, an aerie where they kept caged birds. Once more the audience was raked by the beam of an accusing projector, this time a giant lamp used in the photographer's work. The play again ended without the comfort of catharsis, concluding instead in a fistfight between Gregers and a "drunken but discerning" Doctor Relling.)

The stage history of *The Wild Duck* came full circle, as it were, when Rudolf Noelte, the great conservative among German directors, mounted his forcefully traditional revival of the work at the historic Freie Volksbühne in Berlin in 1979. More than twenty years earlier Noelte had staged a highly acclaimed naturalistic performance of the play – ironically enough at the Schauspielhaus in Hamburg, where Zadek, Luc Bondy, and other radical spirits have since flourished. Now, however, Noelte's Berlin revival literally took critics by storm, coming as it did at the close of one of the most boldly experimental and iconoclastic decades in recent European theatre. "Karge, Langhoff, Zadek – all view Ibsen's drama polemically, looking down at it, from the historical distance of the 1970s," Georg Hensel observed in *Frankfurter Allgemeine* (19 February 1979). "Noelte is no polemicist: he is a realist [who] looks the human beings Ibsen has created squarely in the face and invites the audience to share in the observation – not to pass judgment."

Rooted in the naturalistic tradition fostered in the German theatre by Otto Brahm, the carefully balanced objectivity and humanity of Noelte's approach lay at the farthest end of the spectrum from Zadek's rowdy, defiantly arbitrary eclecticism. "Here nothing is exaggerated, nothing is judged. Only what is in the text is acted out here, carried to its ultimate, gruesomely comic consequence," commented Friedrich Luft in *Die Welt* (19 February). "No insistence, not a single false tone, not a trace of opinionated over-emphasis. A tragic, perfidious world is concretely and believably recreated on the stage."[51] In Noelte's hands *The Wild Duck* seemed, to this critic and others, to regain the dimension of a classical tragedy in which every character is "right" in his own terms and his own way. "No character here is distorted or catered to by the director," Luft continued. "Each figure in the drama pleads his own cause."

As a result, enriched by tradition without being reduced to conventionality by it, the individual characterizations in Noelte's ensemble reacquired that elusive sense of psychological complexity and conviction that Brahm's company had also attained in this play, almost three-quarters of a century earlier. The passage of time, of course, made somewhat different human beings of Ibsen's characters. Albert Bassermann, the greatest Hjalmar Ekdal of his day, had created, Polgar

tells us, a sincere, utterly charming, unselfconscious, gracefully vivacious egoist with "the embryonic spirit of the artist" and "the makings
of a poet" about him – a tenor-personality ("Tenormensch"!) who set
female hearts aflutter and whom even the profoundest suffering inspired "to float along on clouds of pathos and fine-sounding
phrases."[52] As Ibsen had demanded and Bassermann demonstrated,
the actor playing this part must never for a moment show he is aware
that what he says or does may be amusing. In Noelte's production,
Werner Kreindl achieved this very result in a quite different way, by
depicting a subdued, pliable, and appealing daydreamer in felt slippers, applying his very considerable physical energy to the preservation of his inactivity ("a typically passive TV watcher before the advent
of TV," *FAZ* called him). His was a Hjalmar "without that 'pathetic'
quality which directors have superimposed on him. Kreindl *is* pathetic. But he is always so through innocence or necessity. He wants only
his own happiness, even though it be an illusion" (*Die Welt*).

Like the convention of the "farcical photographer," the equally
outworn stereotype of a spiteful, one-dimensional Gregers Werle was
also expunged from Noelte's interpretation, as indeed it had also been
from Brahm's. In the latter's renowned production at the Lessing
Theatre, Oscar Sauer had played the role as a virtually Dostoyevskian
visionary nailed to the cross of his obsession, "a somnambulistic aesthete" with "the fulgent glow of the martyr's dedication radiating from
his face." His sincerity was intensified by "his air of painful silence"
when the gulf between him and others became too wide for words to
bridge, Polgar records, while his parting remark about his destiny
"reverberated with the heartfelt suffering of a pious man who has seen
Heaven recede before him."[53] Although far less hieratic and more
simply conceived than Sauer's reading, Peter Fricke's performance for
Noelte likewise succeeded in eliciting sympathy for his character's
position, rather than resentment. "He is not psychoanalytically
traumatized by father-hatred or mother-love. Nor is he a fanatic,"
Hensel observed in his assessment of this mild-mannered, well-
meaning Gregers. "Obsessive he is not, merely misguided: a naive
monstrosity of idealism." Although Noelte certainly did not take his
side, "he restored respect for him. This sensitive spiritual detective's
only fault [was] that he set himself up as judge."

In a general sense, in its intense preoccupation with the inner emotional logic of Ibsen's characters rather than with the ideas they express
or personify, Noelte's production showed a certain affinity with Ingmar Bergman's approach to *The Wild Duck* and to Ibsen as a whole. In
terms of actual production style, however, Noelte's neo-naturalistic

27 H. W. Lenneweit's spacious, open setting for the Ekdal studio in Rudolf Noelte's revival of *The Wild Duck* at the Freie Volksbühne, Berlin, in 1979. Noelte makes effective use of the spaciousness to emphasize the separation between Gregers Werle (Peter Fricke, right) and his father (Kurt Hübner) in their tense third-act encounter.

revival represents the antithesis both to Bergman's method and to the contrary tendency to "modify" realism by mixing it with symbolic abstraction – as, for instance, in the production of the play mounted by director Christopher Morahan and designer Ralph Koltai at Britain's National Theatre in 1979. Bergman's starkly simplified, shallow platform-stage in *The Wild Duck*, which existed only as an acting area and not as a functional "environment" in its own right, was neither symbolic nor abstract. In Koltai's highly conceptualized design for the open-stage production at the Olivier, on the other hand, a huge symbolic tree and a giant photo montage of a forest in receding perspective hung portentously over an otherwise perfectly realistic period setting. Rejecting both such possibilities, Noelte's *mise-en-scène* returned the play without apology to its naturalistic origins – and demonstrated in the process that this mode was still a viable and highly malleable one in the theatre. H. W. Lenneweit's spacious setting for Werle's salon consisted of no fewer than three (rather than the customary two) sumptuously appointed rooms, filled during the party scene with bustling movement, the clink of glasses, the sound of piano music, and the swirl of cigar smoke. The virtual emptiness of the Ekdal studio presented the sharpest possible contrast. The bare, open expanse of this wood-paneled attic receded into the depths of the mysterious interior loft that lay beyond. In itself, this evocative setting represents a perfect illustration of Noelte's modification and redefinition of the whole concept of "realistic" environment in Ibsen's drama.

In terms of the strength of the emotional appeal it exerted, Noelte's performance in Berlin calls to mind Shaw's warm response to the "poetically realistic illusion" of Charles Charrington's revival of *The Wild Duck* at the Globe Theatre at the end of the last century. "To sit there getting deeper and deeper into the Ekdal home, and getting deeper and deeper into your own life all the time, until you forget that you are in a theatre, to look on with horror and pity at a profound tragedy, shaking with laughter all the time at an irresistible comedy" was for Shaw "an experience deeper than real life ever brings to most men, or often brings to any man."[54] Shaw's justly famous tribute has sometimes been used to define the play as a comedy in which a tragedy occurs. Such a definition seems, however, almost as inadequate as its presumed opposite – that *The Wild Duck* is a tragedy in which some sort of "comic relief" occurs. The truth, at least in terms of theatrical performance, seems rather that the "new method" introduced by Ibsen in this play is rooted in the verbal and visual juxtaposition and *collision* of moods and impressions, comic and tragic alike. It appears clear from its stage history that the play's most effective interpreters in

28 The last scene in Christopher Morahan's production of *The Wild Duck* at the National Theatre, London, in 1979. Stage design by Ralph Koltai.

the theatre, from Bloch and Bjørnson in Ibsen's time to Bergman and Noelte in our own, have been those capable of understanding this basic structural dynamism and controlling its effect on the perception of the spectator, who is abruptly taken by it from one level to another, totally unexpected one and must himself supply the bridge between them. To the mood induced by this collision of opposing emotional states, Vsevolod Meyerhold applied the term "the grotesque." As Meyerhold well knew, and as Ibsen's later plays came to demonstrate, it sets in motion a process that eventually blurs and in the end renders invisible the line that divides the real from the fantastic.

6

Messenger from a closed country:
Hedda Gabler

The actors and audiences of the 1890s were generally bewildered by *Hedda Gabler*, the last play Ibsen was to write before finally returning to Norway to live. "'Subterranean forces and powers' are what it is about," reads one of the numerous notes and jottings he made while working on it: "Woman as a mine-worker. Nihilism."[1] Although the importance of undertext and symbolism is hardly less pronounced in the two preceding plays of his Munich "trilogy," the black outlook of *Hedda Gabler* seems to set it decisively apart from both *Rosmersholm* (1886) and *The Lady from the Sea* (1888). The latter ends optimistically (or so it would seem), with the recognition of Ellida Wangel's freedom to choose; the former, while darker in tone at the end, nonetheless concludes on a note of tragic affirmation, with the mystical death-marriage of Rosmer and Rebecca. By contrast, Hedda's suicide affirms nothing, least of all an uplifting tragic vision. "Life is not tragic – Life is ridiculous – And that cannot be borne," reads another of the play-wright's notes. Even Nietzsche, philosophical nihilist that he was, might well have been troubled by Hedda's psychological nihilism, contending as he did that such an uncontrolled and subjective im-pression of life's futility and meaninglessness arises from a disarray of the instincts, a diseased condition that can and must be remedied by the objective philosophical knowledge that life *has* no higher purpose than the one we assign it. Small wonder, then, that minds made of less stern stuff might view the play as simply a "hideous nightmare of pessimism" (to borrow a typical phrase from London's *Pictorial World*). To its contemporaries, its sole message seemed to be unconditional despair. "Puzzling," "improbable," and "incredible" were the adjec-tives most commonly used by the Scandinavian critics to describe the central character. And to make matters worse, Ibsen appeared to be introducing alarming touches of black comedy and even parody to produce a dissonant clash of tones, culminating in the ambiguous juxtaposition of Hedda's suicide with (what Ibsen's notes call) the "grotesquely comical" vignette of "those respectable people" Tesman and Mrs. Elvsted, busily piecing together their absurd "monument" to a man "who so thoroughly despised the whole thing."[2]

Faced with this air of confusion – and fostering more of it all the time – productions from one end of Europe to the other ended in disaster. At the world premiere at the Residenztheater (31 January 1891), Ibsen was deeply distressed to see the heavily declamatory Hedda created by the popular Munich actress Marie Conrad-Ramlo, in a play whose tight, staccato rhythm indicates the very antithesis of such a style. (Edmund Gosse was perhaps the first to draw explicit attention to the utterly new problem posed by this play's "hissing conversational fireworks, fragments of sentences without verbs, clauses that come to nothing, adverbial exclamations and cryptic interrogations."[3]) Nor was naturalism the solution, despite the play's ostensibly naturalistic external trappings. William Bloch's subdued and rather colorless production at the Danish Royal Theatre a month after the Munich opening was, by general agreement, a total failure. Stanislavski himself likewise admits that the Moscow Art Theatre fared scarcely better when it tried in its very first season (19 February 1899) to stage the play in a conventionally realistic manner. In Paris, meanwhile, where *Hedda Gabler* was put on at the commercial Théâtre Vaudeville in the wake of Antoine's private productions of *Ghosts* and *The Wild Duck*, naturalism never entered the picture. At the single matinee performance (17 December 1891), the comedienne Marthe Brandès – who had been careful to publicize her utter incomprehension of Hedda's character – took refuge in one of the period's favorite stereotypes, the sophisticated, elegantly attired *femme fatale* from the pages of Dumas or Flaubert, "a Madame Bovary who gets her frocks on the Rue de la Paix."[4] Even a partisan like Lugné-Poë was obliged to concede that the experiment was a crushing defeat for Ibsen's cause in France.

Some helpful light was shed on the general confusion, however, when Elizabeth Robins and Marion Lea, two intrepid American actresses, grasped the opportunity to produce the first London showing of *Hedda Gabler*, only five weeks after Grein's beleaguered performance of *Ghosts* at his Independent Theatre. Although the new play was greeted with the same predictable howls of outrage, the production itself at the Vaudeville Theatre (20 April 1891) was, even in the opinion of some of Ibsen's bitterest opponents, a convincing and long overdue demonstration to English audiences of his theatrical power. "An extraordinary process of vivification takes place," marveled Henry James, one of Robins' most powerful supporters. "It was a proof of

Ibsen's force that he made us chatter about him so profusely without
the aid of the theatre; but it was even more a blessing to have the aid at
last ... The play, on perusal, left one comparatively muddled and
mystified, fascinated, but – in one's intellectual sympathy – snubbed.
Acted, it leads that sympathy over the straightest of roads with all the
exhilaration of a superior pace."[5]

This influential essay by James, "On the Occasion of *Hedda Gabler*,"
is in fact quite vague about details of actual performance – whereas
some less "exhilarated" witnesses like Justin McCarthy or even
Clement Scott provide more revealing hints about the dynamics of
Robins' intense and alert portrayal of Hedda. The incorrigible Scott,
who detested the play, still confessed his "morbid attraction" to
Robins' "sublime study of deceit and heartlessness": "What changes
of expression! What watchfulness! ... She has fascinated us with a
savage."[6] An even stronger impression of a highly colored and broadly
pantomimic performance is conveyed by Justin McCarthy, who deplored what he regarded as Robins' attempt to bend Ibsen's conception
to suit popular taste: "The result is that her Hedda Gabler is a very
melodramatic, highly effective creation, ingeniously calculated to interest, even to appeal to the sympathies of London audiences, but far
too obvious, too harsh, too showy for the super-subtle 'White Devil' of
Ibsen's drama."[7]

Robins would probably have answered McCarthy's objection with
the same argument that she later advanced in *Ibsen and the Actress*,
namely that there *is* no single "right" approach to this role. "Ibsen was
by training so intensely *un homme du théâtre* that, to an extent I know in
no other dramatist, he saw where he could leave some of his greatest
effects to be made by the actor, and so left them," she writes in her
memoir of the *Hedda Gabler* production. "Whatever direction the individual gift and temper of the actor inclines to, the effects that Ibsen
leaves him are Ibsen effects."[8] Her impressionistic analysis of Hedda
(presented first as a public lecture almost forty years after the fact) is a
psychological character study that shares the James view of the play as
essentially "the portrait of a nature ... and of a state of nerves as well as
of soul," the dramatization "not of an action but of a condition."[9] Seen
in this way, Hedda became a (novelistic) character of enigmatic complexity and secret thoughts, governed by the shifting, vacillating tides
of unconscious motivation. Holding this character-mosaic together,
however, was what Robins called the playwright's "master-key" to the
role: "Ibsen's unwritten clue brought me close enough to the 'cold-
blooded egoist' to feel her warm to my touch; to see Hedda Gabler as
pitiable in her hungry loneliness – to see her as tragic" (26). As such,

Hedda's suicide was to Robins an act of courage, the final rebellion against the ignominy of a life that had failed her utterly.

In her exegesis of the text, this emphasis on Hedda's "tragic loneliness" takes Robins in two different directions. In conventional naturalistic terms, the actress describes her character as the victim of her upbringing and her social circumstances, "a bundle of unused possibilities, educated to fear life," with "no opportunity at all to use her best powers": "Well, she wasn't on the scene sixty seconds before it was clear she knew there was joy in life she hadn't been able to grasp, and that marriage only emphasized what she was missing" (20). In direct juxtaposition with this "sympathetic" view of Hedda's frustration and longing, however, one encounters the harsh and savage side of Hedda's temperament that Scott and McCarthy (among many others) found so predominant in performance. "I had the best of reasons for not trying to mitigate Hedda's corrosive qualities," Robins declares with disarming frankness: "It was precisely the corrosive action of those qualities on a woman in Hedda's circumstances that made her the great acting opportunity she was" (21). The conscious emphasis on the "demonic" in Hedda's character is clearly evident in Ibsen's own thinking, both in his private notes ("The demonic thing about Hedda is that she wants to exert influence over another person") and even in his letter to Hans Schrøder at Christiania Theatre, urging him to cast Constance Bruun since she could presumably be relied on "to find a way of expressing the demonic aspect of the character."[10] For Robins, the "corrosive" essence of Hedda's nature resided in her scornful revolt against her commonplace surroundings, her selfishness, her open contempt for "so-called womanly qualities," but most of all "her strong need to put some meaning into her life, even at the cost of borrowing it, or stealing the meaning out of someone else's" (21).

In a letter to Robins written immediately after the opening, Shaw had praise for her efforts to amalgamate these two potentially contradictory tendencies, the tragic and the demonic, in her interpretation: "you were sympathetically unsympathetic, which was the exact solution of the central difficulty of playing Hedda."[11] Most of the reviewers, however, were led by her performance to focus solely on the darker side of the portrait – "a most lifelike embodiment of the 'moral insanity' of the medical textbooks" (*The Times*). The deliberately level and rather bland matter-of-factness of the other performances in Robins' ensemble also served to heighten the diabolical intensity of what the *Daily Chronicle* called "the captious, perfidious, and thoroughly detestable Hedda." In particular, Marion Lea's gentle, sweet-faced Thea Elvsted ("fair as a lily, with her glory of yellow hair and frightened eyes, weak as water") appeared like an irresolute lamb in the presence of what more than one observer described as a cunning and rapacious tigress.

This quality of "demonism" in Robins' portrayal of Hedda – supported in turn by Ibsen's own perception of the character as seeking "to exert influence over another person" – finds an interesting and revealing corollary in the intense, even savage vitality she brought to the role of Hilde Wangel in *The Master Builder*, which she took up with great success less than two years later, early in 1893. In fact, of the seven Ibsen heroines Robins played, the ambiguous figure of Hilde in this play remained her favorite. Subsequently, in comparing her characterization with the considerably blander, more "subjugated" Hilde of Suzanne Desprès in Lugné-Poë's production, Shaw succinctly described the "appalling force" of Robins' ruthlessly insensible youthfulness as "more dangerous than a lion in the path," utterly "grief proof" (*Saturday Review*, 30 March 1895). More than once in her career, the Ibsen interpretations of this gifted actress thus pointed up subtle character affinities and interconnections that had not occurred to literary critics.

A clearer impression of the actual practical dynamics of Robins' performance in *Hedda Gabler* is provided by her marked acting script for the production (actually a side-book containing only Hedda's own lines and cues), which in some ways shows us a less intellectualized and certainly a far less idealized character interpretation than that suggested by the actress's later theoretical analysis of the role.[12] In the opening acts, this Hedda kept a tight rein on herself and her emotions, concealing her nervous tension behind a façade of composure and indolence. Glancing from time to time in a French novel she carried, she drawled her lines "languidly" and "indifferently" and moved "listlessly" and "lazily" within the confines of the conventional drawing-room setting.[13] Nevertheless, turbulent currents ran close beneath the apparently calm surface. "Sharp, secret looks" and "keen, nervous glances" were cast, particularly at Thea. When Hedda learned from her of Eilert's presence in town, her stifled exclamation ("Is Løvborg –!") was "low" but "emphasized with a *keen light* in her eyes." Similarly, Thea's reference near the end of their conversation to "the shadow of another woman" in Løvborg's life was marked by a "wild flash of joy" in her interrogator's eyes. It was not really until the end of the second act, however, that Hedda's sneering sarcasm and thinly concealed hostility suddenly erupted into a frenzy of passion and angry spitefulness. Grasping Thea's hands as she again prophesied Løvborg's triumphant return ("with a crown of vine-leaves in his hair!''), she dragged her understandably terrified companion toward the open door and the tea Berte had laid out in the next room. To play up this tense moment, Robins composed a graphic curtain tableau in which Hedda "draws her breath in through clenched teeth and lifts her hand to Thea's hair."

In the third act, the tigress in Hedda was set loose. Even as Tesman took Løvborg's "precious, irreplaceable manuscript" from his coat pocket, Hedda fixed "greedy" but "calm" eyes upon it – and at this moment, Robins notes, "her purposes begin to take force and grow." The demonizing process, which now colored virtually all of Hedda's actions, reached its high-point with the climactic burning of the manuscript, following Arthur Elwood's "really fine exit to his death" (Clement Scott). Here, Robins struck out Ibsen's own very detailed stage directions and substituted her own lines and action, the tone of which speaks for itself:

Hedda holds out her hands, wavering a little as [Løvborg] goes out. She utters a broken cry, grasps curtains, looks back at desk where manuscript is and whispers hoarsely, "*Thea! Thea!*" – again and again as she crosses the room, takes out ms with eager hands, catches sight of stove, glides to it and drops before it opening door and muttering, "*Who? child, the child*" – crushes some leaves and burns them during "*How I love burning your child.*"

In itself, the characteristic rewriting of Ibsen's curtain line ("Now I am burning the child" in the original) bespeaks the quality of pathological destructiveness with which Robins invested this action.

In the play's final movement this Hedda seemed to cross the line from malice to a madness that showed itself in her swift and violent changes of mood and tone. Staring at the stove, she told Tesman of her deed with "a concentrated hatred of the work she'd had no hand in." Using Scott Buist's conventional "fool of a husband" as a foil, she ranged from "quite still and passionless" composure to "palpitating disgust" when Tesman shouted for joy at the news of Hedda's pregnancy. Also during Brack's prolonged recounting of Løvborg's misfortune, Robins ran the gamut of emotion from exultation to distraction and despair. As Thea and Tesman moved into the rear alcove to begin their pointless reconstruction of the lost manuscript, she started toward them "as if to say 'I'll soon put a stop to that' – then a quick thought – 'Why should I? – I don't care' – then the thought of Eilert – turn and go swiftly to chair uttering 'ho ho' in low-voiced laugh. Sink into chair in relief." This relief was soon shattered again. Hedda demanded the truth from Brack with "fierce impatience," and when she learned it she buried her head in her hands in weary revul-

29 Ibsen on Broadway, 1903: a Byron photograph of Minnie Maddern Fiske's revival of *Hedda Gabler* at the Manhattan Theatre. What William Winter called the "velvet duplicity and stealthy elegance" of George Arliss's Brack is met with mordant sarcasm by Mrs. Fiske's Hedda.

sion ("What curse is it that makes everything I touch turn ludicrous and mean?")

Robins and her advisers took great care to make Hedda's final moments theatrically effective – and naturalism be damned. Her last scene with Brack was planned to be played "rapidly," in a state of "high tension" but after a few performances William Archer, who had helped Robins rehearse the play, urged her to speak her lines more loudly, "at whatever cost of verisimilitude," because the audience must be enabled to hear the motives leading up to her suicide. "I have never had a more tremendous experience in a theatre than that which began when everybody saw that the pistol shot was coming at the end," exclaimed Shaw in his impulsive letter to the actress. Archer was particularly intent that the suicide tableau itself should leave no doubt that Hedda had indeed "done it beautifully." Accordingly, just as Alice Wright had made it plain to her public that Mrs. Alving never intended to administer the fatal morphine, Robins chose a posture that would demonstrate Hedda's triumph over life's baseness: when Tesman drew aside the curtains of the inner room, she was discovered lying with her head back, her face up but slightly averted, holding a metal-white pistol in the hand that had fallen across her black dress. This poignant tableau was enhanced by localized lighting from a hanging lamp, "artificially helped out if necessary," Archer advised, "though of course without any sort of William Barrettish limelight effect."[14]

(The urge to end this play with a suitably expressive closing picture has remained strong. In 1904, for example, when Blanche Bates played the part in Philadelphia, a green "special" on the face of the dead Hedda caused considerable comment, while even in 1948 at the Bristol Old Vic, Alan Davis was still invoking the old custom of revealing the body in a single pool of light. Three years later, in a creditable production at Nationaltheatret in Oslo, critics were again busy debating the use of a spotlight in the final tableau, trained this time on the face of General Gabler in a large portrait that hung portentously above Gerd Grieg's prostrate form.[15] Probably the most unusual visual climax of all occurred, however, in Charles Marowitz's expressionistic *Hedda* collage when, after a thunderous gunshot, the empty white stage divided in two, "like a split egg," leaving "everyone on one side, Hedda on the other," the spiritual outcast of her listless society.)[16]

The early, highly successful *Hedda Gabler* staged (and later revived and toured) by Elizabeth Robins epitomizes an approach that has persisted from her time to our own. Its essence is the (naturalistically grounded) assumption that a sufficiently subtle psychological analysis

30 "A souvenir to take with you": watched by the portrait of General Gabler, a seductive Hedda of the 1920s (Betty Nansen) hands a mesmerized Løvborg (Henrik Bentzon) the fateful pistol. At the Betty Nansen Theatre, Copenhagen, 1924.

of the central character's personality traits and past experiences yields the key to the play's credibility in performance. Minnie Maddern Fiske, whose influential New York productions of the play in 1903 and 1904 followed Robins' single Manhattan matinee in 1898, summed up this assumption very succinctly: "I must know all that Hedda ever was. When I do, the role will play itself." In Ibsen's plays, she subsequently told a learned gathering at Harvard, "the actor must of necessity have studied all that has, in the past lives of the characters, led up to the final scene."[17] "What demon winds blew her about? What did she get hurt by? What defensive about? What did she love? What bored her? What excited her?" These and similar questions are Janet Suzman's, posed in *her* lecture on Hedda's character as she portrayed it in London in 1977, but they could as easily have been framed by Mrs. Fiske or Elizabeth Robins.[18] Unhindered, of course, by the Victorian reluctance of her forebears, Suzman's sensitive, careful analysis examines issues they tactfully avoided – Hedda's pregnancy, for example, and her suppressed sexuality – but her avowed aim of discerning in the character a coherent psychological pattern of motivation is no different from theirs. To reveal the shifting currents of this inner life, she even speaks of devising "silent soliloquies" that are models of the naturalistic method of transforming psychology into life-like behavior. Her invention of a "complete honeymoon itinerary" to clarify in her own mind "that foggy time before the play actually begins" corresponds directly to Mrs. Fiske's advice (and anticipates in turn Marowitz's own curious inclusion of imaginary "Random Notes from the Diary of Hedda Gabler" in the published text of his collage). Like Robins, then, Suzman continued to seek vindication for Hedda and sympathy for her tragedy by rendering her "triad of crimes" against Løvborg – the drink, the pistol, and the burning of the manuscript – psychologically believable and even excusable. By 1977, however, this aspiration to psychological credibility was bound to be frustrated, rather than supported, by a conventionally "realistic" period environment and a style of production that inadvertently turned the play into "a high Victorian tragicomedy of manners: Pinero would have been proud of it."[19]

The nearly century-long search for an "explanation" of Hedda's character and behavior has, by its very nature, yielded not a single portrait of a troubled personality but a whole gallery of variants. Hence, while Mrs. Fiske was frosty and remote in her sarcasm (Winter describes her "watchful wickedness" and "icy, piercing, stridulous, staccato speech"), her greatest rival, Alla Nazimova, was smouldering and passionate in the role she played for over thirty years ("a high-bred exotic, an orchid of a woman, baleful, fascinating" is how Walter

Prichard Eaton first saw her in 1906). The intense quietness and resignation of Duse's legendary portrayal of "a weary soul in a languid,
worn-out body" inspired Eva Le Gallienne's aspiration to "natural-
ness" in the part, which she first played in modern dress at her newly
founded Civic Repertory Theatre in New York in 1928. On the other
hand, the Duse style held little appeal for the English temperament;
the Italian star's *"simpatica morbidezza"* had been promptly challenged
in 1907 by Mrs. Patrick Campbell's own actively malignant, emphatically pregnant version of Hedda. Fifteen years later, a much stouter
Mrs. Pat filled the role with an even more extravagant grandeur that
made Agate think of "the canvases of Goya" ("a magnificent portrait of
somebody else . . . not in the least like Ibsen's Hedda"). Meanwhile,
Heddas across Europe in the mid-1920s had become vamps and Circes,
seductively taunting bewildered Løvborgs – though, as the gifted
Danish actress-director Betty Nansen demonstrated forcefully in her
1924 production, the mask of the temptress might well conceal, as one
critic put it, "a poor woman whose aberrations are due to her spiritual
impoverishment and loneliness." Eventually, at the Arts Theatre in
London in 1931, Jean Forbes-Robertson attempted a "redistribution"
of emphasis: consciously playing for laughs (rather than in fear of
them), she endowed her Hedda with a relentlessly mocking sense of
humor that remained, even in her third appearance in the role in 1951,
"as bitter as a distillation of poison ivy." Taking a similar tack in Peter
Ashmore's popular 1954 revival, Peggy Ashcroft admits she went on
the assumption that Ibsen's heroine "lacks tragic intensity but is rather
grimly amusing." Kenneth Tynan was among those who heartily
approved of *Hedda Gabler* played as parlor comedy: "Your weather-
beaten British playgoer, who likes his entertainment warmed by the
blue skies of Verona, Nice or Siam, has immemorially shunned Ibsen,
with his grim galoshes and abiding rain." Although Ashcroft makes
passing reference in an interview to "the existentialist insistence on
choice" as a force in the play, her depiction of an "unnatural," sexually
inhibited Hedda was clearly shaped by the same search for recognizable personality traits and credible motives that Elizabeth Robins had
initiated. "All of that [psychological and hereditary background] is of
the utmost importance," Ashcroft insists, in terms that could as well
have been used by Robins: "The actress has to present the character,
strange as she may be, so that . . . the audience will believe in her."[20]

   This simple but revealing statement actually epitomizes the "theatre
of characters" which has – particularly in England and North America
– almost invariably approached *Hedda Gabler* in the very terms first
suggested by James, as "the portrait of a nature" – a potentially melo-

dramatic, inherently comedic character study of "a permanently con-
founded misfit" (to borrow at random from a description of Glenda
Jackson in the role in 1975). Whatever the differences in shading or
detail have been, the underlying consistency of the "characterological"
approach is best appreciated by considering its antithesis: a "theatre of
situation" (as Jean-Paul Sartre called it) defined not by a preoccupation
with "character" as the sum total of psychological traits, but rather by
its concern with the dramatic situation that ultimately defines the
characters in a play, with the choices it affords (or denies) them, and
with the limits within which they are confined on all sides.[21] Although
the productions of Ingmar Bergman have become synonymous with
the application of this "existentialist" view to Ibsen, the determination
to reveal the inner governing shape of *Hedda Gabler*, rather than the
fortuitous psychological or social aspects of its central character's personal plight, finds its genesis in the work of Vsevolod Meyerhold,
undertaken (though they never knew it) while Minnie Maddern Fiske
and Stella Campbell were still in their first prime, nearly sixty years
before Bergman's astonishing theatrical reinterpretation of this particular play.

FROM PORTRAIT TO IMAGE

Reinhardt's *Ghosts*, Gordon Craig's *Rosmersholm* and Meyerhold's
Hedda Gabler, all produced in 1906, are very distinct but analogous
manifestations of the same anti-naturalistic tendency, characterized by
Craig's avowed determination to "leave period and accuracy of detail
to the museums and to curiosity shops." Through the medium of
Edvard Munch's expressively focused designs, Reinhardt evoked a
palpable atmosphere of oppressiveness and dread overhanging the
Alving household. Using quite different means, Craig created an impressionistic "house of shadows" for his *Rosmersholm* ("a vision of
loveliness," thought Duse) that consisted only of vast greenish-blue
space, soaring lines, and an immense window in the background that
conjured up that "profound impression of unseen forces closing in
upon the place" which he felt governed the play. By comparison,
Meyerhold's *Hedda Gabler* (10 November 1906) represented a far more
radical and comprehensive deconstruction, the aim of which was to
reveal Ibsen's play to the spectator in a new and deliberately unfamiliar
manner, shorn of all the intrusive "parenthetic details" so dear to
Stanislavski. At the heart of all three of these innovative Ibsen productions, meanwhile, was the adamant rejection of the photographic
reality of surfaces and the shared objective of creating a heightened

conceptual image of the inner thematic rhythm and spirit of the work at hand. Craig might have been speaking for all three men when he wrote (in the program for *Rosmersholm*): "Realism has long ago proclaimed itself as a contemptible means of hinting at things of life and death, the two subjects of the masters. Realism is only Exposure, whereas art is Revelation; and therefore in the mounting of this play I have tried to avoid all Realism."[22] ("I simply cannot see painted sets, no matter how hard I try. Nor can I see constructed sets," observed Eugene Vakhtangov, the other great Russian innovator, when he in turn staged his Craig-inspired *Rosmersholm* in Moscow in 1918. "The major idea should never be obscured. Everything auxiliary can be removed ... without harming the main idea.")[23]

Following these same general lines, then, Meyerhold's interpretation of *Hedda Gabler* attempted (in the words of his assistant director, Pavel Yartsev) "to give primitive, purified expression to what it senses behind Ibsen's play," by utilizing colors, shapes, and movements to create a sensual theatrical impression (rather than a naturalistic representation) of a cold, regal Hedda seen against a vast, blue, receding expanse that suggested her aesthetic longings.[24] Meyerhold's production, which inaugurated his brief but extremely important association with Vera Kommisarjevskava in St. Petersbsurg, boldly set aside all considerations of actual period and place. Instead, inspired by the modernist theories of Georg Fuchs, the director adopted a purely symbolic scheme of chromatic values for costumes and setting alike, designed to influence the intuitive responses of the spectator. Tesman, the living emblem of "Tesmanism," wore a dull gray jacket and broad trousers cut in a style reminiscent of the 1820s, while the color signs of the other characters ranged from earth brown (Løvborg) and dark gray (Brack) to pale pink (for Thea) and cool, shimmering green (for Hedda herself). Kommisarjevskaya's costume as Hedda ("like the waters of the ocean, like the scales of a sea-creature," in the words of one observer)[25] blended in turn with the dominant shades of a luxuriously decadent Art Nouveau decor, designed by the noted painter Nikolai Sapunov. An eyewitness account evokes the subtle correspondences of moods and colors found in Sapunov's extraordinary stylization of Ibsen's "handsomely and tastefully furnished" drawing-room:

The basic color of the backcloth – blue. On the right a large window the full height of the stage. Outside the window, green-blue sky with (in the last act) glittering stars. Beneath the window – black rhododendron leaves. Surrounding the window itself – intertwining vines. On the left side of the same backcloth – an indigo tapestry: a shining silver and gold woman with a reindeer. Along the sides of the stage and overhead – silvery gray lacework. On the floor – a greenish blue carpet. White furniture. A white piano. Greenish white vases. White chrysanthemums standing in them. And white fur on a strangely shaped divan.[26]

A focal point in this strange room (put together by Judge Brack, we are told, to suit the tastes of the new chatelaine) was a huge armchair also covered in white fur, intended as a kind of throne for Hedda, around which most of her scenes were played. ("The spectator is intended to associate Hedda with her throne and to carry away this combined impression in his memory," Yartsev notes.) The deliberately flattened, two-dimensional effect created by the painted backcloth and its cut-out window was reinforced by the absence of doors in the set; instead, the actors made their entrances and exits through net curtains that hung at the sides of the stage.

The purpose of such stylization, Fuchs had maintained in *Die Schaubühne der Zukunft* (1905) was to subject the decorative and pictorial elements of the theatre to the "inner" voice of the play, by facilitating the plastic and spatial movements of the human body upon which dramatic art ultimately depends. For him as for Meyerhold, the spoken text alone is never enough to reveal the inner emotional texture of the play – the "subterranean forces and powers" Ibsen himself alludes to in his notes. Rather, the director must enable the actor's movements, gestures and mime to probe and reveal an area beyond the spoken word, and to do so the closest possible rapport must be established with the spectator, whose direct emotional participation in the inner action of the drama is essential. This "intensification of our existence" is the theatre's chief task, Fuchs argues, yet its accomplishment is hindered rather than helped by Ibsen's literary stage directions, prescribing the "reproduction of a particular place, with its necessary depth of stage":

This meticulous reproduction of a specific environment, which is revealed to the spectator at the rise of the curtain, exists for his eyes and for his consciousness only so long as the action itself has not yet taken possession of him. From the moment when he is carried away by the acting, that detailed illustrative setting disappears from his consciousness, and if in the further course of the play it ever bobs up again, it is either to annoy him or to indicate to him that the performance has begun to drag.[27]

Probably no more interesting or provocative refutation of the naturalistic faith in the power of "environment" in the theatre has ever been offered.

Fuch's advocacy of the bas-relief stage, both as a compositional alternative to naturalistic (in-depth) pictorialism and as a means of bringing the actor into closer contact with the spectator, was thus the direct inspiration for Meyerhold's *Hedda Gabler*, which he presented on a platform almost four times as wide (15 m.) as it was deep (4 m.). This exceptionally wide, shallow stage facilitated non-realistic, lateral patterns of movement – in particular, widely spaced groupings – that undercut the very idea of "life-likeness." At times, long stretches of dialogue were acted without movement or gesture of any kind, "with the emotions concealed and manifested externally only by a brief lighting of the eyes or a flickering smile" (Yartsev). Hedda and Løvborg played their first crucial scene together looking straight ahead, never once shifting their gaze or position, delivering the lines straight to the audience or else sitting in motionless silence, each lost in a private world. "Their quiet, disquieting words fall rhythmically from lips which seem dry and cold," reads the assistant director's account of this scene:

> The spectator hears the lines as though they were being addressed directly at him; before him the whole time he sees the faces of Hedda and Loevborg, observes the slightest change of expression; behind the monotonous dialogue he senses the concealed inner dialogue of presentiments and emotions which are incapable of expression in mere words. The spectator may forget the actual words exchanged by Hedda and Loevborg but he cannot possibly forget the overall impression which the scene creates.[28]

As in the case of Meyerhold's subsequent production of *A Doll's House*, some critics were better prepared than others to recognize the iconoclast's ability to liberate the actor's inner resources and to exploit the power of suggestion and understatement in Ibsen's drama. Among the least enthusiastic reviewers of his *Hedda Gabler* was Alexander Kugel, whose views are of interest because they reflect so concisely the familiar characterological bias that Meyerhold's theatre decisively rejected. Writing in *Teatr i iskusstvo* (*Theatre and Art*, 1906/47) Kugel professed himself ready to dissociate this play from a *specific* milieu of Norwegian fjords and local color, for, he argues, this is not what constitutes its effectiveness: "But one cannot tear it loose from true psychology, from the 'outer circumstances,' from the world of reality, from the surrounding objects which weigh down on the mentality of the characters acting within it, and without the presence of which the drama becomes incomprehensible." Hedda struggles against the pressure of bourgeois existence, Kugel continues, but this pressure resides not only in the people around her but also in the reality of her environment, which cannot be eliminated without damaging the action and idea of the play. "Meyerhold, with his incorporeality, his rejection of realism, and his contempt for life, is a very great and innate enemy of the theatre," this fanatical opponent of a "director's theatre" declared in a follow-up article in which he describes the Moscow Art Theatre and Meyerhold's theatre as two opposed but closely related extremes: the one is determined to render everything "as in life," the other is equally convinced that nothing should be "as in life," but in both cases "the artistic balance of the performance is shifted from the art of the actor to the regime of the director" (*Theatre and Art*, 1907/7). With a curiously inverted logic, Kugel denounced Meyerhold's stylized *Hedda Gabler* for having deemphasized the actor's importance but simultaneously criticized Nemirovitch-Danchenko, when he attempted a simplified, non-realistic *Rosmersholm* a year later, for having laid *too much* emphasis on his Moscow Art Theatre actors, whose naturalistic training required the support of a detailed physical environment to bring out the "humanity"in the characters.[29]

The Kugels of the world notwithstanding, however, the great Ibsen experiments of Meyerhold, Reinhardt, Craig, and other directors at the beginning of the century compelled the modern theatre to reconsider the playwright's work in a decisively new and sharply contemporary light. With very much the same kind of impact, Ingmar Bergman's production of *Hedda Gabler* at Dramaten in 1964 seemed to rediscover this particular play for our own time, and to define in the process a new way of looking at all of Ibsen's so-called realistic plays in the theatre, although Meyerhold in particular would have recognized some of his own aims and methods in it. In retrospect, the Stockholm premiere of Bergman's tightly controlled distilation (17 October 1964) has remained one of the truly revolutionary and influential Ibsen productions of this century. "He illuminated the drama in a light that was not of this world," wrote Siegfried Melchinger at the time in *Theater heute*. "His inspiration transformed the mathematical reality of the play into the workings of a dream, over whose outcome one has no control."[30] Almost fifteen years later, when Bergman restaged this favorite play of his in German at the Residenztheatre in Munich (11 April 1979), the result was not a duplication but an even more precise formulation of his concept of it, played now as a chamber play in one fluid and unbroken movement, without an intermission. (During the intervening years a third production of Bergman's version of *Hedda Gabler*, this time in English with Maggie Smith in the title role, was seen in London in 1970, but, for reasons we have made clear elsewhere, it remained an unfinished effort, bearing hardly more than a superficial resemblance to what Bergman had actually intended.)[31] In essence, meanwhile, all

31   Photograph of the stripped, non-representational setting designed by Mago for Ingmar Bergman's first production of *Hedda Gabler* at Kungliga Dramatiska teatern, Stockholm, in 1964. The small movable screen bisecting the stage is visible to the left of the prompter's box.

of Bergman's renderings of *Hedda Gabler* have projected a fundamentally identical vision of the play as a drama of destiny and entrapment, of ghost-like figures ("dead souls in the ashes," *Süddeutsche Zeitung* called them) caught in a world where there are no second chances or alternatives.

Bergman purposefully translated the play into a new theatrical dimension by freeing it of its heavy mosaic of realistic details – the thick carpets, the "necessary" porcelain stove, the traditional French windows, and not least the portentous portrait of Hedda's father, General Gabler (a pointer that Meyerhold was the first to discard). Instead, the director and his designer (Mago, in all three cases) transformed the entire stage space into an immense, non-representational box that suggested the prevailing atmosphere of claustrophobia, rather than illustrating it in a photographic manner. Uniformly lined with a dark red, velvet-like fabric, this confined mausoleum–stage radiated an oppressive sense of timelessness and lifelessness. "One looks into this strange locale and wonders how human beings can breathe there. It is as though there is no air at all in this red chamber of horrors," wrote *Stockholms-Tidningen* (18 October 1964) of this "ghostly vision." Having neither windows nor walls, the Tesman "parlor" consisted only of seven simple rehearsal screens, each covered in the same dark red velvet, which demarcated a shallow playing area within the empty space.[32] Only the barest minimum of stylized period furniture – a dark red sofa, a pair of red chairs, a black bookcase, a black piano on which stood a bouquet of dark red roses, a large mirror – dotted the monotonous landscape of Hedda's prison–world. Now and then during the course of the action, the wall-screen in the background slid open, as if moved by a ghostly hand, to reveal a dark void beyond, where supposedly offstage characters were seen to linger and to eavesdrop on the proceedings that concerned them. The result, wrote Christopher Porterfield of the London production, "shifts the emphasis from actual events to the manner in which they are apprehended by the characters; above all, to the way in which they are apprehended by Hedda, who overhears far more than anyone else."[33]

The most startling and most discussed aspect of Bergman's stage composition was the fact that his set defined not one place, but two. A smaller, movable screen – sometimes a door, sometimes a barrier in the central character's mind – bisected the stage into two equal and adjacent spheres of simultaneous action. To the audience's left, remorselessly exposed to view, was the "inner room" of Ibsen's stage directions, the physical and psychic retreat where Hedda keeps her piano and the General's pistols. Never allowed to disappear from view in this version, she stood trapped before us, caught in a Pirandellian situation of having to watch her own innermost spiritual agony dragged into the spotlight of public scrutiny. Even when not directly involved in the action, she remained a visible, restless, solitary presence, isolated but never private, on her own side of the middle divider that acted like a glass wall separating her, the defeated human being, from the others. "One might have thought that Hedda was spying," Melchinger remarked, "but the impression produced was rather that the stage spied on Hedda, that she was being dissected by it against her will."

Perceived in the eerie unreality of this airless, timeless red inferno, illuminated by a uniformly cold light that tampered with contours and erased any secure sense of spatial dimensionality, all the characters in the drama appeared like figures suspended in a void. Each was dressed (*without* any symbolic connotation) in a muted, unrelieved monochrome: Hedda in dark green, the others in yet more subdued color values that ranged from pale gray and olive to black. A hint of period flavor in the costumes – pointedly simplified and stylized – completed the impression of characters that existed independent of any material surroundings, in an atmosphere in which the world outside, the world of reality, had no place whatsoever. "It exists only as a quotation," observed Hans Schwab-Felisch in *Frankfurter Allgemeine Zeitung* (18 April 1979). "It impinges on what happens, and it even has the power to affect events, but it has no real meaning." Inevitably, perhaps, the impact created by these isolated human figures, seen against a ground of strangely menacing vacancy, evoked allusions both to Bergman's own somber vision as a film-maker and, repeatedly, to Edvard Munch's muted, brooding mood studies of spiritual desolation and paralysis.

Another equally crucial aspect of Bergman's arrangement of the stage was his determination (emphatically shared by Meyerhold) to bring the play as close as possible to the theatre audience, in order to render the spectator an initiated partner in the emotional process. Even before the play began, he invited the establishment of the strongest possible imaginative rapport between stage and auditorium. In the earlier production at Dramaten, the theatre's ornate front curtain rose – but only halfway – several minutes beforehand, allowing the audience a chance, as it were, to breathe in the atmosphere. ("Everything is quiet. We experience the theatrical space as a unity. We are made to understand that actors and not real people from the nineties are about to make their entrance. The screens are not walls in a house but rather the kind of screen the Chinese put up to force evil spirits to

alter their course," *Arbetarbladet* told its readers.) In Munich, where the
production was played entirely without a curtain, Bergman accomplished his purpose even more effectively, by thrusting the stage of the
cavernous Residenztheatre so far forward into the auditorium that
virtually all the scenes were played in front of the curtain line. In both
productions the house-lights were dimmed only after the play had
begun, and later a glaring projection of light from the back of the
house, sweeping just above the heads of the audience, further obliterated the separation between stage and auditorium. Thus deprived of
the comfortably detached naturalistic notion of an invisible fourth
wall, the spectator felt himself to be in the Tesman "home," virtually
face to face with its inhabitants.

Ultimately, however, all these technical strategies were only means
to an end for Bergman, which was the revelation of the inner essence of
Hedda's situation – a situation in which she is icily aware of, even
sometimes appalled by, what she says and does, yet remains helpless
to alter its course. ("In a tragedy, nothing is in doubt and everyone's
destiny is known. That makes for tranquility," the Narrator in
Anouilh's *Antigone* reminds us. "There isn't any hope. You're trapped.
The whole sky has fallen on you and all you can do about it is to
shout.") In Munich, Christine Buchegger established an unhysterical
Hedda characterized not by frantic desperation, but rather by a
strangely detached sense of composure, of authority and control
blended with an almost cynical disdain for the destiny she knows she
has chosen for herself. At Dramaten, Gertrud Fridh drew a more
mature and strikingly aristocratic portrait of General Gabler's daughter, possessed of an even greater degree of self-control and displaying
an ironic remoteness from everything and everyone around her. (An
ideal Phaedra, a role she in fact played earlier in 1964.) The common
denominator of both these interpretations was the accumulating
sensation of isolation, alienation, and entrapment that they projected –
a quality of otherness that set this messenger from a closed country
inexorably apart from the world in which she found herself.[34]

Bergman's productions have all begun with a wordless, dream-like
visual overture. Others, of course, have opened *Hedda Gabler* with a
"telling" pantomime: Ralph Richardson has, for example, recorded his
boundless admiration for the "Clytemnestra" opening with which Mrs
Patrick Campbell liked to preface her performance, in which she stood
practicing pistol shots alone in the darkened Tesman parlor, counting
to seven before each shot.[35] The complex visual image conjured up by
Bergman's Hedda was not a titillating plot *hors-d'œuvre* of this sort,
however, but rather a painful, time-stopped instant of spiritual naked-

ness, in which the audience was given a glimpse of Hedda's inner anguish that foretold her doom, before a single word had been spoken. Silently, like a sleepwalker, she came on to the empty stage, her features locked in a death mask of mortal despair and frustration. "We do not experience her as a human being of flesh and blood," *Stockholms-Tidningen* said of Fridh in 1964: "It is a damned soul who is stirring in this strange abode, before Ibsen himself starts to speak and the intricate clockwork mechanism begins to operate." Buchegger, added *Frankfurter Allgemeine* in 1979, likewise seemed "a woman whose despair manifests itself only as a last and, as we know, a vain protest against circumstances. She is defeated from the very beginning." As the light focused on Hedda and the auditorium gradually darkened, she moved noiselessly toward the audience. At the very front of the stage she stopped and, for a frozen moment, she stood utterly immobile and expressionless, staring with wide open eyes into vacant space. Melchinger has provided a vivid description of this moment: "For a long time to come, I will see Hedda Gabler before me: standing at the front of the stage, aristocratic, with her chin tilted slightly upwards, the Titian-red hair outlined against the dull red of the stage space, with her sarcastic, tense mouth and those eyes that stared into the darkness, where we sat." Turning away, she walked over to the (empty) mirror and began a critical examination of her person – first of her face, then her figure, letting her hands run slowly down her body to her stomach. Then, in a violent reaction of revulsion and despair, she suddenly bent double and pressed her hands to her abdomen, pounding it several times with the full force of her clenched fists. (The risible morning sickness antics that crept into the English performance were confined to that occasion.) At last, in an effort to regain control over herself, she walked to the piano, lit a cigarette, stubbed it out at once, and then settled herself in an armchair. Meanwhile, the intrusion of the outside world, in the persons of Aunt Julle and the maid, began, as their expository small-talk broke the silence for the first time.[36]

Once established, the pattern of Hedda's alienation and spiritual nausea proceeded to grow and develop through a continuous sequence of peripheral actions, performed as she listened, or pointedly refused to listen, to the conversation taking place on the other side of the dividing screen. The spasmodic movements of Hedda in her cage – lighting and extinguishing cigarettes, biting her own hand in a sudden neurotic gesture of self-contempt, or ironically perusing a book in a parody of the manners of the well-educated nineteenth-century woman, only to let it fall to the floor a moment afterwards – were signposts making her inexorable progress toward destruction unmistakable. Accordingly, attention was fixed not on the act of Hedda's suicide itself – for that was a foregone conclusion from the outset – but on the existential *process* of the act, as analyzed by the character who commits it. (Tragedy has nothing to do with melodrama, Anouilh's Narrator points out: "Death, in a melodrama, is really horrible because it is never inevitable.")

Out of self-reflection arose Hedda's consuming soul-sickness. Humiliated by the superimposed identity that Tesman's world has prepared for her, she searched in vain for some reliable evidence of her elusive self. Tormented by the thought of this incarceration in a role, she found herself drawn to the mirror – the most central of all props in Bergman's art – in which she would watch herself live and watch herself prepare to die. She was "continually shown before the imaginary mirror, striking poses, testing attitudes, examining her fading complexion, trying as it were to convince herself that she is truly real; now and then she stands so close to the mirror that it seems as if she wants to breathe away her human features," remarked Per Erik Wahlund in *Svenska Dagbladet*.[37] Even more important than as a device for reassuring Hedda of her reality, however, was the mirror's function as a glass in which *the actress* observes her own performance. Standing before the mirror at the end of the first act, staring at a reality that is already fixed forever, she coolly and dispassionately rehearsed the aesthetically pleasing suicide she had prepared for herself. She removed her high-heeled pumps carefully, both as a gesture of fastidiousness and as a practical measure that allowed her to stand more steadily when she fired. And she again stood before the mirror when, with the utmost composure, she actually pointed the pistol to her temple and squeezed the trigger at the end.

From her first entrance into the world of the others, Bergman's Hedda stood demonstrably alone, dissociated from everyone about her. The fact that she alone seemed aware of the stifling, hermetically sealed atmosphere ("the odor of death" which she tries to describe to Brack) in which they moved and in which she was a prisoner heightened the sense of her dislocation. From the beginning, whether reacting with disdain or thinly disguised disgust to the insinuating conversation between her husband and his precious Aunt Julle or coldly contemplating the bleak autumn landscape outside ("so golden – and withered"), her entire behavior emphasized that she was the outsider, the alien who acted and reacted on a different level and with far greater intensity than these ordinary, and in this case actually paler, figures around her. Tesman, by no means the stereotypical bumbling idiot in

Bergman's version, was an affable, middle-aged pedant whom Hedda treated with bored, impatient politeness, and whose ceaseless pursuit of data from a dead and meaningless historical past epitomized the futility of her own situation. Both in Ingvar Kjellson's discreetly comic performance in Stockholm and in Kurt Meisel's very sympathetic portrayal of the character in Munich, Tesman's contentedly self-centred preoccupation with his own small world lent him a certain child-like innocence that, in itself, deepened the impression of the gulf between him and Hedda. Judge Brack – who made all his entrances and exits through a concealed door in the proscenium, like a spy or a villain in a melodrama – was a smiling, insolent blackguard who offered her an alternative she had certainly considered and had long since rejected. As a kind of male counterpart to Hedda, Brack was the only one to whom she could actually communicate her boredom, her painful perception of life as one unending and tedious railroad journey that one spends locked in a compartment with a solitary travelling companion. But, as she well knew, this detached and cynical libertine was also the only one who saw straight through her at all times. He recognized the potential danger when she threatened him with her revolver, yet he remained at the same time maddeningly unwilling to treat her threat as more than an empty theatrical gesture ("People don't do such things"). Eilert Løvborg, the third man in Hedda's life and, in Bergman's interpretation, so obviously her former lover, was from the beginning a man who had reached the end of his rope. This deromanticized Løvborg – played with particularly moving and passionate desperation by Martin Benrath at the Residenztheater – was no free-spirited Dionysian visionary. He possessed neither vine leaves nor a future any longer, and the "masterpiece" containing his prescription for the future of human civilization was nothing more than painfully few sheets of paper.[38]

The strong suggestion of the perceptional and emotional gulf that separated these other characters from Hedda was visually reinforced by the spatial and compositional patterns that Bergman developed, chief among which were the expressive bas-relief effects that recalled the work of Meyerhold and Fuchs. Taking the fullest advantage of the width of his stage – emphasized by the distinct impression of shallowness created by the barricade of low screens enclosing the playing area (and by the half-lowered curtain at Dramaten) – Bergman stressed widely separated groupings, conversations conducted from opposite ends of the stage, and vivid images of Hedda seated apart or faced away from the other characters during even the tensest of confrontations (in, for instance, the second-act scene in which she so ruthlessly destroys the relationship between Thea and Løvborg). A sinuous inter-play of colors, lighting changes, and figure compositions produced at times a distorted, impressionistic, even dream-like quality in the many scenes in which silhouette or bas-relief effects predominated. Both in Stockholm and in Munich, critics singled out the chilling physical sensation of staleness and futility conjured up in the moment at the opening of the third act when Thea and Hedda awaken from their anxious all-night vigil. Here, low-angle projectors (so-called Bergman lamps) that hung at the back of the auditorium illuminated the fore-stage so glaringly and piercingly that the plastic contours of the charac-ters' faces were momentarily obliterated. ''There they sat, facing the front of the stage, opening their mouths, carefully choosing their gestures, now and then looking at each other in profile,'' wrote Mel-chinger, who compared Bergman's emphasis on unmitigated frontal playing and severely linear, flattened picture compositions to Cezanne's revolutionary redistribution of the elements of pictorial space. In every such instance, each choreographic nuance was in turn blended into a broad, firmly conceived sculptural plan, in which the revelation of the unspoken undertext and inner rhythm of the play was the objective, and the creation of an illusion of life-like reality played no part at all. (This, more than anything else about Bergman's approach, was what seemed hardest for the critics or cast of the London *Hedda Gabler* to comprehend, even in 1970.)

Like space and physical contours, time was also purposefully man-ipulated by Bergman, both in order to create a precise atmosphere and to direct audience response toward a specific emotional stimulus. ''One second of reality can be two minutes on the stage,'' he told the cast of the Munich production, and his consequent application of a kind of theatrical slow-motion at times added a striking extra dimen-sion of suspended animation to the finished performance. This dimen-sion was forcefully projected in the first face-to-face encounter be-tween Hedda and Løvborg, in which a sense of time and motion in suspension governed the expressive vocabulary of signs and gestures in the scene. The result was, however, entirely different from, say, the ''static'' staging of this episode in Meyerhold's production. As Løv-borg's arrival was announced, mid-way in the second act, Hedda's forcible effort to conceal her apprehension and to remain, as always, in control of the situation found its expression in languid, automaton-like movements – watched narrowly by the cynical Brack who, as usual, lost no time in signifying that he had taken note of her agitation. When Løvborg came in, he stopped at once to search out Hedda; looking fixedly at her – and completely ignoring Tesman, who stood right beside him – he walked slowly toward her and took her hand, which he held "a little too long." The almost mesmeric influence that the mere physical presence of Løvborg exerted on Hedda overshadowed his subsequent conversation with Tesman about his new book, an enterprise whose vision of the future held, it was obvious, as little interest for Hedda as her husband's empty pursuit of a dead past.

The crucial scene that follows when Hedda is left alone with Løvborg is a touchstone in any production of *Hedda Gabler*; Bergman's richly textured orchestration of it is worth examining in some detail, as a vivid example of the rhythm of emotional expression and response that characterizes his Ibsen style. In this instance, with steadily accelerating force, his staging articulated the essence of the total impasse between the two characters – not as a "breakdown of communication" in conventional terms, but rather as a situation in which the unspoken communication that passes between them is all too audible and clear. The passionate emotionality of Løvborg's first impulsive outburst ("Hedda. Hedda – Gabler!") was coupled with a conviction of his own strength in this encounter ("he knows he is dangerous to Hedda," Bergman notes). She, in turn, met this with her own determination to avoid an emotional scene altogether and, above all, to regain her dominance over him. In the initial phase of this power struggle, her perfect aloofness was buttressed by a range of strategies: her calculated formality, her avoidance at first of any eye-contact, the ferocity with which she displayed the honeymoon photographs ("These are the Dolomites, Mr. Løvborg"), and the exaggerated amiability with which she met Tesman's interruption of their *tête-à-tête*. Gradually, however, as Løvborg insistently demanded to know whether there had not been a trace of love between them, the mood of the scene began to change. Hedda's stinging retort – that their relationship had been that of "two good friends who could tell each other everything" – was spoken "to herself, full of sarcasm," and this marked the beginning of an emotional transition in her behavior. From this point on, as their conversation drifted to remembrance of things past, she became both more responsive and also increasingly more aggressive. Her realization that "you think I had some power over you" even prompted her to smile.

As the scene began to take on the character of a virtual reenactment of similar scenes between them in the past, Bergman's groupings and lighting effects established an eerie visual adumbration of unreality and *déjà vu*. Much as the presence of General Gabler had hovered over their intimate meetings in the past, so too the figures of Tesman and Brack could now be seen through the open screens, as menacing presences that loomed in the background. By the time the scene had reached the point at which the stage directions indicate that it has begun to grow dark, Bergman's lighting scheme – which was, of course, completely independent of Ibsen's naturalistic planning, as there were neither windows nor other obvious sources of light in the setting – had undergone a subtle and marked change. The penetrating light that fixed the two characters on the forestage had dimmed, and long, oversized shadows began to be cast upon the wall-screen behind them. The contours of the figures themselves were erased, and for a moment the distinction between the living characters and their own ghostly silhouettes seemed actually to be obliterated.

Immersed in this dream-like atmosphere of brooding shadows, Hedda and Løvborg pursued their futile journey into the past with a bitterness and an increasingly overt aggressiveness that drew the scene several degrees closer to Strindberg's vision, or to the more harrowing sexual confrontations in Bergman's own films. "But tell me, Hedda – the root of the bond between us – was that not love?" cries Løvborg – and that outcry became the explosive juncture at which he decisively lost his serenity and the balance of power reverted inexorably to Hedda. Their discussion of Løvborg's new relationship with Thea Elvsted was suffused with a savage, menacing belligerency on his part that communicated itself directly to Hedda and conditioned her own response. When he pronounced Thea "too foolish" to understand such a thing as human sexuality, her defiant rejoinder – "And I am a coward" – erupted into a sudden outburst of hatred, expressed both in her harsh tone of voice and in her abrupt movement as she sprang to her feet. The struggle reached its climax when Løvborg, in a final and erotically charged gesture, embraced Hedda from his seated position, pressing his face passionately against her. For a single instant she seemed about to relax her steely self-control. Then, brutally reasserting her dominance, she thrust him away with both hands. Immediately afterwards Thea entered – "as in a dream," Bergman had observed during rehearsals, "because when you want something to happen in a dream, it does. And Hedda wants a showdown with Thea."

Hedda's unyielding determination to have, for once in her life, "power over a human destiny" (as she tells Thea at the end of the second act) stood remorselessly exposed in Bergman's interpretation as a crucial, irrevocable step in a progression that led with relentless dramatic logic to her own destruction. To recognize the precise nature of this progression is to understand what sets Bergman's so-called existential approach to Ibsen so decisively apart from the naturalistic productions of the past, with their abiding concern with the case-study documentation of reasons and motivations for "deviant" human behavior. In an essay entitled "Psychology and Form", Kenneth Burke has suggested a useful distinction between "syllogistic progression" in a literary composition, in which the reader is led from one point of it to another by means of logical relationships, and "qualitative progression," in which a pure "logic of feeling" leads the reader, by means of association and contrast. Francis Fergusson uses Burke's idea of qualitative progression to describe the compositional principle at work in Wagner's music-dramas.[39] The analogy might, however, be as validly applied to Bergman, for whom cinematic or theatrical art is always "a matter between the imagination and the feelings," never a rational phenomenon to be comprehended by logical analysis and confined within a closed framework of "meaning" (be it Freudian, feminist, political, symbolic, or whatever). Expressed with the utmost economy of means, often compressed into an arresting sensory image, each emotional unit or suggestion in his *Hedda Gabler* sought, as it were, to implicate the spectator in this spontaneous and direct way, through a rhythm of feeling, without any intermediate landing in the conscious intellect. (The presence in the text itself of an inherent imagistic rhythm of emotional expression is emphasized by its successful adaptation as a ballet, choreographed by Kari Blakstad and performed at Den Norske Opera in 1980.)

Viewed thus, Hedda's actions against Løvborg are important not as a "triad of crimes" for which some psychological motive must be found or invented, but rather as a deadly pattern of choices that all prefigure, with mounting emotional intensity and certainty, the fate that awaits Hedda herself. The first of them, when she goads the reformed alcoholic to drink again, was not simply an act of deliberate, malicious irresponsibility; it was a violent metastatic eruption of the deadly cancer, the perception of entrapment and interment, that fed on Hedda's inner being. The emphatic slow-motion effects that Bergman introduced again at this moment lent it both an hallucinatory intensity and a mythological signification that several reviewers associated, of their own accord, with the sombre finality of the gesture with which Isolde seals her own and her lover's destiny in the first act of Wagner's *Tristan und Isolde*.

The second destructive encounter between the two, when Hedda sends Løvborg away in the third act with her "souvenir" in his pocket, was presented by Bergman and his actors in the Munich production in a manner that eliminated all exposition and "realistic" evasiveness to reveal the raw emotional core of close, unspoken violence in the scene:

LØVBORG. This? Is this the souvenir? (*Puts the pistol in his breast pocket*) Thank you.
HEDDA. Beautifully, Eilert Løvborg. Promise me that.
LØVBORG. Goodbye, Hedda Gabler.[40]

The speed with which Ibsen lets Hedda proceed immediately to her third act of destructiveness, the burning of Løvborg's manuscript, heightens our sense of its brutality. The deed seals her own doom, by finalizing her willful rejection of the future and her election of the past and of death. Unquestionably the most intense emotional gesture in Bergman's productions of the play, it was positioned by him at the very center and forefront of the stage, where the true reality of the situation was created (as the reality of the attic in *The Wild Duck* had been created by him) solely through the physical presence of the performer. Facing the audience directly, Hedda slowly knelt before the hooded prompter's box itself, which thus became the "stove." Every nuance of facial expression was remorselessly disclosed in the searching light that flooded the stage at this point. With icy determination, her face frozen now in an immutable mask-like expression, she fed the "fire" with page after page of the manuscript – Løvborg's vision of the future, his and Thea's spiritual child. Then, just when her act of wanton destruction had been completed, the sorrowing figures of Tesman and the black-clad Miss Tesman, in mourning for her dead sister, appeared behind her, and, in a single, startling moment of juxtaposition, the image of physical death merged with the image of Hedda and the motif of death-in-life, emotional sterility, and inhumanity that she embodies.

In this interpretation Hedda's implacably exposed public suicide, which Bergman considers "the most consequent of any in dramatic literature," became as logically inevitable as the solution to a mathematical problem. Nothing was permitted to mitigate the harshness or obscure the clarity of this final scene. The "frenzied dance melody" which Hedda plays on the piano in Ibsen's text was reduced to a few dissonant, non-musical chords hammered out in frustration. As she stood before the mirror and quietly prepared to put a bullet through her head, her husband and the self-possessed Mrs. Elvsted sat motionless at the other end of the stage, totally absorbed in their absurd task of reassembling the dead Løvborg's notes – a deadly picture of hollow people trying to paste together a vision whose spirit they do not comprehend, clinging to a meaningless past that completely overshadows both the future and the present.

"Life for Hedda," Ibsen says, "resolves itself as a farce that isn't

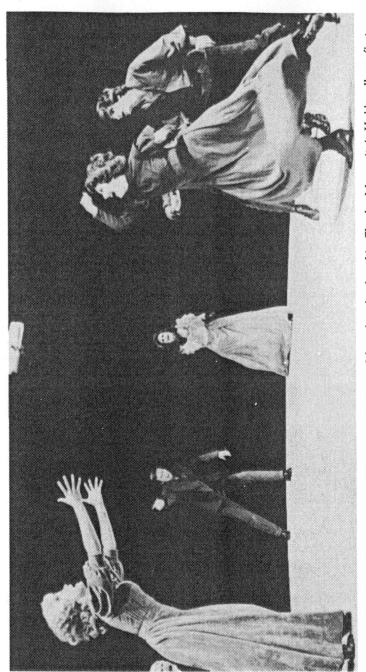

32　A bewildered Løvborg sees his manuscript tossed from hand to hand in Charles Marowitz's *Hedda* collage, first performed at the Bergen Festival in Norway in 1978.

worth seeing through to the end." In Bergman's productions, her last act before withdrawing into the ultimate isolation of death was to remove her high-heeled shoes carefully, in a final irrational attempt to control and transcend a reality that had become a farcical nightmare. "The only thing she wants is to die a beautiful death," Bergman has said in an interview. "She has rehearsed the last gesture before the mirror. She knows how to use the pistol so that it becomes aesthetic. Perhaps she also takes into consideration that she wants to fall nicely. It is an uncontrollable moment that she subconsciously tries to control by taking off her shoes."[41]

Judge Brack had the last word, as of course he does in Ibsen, in all three of Bergman's productions of the play. In Munich, however, his line was reinforced by an astonishing gesture of sheer brutality. Standing nonchalantly over Hedda's outstretched corpse, Brack seized her roughly by the hair and lifted her head, as though to assure himself that she was dead, before pronouncing his cynical verdict that "people don't do such things." Then, with an aesthetic fastidiousness of his own, he surreptitiously wiped his hands on his handkerchief as he left. Like Eilert, Hedda had found only a harsh and unlovely finish. "The irony in all this," Bergman remarks, "is that she dies such an ugly death anyway – that she ends up lying there with her rump in the air."

During the 1970s the influence of Bergman's renewal began to be felt widely in Europe, in performances of all of Ibsen's prose plays. In some quarters, notably in Britain, the effect of his influence was largely negative. Anthony Page's revival of *Hedda Gabler* at the Royal Court in 1972, "adapted" for the occasion by playwright John Osborne, was a welcome opportunity for the most tradition-minded London critics to hail the restoration of a faithfully detailed naturalistic approach to this play, adorned with "some splendid chips-off-the-old-Osborne" such as Hedda's complaint about her husband's "snorting around in libraries" and Tesman's claim that he could never ask his wife to settle for "a petty bourgeois pottage."[42] The only proper style for *Hedda Gabler*, the director and self-named "counterfeit critic" Charles Marowitz proclaimed in his own indignant denunciation of Bergman's method, is "the most diligent application of a Stanislavski-based realism."[43] At first blush at least, Marowitz's own "free adaptation" of the play in 1978 hardly seemed a logical extension of this proposition. Rooted in his theory that a classic can be reconstructed into a *new* work of art while still retaining the spirit of the original, his *Hedda* collage (the complete script of which he published in 1982) juxtaposed familiar segments of Ibsen's text with invented scenes and Freudian fantasy sequences used mainly to illustrate Hedda's psychosexual repressions

– notably the Electra complex that has made her an emotional cripple in her relations with other men. In this sense, perhaps, Stanislavski's preoccupation with psychological motivation is not so remote an impetus after all. The performance itself, however – played on a huge, white, empty disc that denoted Hedda's inner life – focused on graphic expressionistic images that left little room for the subtleties of naturalistic character analysis. At one point Hedda appeared astride a giant phallic pistol that had descended from the flies, while a reincarnated General Gabler fired his own cocked revolvers at everyone in sight. In the "sexual ballet" in Mademoiselle Diana's brothel (the scene for which this unusual theatre event is chiefly remembered), the half-naked prostitute knelt before Løvborg to perform fellatio, only to be replaced in a flickering blackout by Hedda herself in the same position, kneeling first before Løvborg and then before the rambunctious old General. Finally, in a trial scene viewed through Hedda's terrified eyes, she was condemned by a whispering, Kafkaesque tribunal presided over by none other than her ubiquitous father. If Marowitz's creation reveals only a passing resemblance to Ibsen's text (and none at all to Bergman's stage version of it), it does have an interesting and rather characteristic forerunner in Raymond Rouleau's French television version of *Hedda Gabler*, from 1967. Here, Rouleau tried consciously to transform the play into a drama of guilt by introducing a dream sequence of his own invention, during which Hedda fantasizes about Løvborg and Tesman at the stag party, at which her father, too, appears and criticizes her severely.

In Norway, where it was first performed in conjunction with the playwright's sesquicentennial, Marowitz's attempt to contemporize and activize our perception of Ibsen's masterpiece was seen against a background of a domestic (indeed, a Scandinavian) performance tradition confident, as we have already seen, of its ability to absorb change and renewal without thereby rendering Ibsen artificially rootless in the process. (To take just one more example, this blend of tradition and contemporaneity was perfectly revealed in a New Norse production of *Hedda Gabler* staged by Tormod Skagestad at Det Norske Teatret in 1971, in which the performance's modern speech rhythms and intimate, almost Chekhovian tone of understatement found support, rather than contradiction, in a Walentin setting redolent with period flavor, ironically dominated by an outsized portrait of General Gabler on horseback.) In Germany, meanwhile, where deconstructions and "quotations" of Ibsen's plays have become the rule rather than the exception, the expressionistic Marowitz collage would hardly have shocked or even surprised audiences who had experienced Niels-Peter

Rudolph's notorious *Hedda Gabler* the previous year. Given at the Schiller Theatre in Berlin, Rudolph's harsh, angry parody was a denunciation of Ibsen's text more radical than anything Fassbinder or Peter Stein might have conceived. "The play is not performed; it is *farciert* [hacked to mincemeat], drowned out in farce," quipped Friedrich Luft without enthusiasm in *Die Welt* (11 February 1977). Grotesquely padded like sinister sideshow freaks – an enormous cotton-wool bosom for Thea, phoney Charles Atlas muscles for Tesman – the characters in the drama became cartoon-strip caricatures of bourgeois folly, continually stumbling over the furniture and themselves while a live pigeon flew aimlessly about in the chaos. In the grotesque emulation of the bird, Hedda herself (Gisela Stein) sprang on to the piano or perched atop the wardrobe in parodic demonstrations of her desperation. Her "tragic" suicide gave the director his final horror-show flourish: without warning, Hedda's body came crashing through the drapes that concealed the inner room where she had shot herself.

By contrast, the suicide in Peter Zadek's *Hedda Gabler* was played in full view of the audience, beneath the stern, forbidding picture of Hedda's progenitor. In general, the German critics tended to discuss Rudolph's slapstick travesty in Berlin as an instructive contrast to Zadek's no less tough-minded but far more effective critical quotation of the play, presented by him at the Schauspielhaus in Bochum only one week later. The implied "dialogue" between these two simultaneous productions yielded a useful distinction. While Rudolph exhibited "the inner deformity of the characters by displaying their outer deformity," Zadek chose "Ibsen's way," Georg Hensel suggested in *Frankfurter Allgemeine Zeitung* (18 February 1977): "the monstrousness that exists behind the outward features of the characters emerges gradually, through their apparent harmlessness ... He exhibits the absurdity in Ibsen's human beings without ridiculing them. We laugh at them as we laugh at ourselves, with a complicated understanding that also involves fear. Zadek plays up the comedy that almost inevitably underlies every tragedy."

In the manner of Dieter Giesing's influential stylization of the play at the Munich Kammerspiele almost nine years before, Zadek's staging sought to project not a distilled Bergmanesque image of the play's inner landscape but a pointedly ironic illustration (not caricature) of its social context. At the Kammerspiele in 1968, Jürgen Rose's stage design had contributed a concise emotional impression rather than a period picture of the Tesman milieu, elegant but cold and empty to the point of barrenness. Reflecting the much more polemical spirit that

33   The Tesman environment as it was presented in Dieter Giesing's coolly
stylized production at the Munich Kammerspiele in 1968. Setting designed by
Jürgen Rose.

ruled Zadek's version, the setting which Götz Loepelmann created for
him in Bochum ("an orgy of velvet, glass, and marble," as Hensel
described it) made a more sarcastic critical comment on the bourgeois
pomp of the society inhabited by Ibsen's characters. Indeed, to Horst
Ziermann of *Die Welt* (19 February 1977), Loepelmann's dazzling set
seemed "a symbol of the sort of sarcophagus in which men, to this day,
seek to domesticate women." Presumably to enhance this perception
of relevance, Zadek and his designer deliberately fractured the stylized
period framework by interjecting not only contemporary costumes but
also such ironic anachronisms as a modern telephone and a radio that
played dance music from our own time.

Zadek's Hedda (Rosel Zech) was likewise a curious mixture of old
and new. Dressed as a fashionable society woman, she became once
again the menacing Circe, with an evil laugh and a red wig to match it –
a *femme fatale* of mythical dimensions, compared by the director (in one
breath) to Mérimée's Carmen, Dumas' Marguerite Gautier, Tolstoi's
Anna Karenina, and Wedekind's Lulu. Yet at the same time she conveyed a distinctly modern impression of the eternal outsider, "the
stranger in the midst of a masculine world that can be overcome only in
dreams," as Ziermann phrased it in *Die Welt*. To this critic and others,

she seemed disturbingly disengaged and hence "totally soulless," without a past and without any link to the society around her. "Why she considers herself doomed to lifelong boredom, why she takes such pains to drive Mrs Elvsted and Løvborg apart, why she drives him to drink and suicide, why she burns his manuscript, and why she finally kills herself remain unanswered questions." These were, of course, the very questions which Elizabeth Robins and the actresses who came after her ceaselessly posed in their search for a psychological "explanation" – and extenuation – of Hedda's behavior. In Zadek's interpretation, however, it was the absence of answers – or, perhaps, the absurdity of such questions – that delineated the true modernity of Hedda's protest against life.

In this sense, the challenge of *Hedda Gabler* appeared to change Zadek's whole attitude toward Ibsen, as surely as it had changed Bergman's. His earlier polemical deconstructions of *A Doll's House* (1967) and *The Wild Duck* (1975) had bordered on travesty in their denunciation of the bankruptcy of the moral and social assumptions underlying these Ibsen plays. By contrast, although still a critical "quotation," Zadek's *Hedda* approached the central character's fate as more than simply a predictable result of the bourgeois social equation. With his production of *The Master Builder*, presented at the Residenztheater in Munich in 1983, this shift to a more ambivalent, less socially defined point of view became unmistakable. To the surprise of many, in this subsequent work the committed iconoclast ("der Schrecken einer ganzen Abonnenten-Generation," as one Munich critic called him) laid aside shock tactics altogether in his exploration of the paradoxes that grow, in both these plays, out of the dislocated individual's despair over human existence. Again, Götz Loepelmann provided a stage design that was a forceful visual signifier of the director's intent, but this time his setting incorporated a calculated transition from period specificity to the virtual abandonment of actuality. From the spacious and rather gloomy Victorian surroundings of Solness' office–workroom in the opening act, the action moved first to a living-room from the 1930s, mid-way in time between Ibsen's past and our present, and then to an open, timeless space overlooked by a threatening, ice-covered mountainside and defined only by a rough approximation of the veranda and railing described in Ibsen's directions. No crowd and no brass band were on hand to bear witness to Solness' silent fall and Hilde's almost fanatical ecstasy at the end. Rather, as in Zadek's earlier interpretation of *Hedda Gabler*, the key point seemed the dissociation of the individual(ist) from society. This brooding, bourgeois master builder (Hans Michael Rehberg) and his unwitting young

Nemesis in sunglasses (Barbara Sukowa) were both dreamers "in love only with their own illusions," as Hans Schwab-Felisch observed in *Frankfurter Allgemeine Zeitung* (27 April 1983). "Society is still present, but it is no longer a self-contained unit. The human being steps out of it, he finds himself face to face with himself, with nature, with God."

As for *Hedda Gabler* itself, the radical experiments by Marowitz, Zadek, and others during the 1970s have led in turn to even bolder attempts at innovation, including the American Ibsen Theatre's production of the play in drag, with Charles Ludlam in the title role, in 1984. From whatever angle one tries to approach this work, however, the director or actor is inevitably brought back to Ibsen's own well-known observation about it. "My intention in this play has not really been to treat so-called problems," he wrote to his French translator just before *Hedda Gabler* was published. "The main thing for me has been to depict human beings, human emotions, and human destinies against a background of certain prevailing social conditions and views."[44] The present social context to which the playwright refers has long since become the historical past. The correspondence which he perhaps intended between Hedda's fate and the circumstances of her social reality now seems less immediate and far less important than other aspects of the play. Yet the *dramatic* reality of Ibsen's human beings and their emotional life has remained unchanged, as the constant source of energy from which any performance of *Hedda Gabler* in the living theatre, no matter how "deconstructed," must draw its power.

7

On the mountain top:
John Gabriel Borkman

Ibsen's last plays pose a special problem in the theatre. In them the playwright redefines the meaning and capacity of the realistic convention of theatre, without thereby abandoning it entirely, as Strindberg was to do. In the process, Ibsen moves once more from the claustrophobic confines of bourgeois parlors into the open air – and into an arena in which the dividing line between the realistic and symbolic modes of expression is sometimes all but obliterated. Among these last plays, while *The Master Builder* is arguably the most popular in performance, *John Gabriel Borkman* represents an even more striking example of the difficult amalgamation with which the dramatist confronted the theatre at the end of his career. He himself was well aware that his penultimate work made new and even extreme practical demands. "The play presents quite unusually difficult problems both in respect of casting and of scenery and stage machinery," he admits in one of his characteristic letters of advice to colleagues in the Norwegian theatre.[1] Although less frequently performed than the more familiar prose plays we have been considering, *Borkman* has never ceased to hold a magnetic (and occasionally fatal) attraction for directors and actors alike. Within six weeks of its publication, the eagerly awaited work had been performed in the major cities of northern Europe, and by the end of 1897 it had been seen by audiences in London, Paris, and New York. Moreover, after an intervening period of indifference (and indifferent productions), a cluster of notable revivals in recent years has conferred renewed theatrical life on what Edvard Munch once called "the mightiest winter landscape in Scandinavian art."

As we might expect, the early productions were for the most part rooted firmly in the prevailing naturalistic style, with its emphasis on a detailed, particularized representation of a life-like environment. Even so, the play's first critics and performers were by no means blind to the fact that the main characters in Ibsen's most elusive and most substantial artist drama tower above the realistic plane. They are intended, one reviewer of Emil Poulsen's highly acclaimed production at the Danish Royal Theatre observed, "as characters in daily life taken to a higher degree, so to speak, in a spiritual sense of more than ordinary proportions."[2] In pursuit of this idealized dimension, the early interpreters of Borkman sometimes played the role in guises that could be counted on to suggest the quality of greatness which *must* be present if his final anguished anagnorisis on the mountain top is to have its true significance for an audience. August Lindberg, whose intrepid troupe presented the Norwegian premiere of the play at the old theatre in Drammen (19 January 1897), made the title character up to resemble Johan Sverdrup, the former Norwegian prime minister and political reformer whose revolutionary vision of a democratized society must have provided a rather ironic parallel to Borkman's own Faustian dream of the welfare of all mankind.[3] A much more readily accessible association was with the figure of the artist himself, whose suffering and guilt are so obviously at the center of the work. Poulsen acted his Borkman in Ibsen's own likeness, for example, while at the Deutsches Theater in Berlin the character was somehow thought to have resembled both the playwright and his arch rival, Bjørnstjerne Bjørnson. Although the tendency to suggest such literal parallels as these has all but disappeared in performances of the play, the actor's need to locate the character in some kind of mythic or archetypal dimension has not changed. Ralph Richardson's success in Peter Hall's production at the National Theatre in 1975, for instance, was the direct result of his ability to endow his Borkman with a quality of ruined majesty that made him seem, agreed Harold Hobson and other critics, nothing less than "an emperor" who had never accepted his abdication.[4]

Apart from Emil Poulsen's modest "stylization" of the title character's appearance, meanwhile, this Ibsen veteran's authoritative staging of *John Gabriel Borkman* at the Royal Theatre in Copenhagen (31 January 1897) exemplified the naturalistic tradition that seems, on the surface, to govern and support the play's first three acts, if not its fourth. Poulsen's own performance was an imposing fusion of grand passion and truth-to-life in the most intimate detail. From his very first appearance, recorded the reviewer for *Politiken* (1 February), "when he placed himself beside his desk, ready to receive his restitution, one had the complete impression of a man who cannot understand that the world can do without him, because his mind is as keen as ever, his spirit as fervent as ever, and because he still hears the iron-ore sing." This same charged emotionality was in turn imparted by Poulsen, who had become an able director at the end of his career, to such key episodes as the bitter first-act encounter of the estranged twin sisters, Gunhild Borkman and Ella Rentheim. Here, taking Ibsen's very explicit stage directions as his guide, Poulsen envolved a life-like pattern of physical actions and reactions in which, *Politiken* continues, "even Ella's glances at the ceiling as she listened to the dragging footsteps overhead, as she listened to her sister's unpitying words each time the talk tuned to the 'sick wolf,' were of the greatest effect." As a result, this scene in particular was praised by the Copenhagen critics for conveying "the tense atmosphere of death and destruction that lurks beneath the surface of the dialogue."[5] Betty Hennings, who had been cast as Ella Rentheim despite Ibsen's objections, was in fact criticized by some for seeming too unaffected by this crushing atmosphere of loss, all mildness and resignation in the teeth of Josephine Eckardt's passionate and unyielding Mrs. Borkman. Nevertheless, this "elegiac" reading of the role, perpetuated in turn by the performances of Eleonora Duse, was to remain the traditional one, still in evidence to some degree in "the softness of embalmed goodness" with which Peggy Ashcroft met the grimly ironic bitterness of Wendy Hiller's Gunhild in the National Theatre production.[6]

Ideally, at least, the unifying focus of a naturalistic production like Poulsen's was the painstakingly reproduced environment in which Ibsen's characters might, as Antoine would put it, be seen to "live" before the eyes of the audience, in a milieu that both reflected and shaped the personalities of its inhabitants – in this case the desolate Rentheim estate outside Christiania and, in the last act, the windy slopes of Grefsenkollen. The two interiors designed by Thorolf Pedersen for the Copenhagen production were steeped in an atmosphere and a tradition that can only be called Gothic, reminiscent of the romantic *genre sombre* still in favor when Ibsen first visited the Royal Theatre as an apprentice director, nearly half a century earlier. Outside the small windows of Mrs. Borkman's old-fashioned sitting room, blowing snow could be glimpsed during the first act. Upstairs, the walls of the deep, austere, windowless room that Borkman has made his prison were covered with mouldering hangings: "the age of the fabric, the faded greenish-gray color that is so typical of old tapestries was splendidly captured," the keenly interested observer for *Politiken* noted.

Incidentally, the fact that these heavy naturalistic interiors did not always accomplish their intended purpose is obvious from the evidence of other productions of this period. Polgar, whose eyewitness accounts of Otto Brahm's Ibsen performances at the Lessing Theatre usually exude such enthusiasm, deplored Brahm's staging of *Borkman* because he felt it possessed "none of the suggestive atmospheric power" that Ibsen's play requires, and that "harmoniously ties the individual voices together."[7] In London, where the play was first put on by W. H. Vernon (who also played Borkman), its failure was attributed by Shaw partly to the "devotional earnestness" of the typical Ibsenite actor (who "marks the speeches which are beyond him by a sudden access of pathetic sentimentality and an intense consciousness of Ibsen's greatness") but chiefly to the dreary scenery. "for the first scene in the gloomy Borkman home, a faded, soiled, dusty wreck of some gay French salon, originally designed, perhaps, for Offenbach's *Favart*, was fitted with an incongruous Norwegian stove," growled GBS. "In Act II the gallery where Borkman prowls . . . was no gallery at all, but a square box ugly to loathsomeness and too destructive to the imagination and the descriptive faculty to incur the penalty of criticism."[8]

As many a theatre critic has had occasion to point out over the years, meanwhile, it is in the play's fourth act that a fatal crashing of gears may be expected to occur in a conventionally naturalistic production of it. When, at the end of this long, uninterrupted night of reckoning, Borkman rushes forth from the house into the winter air and eventually climbs through the snow to the mountain lookout where he re-creates his great dream for Ella, Ibsen enters new territory that lies beyond the reach of the realistic illusion created by painted drops, cardboard rocks, and canvas trees. Yet countless productions have resorted to precisely these conventional means to represent the strange, shifting localities described in Ibsen's stage notes – first the snowy open courtyard outside the house, flanked by evergreens bent with fresh snow, with steep wooded slopes beyond and a dark, moonlit winter sky with scudding clouds overhead; then, as house and courtyard "disappear," the rugged, sloping terrain that slowly changes to become "wilder and wilder"; finally the summit overlooking the vast landscape described by Borkman, "with fjords and distant peaks, rising one behind another."

Exactly as in the first productions of *Peer Gynt*, the initial impulse in this case was likewise to paint a picture of this unreal realm of dreams. Ironically, Ibsen himself was the most eager of all to do so. For the important premiere at Chrsitiania Theatre, which took place only six days after Lindberg's initiative in Drammen, the playwright pressed the threatre's designer, Jens Wang, to illustrate the oneiric journey of Borkman and Ella by employing a rolling panorama drop – a hackneyed effect that Wang rightly feared would elicit unwanted comparisons with popular potboilers like *Around the World in Eighty Days*.

Despite the designer's best efforts to sketch and paint evocative views of the picturesque Norwegian countryside that Ibsen apparently had in mind, the miscarried stage experiment failed to integrate the actors – who remained on level ground – with the panoramic "motion picture" of a steep climb up Grefsenkollen which unfolded behind them.[9] In the end, Ibsen alone seemed satisfied with the result.

With the more sophisticated stage machinery of the Royal Theatre at his disposal, Thorolf Pedersen, who had previously been dispatched to Norway to consult Wang, created a less primitive but no less pictorialized scenography for the problematic fourth act. His surviving sketch of the dark, brooding Rentheim manor set in wintry Nordic surroundings reflects the robust traditionalism he always favored. (This is, remember, "the old scene painter" Gordon Craig had to contend with when the latter was called to Copenhagen nearly a generation later to design *The Pretenders*.) At the moment in Ibsen's text when Borkman and Ella disappear into the trees ("The two of us belong together. Come!"), Pedersen introduced a blackout and lowered a scrim arrangement in order to fade in a final, hazily defined picture of a rugged mountain scene with a black fjord and distant peaks on the horizon. It was much the same time-honored pictorial convention he was to use, quite indiscriminately, in the third act of *When We Dead Awaken* three years later. Although Pedersen's atmospherics in the *Borkman* production – "the soft beauty of the Nordic winter night in half-light, the blowing snow-clouds that gradually disperse, allowing the pale glow of the sky and the winter stars to emerge" – made a generally positive impression on the critics, his approach still did not persuade them of an organic connection between the fourth act and what had gone before. Some found the play itself anti-climactic and without dramatic tension in the last act, while others, including *Politiken*, blamed the complicated staging it seemed to require: "All the scene changes, the transparencies hoisted up and down, the snow and the moving clouds . . . unavoidably distract attention."

Then as now, one continually encounters a tendency on the part of reviewers to refer to the final movement of *John Gabriel Borkman* as "the 'symbolic' fourth act," as though it existed somehow apart from the other three (non-symbolic?) acts, rather like the dream epilogue in Shaw's *Saint Joan*. Perhaps the most impressive achievement of Peter Hall's 1975 National Theatre production of the play was its clear practical demonstration of the work's organic unity, in style and substance. "The secret of Hall's success is that he perceives neither realism nor symbolism as ever absolute in Ibsen: that they seamlessly merge and intertwine," Michael Billington wrote in the *Observer* (2 February 1975).

34 The wintry exterior of the Rentheim manor in the last act of *John Gabriel Borkman*, as pictorialized by designer Thorolf Pedersen in the Danish Royal Theatre production in 1897.

"Thus Hall sweeps away the pedagogic naturalism that so often mars Ibsen productions and directs as starkly and simply as Pinter and Beckett." This director's own term for his method was "modified realism," which involved the systematic removal from the staging of everything inessential or merely decorative – including the natural details with which so many older productions had tried to illustrate the "spoken scenery" of the concluding scenes in the open air.

Essentially, all of the play's locations were treated by Hall and his designers as expressive manifestations of the inner mental landscapes of the characters themselves. "It soon became apparent," Inga-Stina Ewbank, Hall's translator and dramaturgical adviser, later commented, "that the important locations are not a particular Norwegian living-room, drawing-room, and mountainside, but a cold and isolated house where downstairs and upstairs have come to stand for irreparable alienation, where inside means claustrophobia and outside means freedom – escape, like Erhart's, or death on the mountain, like Borkman's."[10] Seen in this light, then, the "vast, gray, vaguely walled and sparsely-furnished sepulchre of a living room" (*Sunday Telegraph*) defined Gunhild's spiritual space, while the prisoner upstairs in turn bestrode his own "vast empire-style drawing-room like a Colossos" (*Observer*). Accordingly, the final station on Borkman's night-long journey – a snowclad rise of ground that rotated into view, silhouetted againt a black background and crowned by the bench that serves as Borkman's bier – was more desolate but otherwise neither more nor less "symbolic" than the other locations that preceded it. The simplicity of the solution rendered the complex back projections and penumbrascopes of modern technology as unnecessary to Borkman's final self-reckoning as the elaborate pictorial representations of an earlier era.

Long before this, of course, directors and designers had begun, albeit in hesitant fashion, to grapple with the problem of fusing the inner and outer landscapes of Ibsen's "winter's tale" into a unity that transcended realism, without thereby succumbing to the artificiality of imposed symbolism. In some respects like his earlier Kammerspiele experiment, Max Reinhardt's later production of *Borkman* at the much larger Deutsches Theater in Berlin in 1917 was a coordinated and seminal attempt to translate his controlling image of the play into precisely defined conceptual terms, stripped of the illusionistic details of naturalism. In itself the casting of Paul Wegener, fresh from his great success as a terrifying and demonic but deeply human Hummel in *The Ghost Sonata*, was bound to make Borkman into a fascinating counterpart of Strindberg's strange creation. "Of his latest play: *Borkman* –

35 Wendy Hiller's frosty Gunhild Borkman in her final confrontation with Fanny Wilton (Anna Carteret) in the National Theatre production, London, 1975.

36 Borkman's shadowy chamber (Act II) as envisioned by designer Ernst
Stern for Max Reinhardt's production at the Deutsches Theater, Berlin,
in 1917.

there is something fiendish about it," Munch supposedly once said, and
it is precisely this quality that suffused Wegener's interpretation of the
role. "This Borkman needs no forcible effort to make of the former bank
director a man obsessed, conducting his secret dialogue with a world
beyond," the reviewer of *B. Z. am Mittag* (15 March 1917) tells us: "His
eyes stare into empty space. Each of his movements bears witness to
his broken power ... Every word he speaks reverberates heavily.
Fantastic gestures accompany his descriptions of his wild speculative
dreams."

Filled with this same aura of the surreal and the macabre, Ernst
Stern's settings for the Reinhardt production, held in predominantly
gray nuances throughout, evoked a chilling atmosphere of discord and
human desolation from the outset, long before Wegener's imposing
figure appeared on the scene. "The curtain rises, and one is confronted
by a brownish-gray, cheerless, heavily curtained room," records *Vos-
sische Zeitung* (15 March). "Fresh flowers would soon wither here. Even
the great stove is streaked with grayish black ... In this desolate space
Mrs Borkman (Rosa Bertens) keeps herself in hiding from the world."
Stern's surviving designs for the following acts are mood studies
that evoke the ghostly, brooding sense of a dead past by giving prominence to selected visual motifs in the decors. In Borkman's shadowy,
sparingly furnished chamber, lighted in irregular patterns by glaring
globular lamps and dominated by two curtained windows that exclude
the outside, an impression of chill and isolation fills the totally enclosed space, the walls of which appear to dwarf the black, frantically
pacing figure in the center of the composition. In Stern's semi-abstract,

thoroughly deromanticized rendering of the scene on the mountain, the same feeling of bleakness and the same eerie interplay of glare and shadow are translated into outdoor terms. In that sketch, there are two small black figures instead of one in the designer's spatial concept, lost in the middle of an alien universe of black sky, winter-bare trees, and rises of ground that might almost suggest large burial mounds. It is a "busier" design than Gordon Craig might have drawn, but one certainly akin to Craig's now-familiar conception for the barren seacoast in the last act of *The Vikings of Helgeland*, directed and designed by him in London in 1903.

Even in London, where such Ibsen experiments remained rare exceptions in the earlier part of the century, the controversial expressionist designer Theodore Komisarjevsky's untraditional concept for *John Gabriel Borkman*, presented during an Ibsen season at the Everyman Theatre in 1921, seems to have adopted the same interpretative use of space, line, and color pioneered by Reinhardt and Stern in their production of the play four years before. Strongly in evidence was the beautifully graduated lighting effects for which this designer's later productions of Shakespeare became noted. James Agate, who passionately and regularly denounced the "dingy parlours hung with penitential gloom" which he almost invariably found associated with Ibsen in the theatre, harked back many years later to the unusual departure from this norm attempted by Komisarjevsky, who "raised his curtain on total night. Slowly we became aware of something that might be firelight, chairs, tables, human lineaments. It was all rather like the grave giving up its dead." In these dematerialized surroundings, the performance itself took on the character of voices in the air, detached from material reality. "The actors spoke from another world; their features were 'composed,'" Agate's highly colored description continues. The "intellectually magnificent" Borkman created by Franklin Dyall seemed to him ("with his grey beard and his glittering eye") an archetypal fabulist of Coleridgean proportions, "a man 'all light, a seraph-man,' standing on his own corse." His tones resounded, as it were, "from the cellerage of his past."[11]

In the Norwegian theatre itself, meanwhile, it was not until the first of Agnes Mowinckel's forceful revivals of the play in 1938 that a more consistently interpretative approach to its underlying symbolic values was even attempted in performance. This redoubtable veteran's long career at Nationaltheatret extended literally from Bjørn Bjørnson's time to the 1950s (she restaged *Borkman* in 1954, when she was nearing eighty), and as such her *mise-en-scène* tended instinctively to seek thematic expressiveness within the conventional bounds of the realistic tradition, rather than in opposition to it. To take a single example: Mowinckel staged the second act in a dark, cavernous interior pierced by a large window that looked out on a bleak winter landscape whose coldness was thus tangibly linked to the figure of Borkman and his inner state. As August Oddvar, whose compelling mixture of genius and madness in the role (both in 1938 and 1954) established a stage custom, paced the floor of his shadowy chamber, his figure moved from semi-darkness into the bleached light of the moon through the window and back into the semi–darkness again. This effectively choreographed visual touch was, Kristian Elster declared in his review, like "an overture to the entire act – a fantasia on the themes of mines and prisons." Ultimately, however, Elster and others found the unity of the Mowinckel production compromised by the unsteady balance she struck between the realistic credibility of the first two acts and the incongruously abstract form of stylization she attempted to imposed on the last two. Most egregious, in Elster's eyes, was the weakening of Borkman's return to "freedom" that occurred when the crucial third act was moved from the intimacy of Mrs. Borkman's parlor to the eerie precincts of "a mysterious, vaulted room that bore absolutely no organic relationship to the play."[12]

In the Scandinavian theatre as a whole, it was Alf Sjöberg's authoritative *John Gabriel Borkman* nine years later – the first of an influential quartet of Ibsen productions he directed at the Royal Dramatic Theatre in Stockholm – that moved the play decisively out of the realm of the realistic and the domestic, by crystallizing what *Svenska Dagbladet* (13 December 1947) characterized as "the concentrated mood of numbing solitude and ghostly half-reality" that underlies it. Sjöberg's productions of the mid–1940s represented some of the most visually exciting theatre in Europe, and the basic tone of darkness and pessimism in his *Borkman* found emphatic visual expression in the stage designs of Stellan Mörner, one of Sweden's most gifted pictorial artists. Each of Mörner's four decors projected a concise, disturbing image of stasis and desolation, filled (*Svenska Dagbladet* continues) with "cold, immutable joylessness." Inside, the rooms were "real" enough but "thinned out," in the words of *Dagens Nyheter* (13 December), to become starkly transparent metaphors for the dominant atmosphere of "chilling isolation." Mrs. Borkman, who sat arranging old letters and bills in a large ledger when her sister surprised her at the beginning of the first act, inhabited a dark, cheerless interior dominated by a large, ice-fogged window in the background, beyond which one sensed the driving snow Ibsen describes. The perception of intense coldness was even stronger in Borkman's study, a spacious, barren room where funereal dust sheets shrouded the disused furniture and the walls were hung with faded gray tapestries depicting figures forever reaching upwards. Here, a huge window arrangement framed "a round, cold moon, as round as the lamp before the window,"with which Sjöberg consciously associated "the cold and desolate human being."[13] Outside, however, the black exterior of the Rentheim manor seemed hardly a house at all, but resembled instead a funeral chapel (or perhaps Brand's Ice Church) with its tall Gothic windows and spires bedecked with icicles. For the final scene, Mörner's surreal image of a ledge and a dead, twisted tree overshadowed by high, ominous mountain shapes was no "place" as such, but rather a poetic evocation of the sense of death-in-life that Sjöberg saw as the governing force in this play.

The most remarkable aspect of this production was not, however, the director's conceptual stylization of the play's outer landscape but his corresponding intensification (not melodramatization) of its inner lattice of broken emotional relationships – in particular the gulf that separates the two estranged sisters. Tora Teje's remorselessly harsh, bitterly arrogant Mrs. Borkman took on, in the opinion of critics, the proportions of a figure out of Greek or Racinean tragedy. "With the plastic movements of a tigress and the look of a wounded wild animal, Mrs. Borkman seemed, in her dress and shawl from the nineties, like Medea in her *peplos*," Ivar Harrie commented in *Expressen* (13 December). She seemed full of hatred, Agne Beijer observed in his incisive account, "even in the only kind of love that she is able to feel, and which in fact is not love but her maternal desire of domination."[14] Even the virtually musical verbal dynamics of this performance were scored by Sjöberg to emphasize the central dichotomy between the implacable darkness of Teje's monumental portrait of Gunhild and the "imperturbable charm and youthfulness" of Anna Lindahl's conciliatory Ella Rentheim. "The two voices, the one deep and commanding, the other rich and light, formed a tragic duet," Harrie added.

The true *raison d'être* of this interpretation was, meanwhile, its unrelenting exposure of the spiritual bankruptcy of Borkman himself. From Ibsen's hand, the character has a touch not only of Peer Gynt but also of Brand about him, and Sjöberg's *Borkman* – like his controversial production of *Brand* two seasons later – centered on a condemnation of the idealist and the terrible price he exacts from his surroundings. Lars Hanson, at the height of his formidable powers, portrayed a man imprisoned in his own illusions of greatness, no poetic dreamer of dreams but a dispossessed, incurably self-indulgent self-deceiver. (In retrospect, the reading seems an unmistakable foreshadowing of one of Hanson's most famous performances, as the first James Tyrone in the world premiere of O'Neill's *Long Day's Journey into Night* in 1956.) "This Borkman possessed no other greatness than that of the play-actor, and the role of the genius that he played for himself and for Foldal sat as loosely on him as his worn and much too ample morning-coat," wrote Beijer, whose review paints a vivid picture of this counter-feit Napoleon whose "voice lent no power to his grand statements. No matter how much he pulled himself up and threw back his head in imperial fashion, he could not prevent his weak legs from buckling under him during his restless, shuffling march across the room. A wounded bird flexing his wings in the belief that he is still flying."[15]

Yet, despite the intimate realistic touches that Hanson wove into his characterization of Borkman as a grotesque ruin of a human being, there came almost magical moments when his performance appeared, in the eyes of observers, to transcend the bounds of mere reality. "His toneless, straining voice really did seem to come from the tomb: it was a dead man beyond hope, acting out a shadow-life, that one was faced with here," Harrie remarked. "This John Gabriel Borkman was truly the prisoner in the realm of the Mountain King." Finally, in the closing moments of the play, Hanson set aside realistic depiction altogether. The most startling transformation in Sjöberg's densely layered interpre-tation was thus not a scene change but a veritable transfiguration of Borkman himself when, like a mad Peer Gynt in the midst of his imaginary kingdom, he begins to speak in the poet's own voice and deliberately pierces the fabric of the drama (as Molière does at the end of *Dom Juam*, and Shakespeare likewise in *The Tempest*). "Suddenly Ibsen's sorcery colors the drama," Beijer continues. "Just as suddenly, Lars Hanson takes the consequence, throws his great cloak about him with the grand gesture of the magician, and is changed into a new being. Erect and proud, he wanders forth into the bitterly cold night; with a new voice he lends vibrant resonance to the lines which open up an entirely different and broader perspective on the play."

It was precisely this transcendent moment and the "broader per-spective" it invokes which, nearly forty years later, shaped the thinking of Sjöberg's younger contemporary, Ingmar Bergman, in the last and perhaps most forceful of his boldly unorthodox German productions of Ibsen's plays. "In all of Ibsen's work there is no other moment like that," Bergman says of Borkman's great final apostrophe to the hidden and beckoning powers. "And in every word and every phrase, Ibsen is talking about his own poetry, his own life's work – and judging it. Passing a terrible judgment on it."[16]

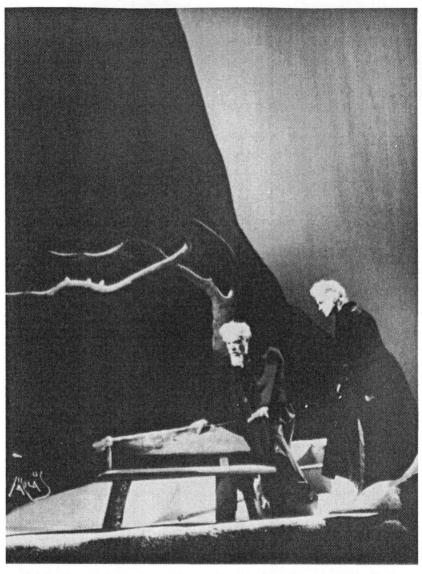

37   The final scene between Borkman (Lars Hanson) and Ella Rentheim
(Anna Lindahl) in Alf Sjöberg's production at the Royal Dramatic Theatre,
Stockholm, in 1947. The dead, twisted tree and overshadowing mountain
shapes in Stellan Mörner's stage picture intensify the prevailing mood of
desolation and entrapment created by this director.

BEGINNING AT THE END

During the period of years between the Sjöberg production at Dramaten and Bergman's revolutionary revival of the play at the Residenztheater in Munich in 1985, only a small handful of directors like Fritz Kortner, Gerda Ring, Erwin Axer, and Peter Hall continued to present significant new approaches to *John Gabriel Borkman*, while at the same time the "comic" performances of Donald Wolfit and others seemed to take the attitude that travesty was the only solution left to the formidable problems posed by this particular play. Even as some London critics were recommending that Wolfit's "impish rendering" of Borkman should become the definitive version, however, the sensitive revival mounted by Fritz Kortner at the Vienna Burgtheater in 1964 restored the balance by reaffirming the play's rightful place in the modern repertory.

Like Sjöberg's earlier attempt, the Kortner production depended ultimately for its success on the strong sense of conceptual unity that its director's interpretation brought to the play. In marked contrast to the deliberately stylized and heightened approach adopted by Sjöberg, however, Kortner chose to make use of an intricately textured mosaic of convincingly life-like details. A "perfect naturalism" capable of illuminating even the smallest nuances in the play was the general description applied by critics to his interpretation. Rather than relying on fragmentary or "modified" realism for suggestive effect, the point-device pattern of surface detail retained in Kortner's neo-naturalistic approach was so complete and intense that it acquired a dimension beyond realism, confronting the audience with an oppressively dark, highly charged poetic image of what the Munich paper *A. Z.* (23 November 1964) called "a drama about the isolation of human beings, about human self-deception."

The period settings designed by Jörg Zimmermann were thus solid reproductions of a perceived reality that also worked, most observers agreed, as large-scale metaphors for what Hilde Spiel described in *Frankfurter Allgemeine Zeitung* (26 November) as "the inner decay concealed beneath the rich, apparently indestructible furnishings from the turn of the century." Nor, in this case at least, did these period environments prove static or unwieldy, thanks to Kortner's innovative use of the flexible elevator stage available to him at the Burgtheater. Implemented by its hydraulic lift facilities, *a vista* scene changes were emphasized as a means of linking the different locations in Ibsen's play so that they became parts of a single continuum, from which the characters never escaped. As Mrs. Borkman's parlor environment disappeared beneath the stage at the end of the first act, Borkman's room above rose into view as a kind of mutation of it, connected to it by a narrow, winding staircase. Even more striking and unusual was the manner in which Kortner compressed the shift from inside to outside into a single, unbroken image, demonstrating (in the words of Joachim Kaiser) his "grandiose mastery of the transition from the real to the surreal."[17] In this streamlined, telescoped version, in which the action of the play's last movement was transferred to a roof garden at the top of the Rentheim estate, Borkman did not leave the house to go "out into the storm of life," to climb through the snow to the mountain lookout. Instead, as the closed room sank into the understage, Ewald Balzer's unheroic, utterly demythologized fabulist made his way up a staircase to the rooftop, from where he could survey the imaginary kingdom he so clearly would never reach. Paula Wessely's vibrant, richly lyrical rendering of Ella lifted their last scene together to a plane that transcended prosaic reality, in perfect harmony with the poetic expressiveness Ibsen's characters achieve at this moment. "As she gave voice, from the very depths of her soul, to her despair over a ruined existence," Kaiser goes on, "the performance outgrew all calculation and reached into an area that is otherwise accessible only to music."[18]

Hence, in spite of the multifaceted touches of realism that shaped the visual tone and texture of his production, Kortner's chief preoccupation was not with the gratuitous creation of realistic illusion, but rather with the use of such touches as a means of stimulating the audience's sensitivity to suggestion and implication – the poetry of environment which Ibsen's stage directions seek to evoke. "Kortner played on his scenic properties as a musical instrument – sparkling crystal lamps; matches that refused to light and were tossed away in irritation; Gunhild's shawl, her crocheting; the mirror in which every entrance and exit was repeated. Everything was toned down, held back, *con sordino*," Hilde Spiel commented (*Frankfurter Allgemeine Zeitung*). So muted and emotionally subdued was Kortner's sordine, in fact, that "Chekhovian" was the adjective repeatedly used to describe a performance in which "every dialogue ebbed out in a lonely monologue." This latter observation, made fully twenty years afterwards by Hansris Jacobi in *Neue Züricher Zeitung* (6 June 1985), was used by this critic to explain the contrast he perceived between Kortner's approach and the fiercely direct emotional intensity of Ingmar Bergman's Munich revival of the play that year.

Above all, perhaps, it was thus the unapologetic emotional directness of Bergman's attack that distinguished his production of *John*

Gabriel Borkman at the Residenztheater (31 May 1985) from both Hall's coolly "Pinteresque" style and Kortner's quiet "Chekhovian" obliquity. Bergman's *Borkman* represented, in many respects, a fresh start, a new and compelling synthesis of this director's ongoing quest for an illumination of Ibsen's œuvre that will penetrate beyond the ostensibly realistic surface to its inner essence. By systematically pruning away what he – in this play and elsewhere – views as conscious symbolic signposting on the playwright's part, he sought to anchor his concise, fast-paced version more firmly in a personal, emotional context, rather than in a vaguely mythic one. The three principal "dreamers and self-deceivers" at the center of the work remain, he would contend, locked within their own individual visions of reality and the past – the inescapable force that deforms them and is, in turn, deformed by them. "Vociferous, wounded human beings pursue their hopes with unswerving intensity," Kaiser wrote in his review in *Süddeutsche Zeitung* (3 June 1985). "That these hopes could be pipe-dreams – destructive, oppressive (or comic) illusions – is something of which they seem to have not the slightest suspicion." Isolated in a loveless world cut off from life, these desperate, purblind believers in a brilliant comeback groped their way from one emotionally intense, fleeting instant of human contact to the next. "I can bear this life no longer," Gunhild Borkman cries out at the end of the first act. Her outcry became the ruling leitmotif in the Bergman production, echoed in one way or another by all the other characters. Borkman himself was the first to express a truth that had been apparent to the audience virtually from the outset: that both he and the two women whose lives he had botched were already dead.

With "that clear, crisp insight born of hatred," Mrs. Borkman taunts her husband during their bitter third-act confrontation: "Give up dreaming about life. Lie quietly where you lie." And at the end of the act in Bergman's vision, in which both sisters rushed outside to pursue Erhart, Borkman collapsed to the floor in a lifeless heap. "It's a dead man who comes out in the last act – a man who knows he's dead," Bergman comments. "Borkman is already far away from everything and everyone. The rest of him has already died. He knows that. And now he just stands there motionless, like a bitter, angry ghost."[19] This allusive observation of his helps to emphasize a crucial point about his interpretation of *Borkman* as an endgame in which, regardless of the possible moves (stories, visions, evasions) left to the players, the process of ending is irreversible and plain to see. In this sense, then, Bergman's approach did not seek to build (as so many others have done) a smooth and convincing "transition" from the first three acts to the fourth. Rather, he *began* with the end as a foregone conclusion, a bleak assumption that colored every move and every tone in the play. Hence, Borkman's death and epiphanic "resurrection" on the mountain top constituted the focal moment of knowledge and self-knowledge toward which everything in this production tended. The elimination of the much-debated closing lines, in which a dubious truce of tigers is reached by the two sisters, further concentrated undivided attention and sympathy on the title character and his dilemma.

In themselves, the radically dematerialized, basically monochromatic settings (designed by Gunilla Palmstierna-Weiss) represented not "modified realism" but fragmentary quotations of a reality of no real consequence, from which the characters were noticeably dissociated in their thoughts and behavior. The raked platform-stage on which the action took place was a dislocated world devoid of stable contours, surrounded by an unchanging, dimly perceived white void that reminded one, from start to finish, of the encroaching presence of Borkman's cold kingdom. At the front edge of the platform, a single permanent feature stood out: the low, simple bench that was to be the final station on Borkman's journey. Mrs. Borkman's "parlor" was delineated only by a painted back-screen, decorated with a faded red pattern, which provided an almost perfunctory indication of its rear wall and part of a ceiling above it. A thick red carpet, a lighted red lamp, and an old-fashioned sofa and armchair upholstered in the same dark red fabric comprised the sole furnishings in a setting which – like the others that followed – stressed a deliberate disjuncture between the three-dimensionality of the actors and the obviously flattened theatrical perspective of the space in which they moved. As a result, the true focus of the composition became not its ground but the figures in it, whose emotional turmoil was literally drawn closer to the audience in what amounted to the theatrical equivalent of a cinematic close-up. Thus, one critic remarked, Bergman and his actors "chiseled out the distinctive features of these roles with a spiritual and gestural precision that has virtually been forgotten in today's theatre."[20]

If Mrs. Borkman's red room suggested a real, albeit highly stylized interior, the space in which Borkman himself existed bore no resemblance whatever to a habitable human environment. Rather, its only true reality was an inner and subjective one, the reality of the central character's tormented sense of defeat and emotional turbulence. The black, slate-hard flooring of the platform-stage reechoed the anxiety of his methodical pacing – six steps in each direction, like a prisoner in a cell. A large back-screen depicted a brutal battle scene, reminiscent of the violent, distorted visions of Hieronymus Bosch and aptly reflective of Borkman's own view of himself as a man struck down from behind by treachery in the midst of his struggle for victory. Above all, the pervading mood of inner turbulence was established and accentuated by the music Frida Foldal played at the opening of the second act – not the customary bars from Saint-Saëns' popular *Danse macabre*, but instead a full two minutes of Beethoven's surging *Tempest* sonata (No. 17 in D minor, also known as the *Ghost Sonata*), to which Borkman sat listening in motionless silence, eyes closed and head leaned against the piano. Apart from the chair he occupied and the black upright at which Frida sat, the only furnishings in this vacuous space were the nine other straight, high-backed chairs that stood arranged in severe symmetry along the lateral edges of the platform, virtually fencing it in. The evocative visual image suggested (but by no means "symbolized") the tribunal which Borkman – acting as his own prosecutor, his own defense, and his own judge – has composed for himself in his solitude, from whose silent verdict there can be no appeal.

Bergman deliberately altered the audience's perception of an observable place in time – the reality of conventional understanding, as it were – in order to refocus attention on the inner emotional design of Ibsen's play. This strategy found its boldest expression in his treatment of the difficult fourth act. His image of the cold winter landscape outside the Rentheim estate was a vast, utterly empty expanse of whiteness that covered the full depth of the platform-stage and the peripheral area adjoining it. In essence, the audience now found itself in the midst of the cold kingdom whose visual presence had been felt in the stage picture from the very beginning. This bleak, colorless world beyond life was illuminated by searing, unpityingly harsh low-angle projectors whose light emphasized, and compelled, intense facial and gestural expressiveness. In the background stood a tall, unearthly tombstone of a house-façade: "a vision of a blanched ghost-house, with black cavities for windows," Jacobi called it in *Neue Züricher Zeitung*. In this movement of the play, the atmosphere of a spiritual and emotional desolation – of "death as the extreme of loneliness," as Bergman puts it in *Cries and Whispers* – was instantly created by a vivid opening pictorial composition. Before the "house" at the very back of the stage one saw the inert, strangely distant figure of Borkman, age-old now and dressed in a heavy black overcoat and hat; at the very front of the platform, a universe away, stood the two sisters, dark, mournful shapes whose long shadows called up associations with the art of Chirico and Munch. Later, as Borkman began his last journey with Ella to the "clearing high up in the forest," even the eerie house-façade vanished, leaving only the interplay of darkness and light, and the poetry of the dialogue, to conjure up the "vast, infinite, inexhaustible kingdom" of his imagination.

Bergman's stark dematerialization of the play's physical locations and his corresponding excision of much of the mosaic of "life-like" stage business and ambient sounds (footsteps heard overhead, sleighbells passing) so dear to generations of earlier naturalistic directors produced what he likes to call a distillation, a clarified, almost musically precise and very immediate expression of the inner emotional rhythm and logic of the drama. This play's greatest strength, Bergman insists, is its tightly compressed structure, the forceful, profoundly musical design of "an octet in four movements" that does not depend on the conventions of verisimilitude for its effect in the theatre. "It's of the utmost importance when working on a play like this that you simplify and simplify so that the strong classical lines of the tragedy remain clear," he goes on to say. "From the moment I began working on this play I had the sense of it as very stark and simple, virtually immovable. They sit there in their chairs – they stand there unmoving – they are rooted to the spot. Everything remains only half an attempt at contact. But there is none. There is no longer any real contact between them."[21]

At the very outset, the disquieting image of the darkly clad, heavily veiled figure of Mrs. Borkman (played by Christine Buchegger), seated motionless on her sofa like a lifeless doll, prefigured the paralyzing sense of desperation and death-in-life which suffused the play in this performance. "The soul-murder had already taken place, even before the dialogue had begun," observed *Nürnberger Nachrichten* (3 June). As abruptly and soundlessly as a figure in a dream, Christa Berndl's pale, ghost-gray Ella Rentheim appeared without preamble in the open doorway, as the ominous manifestation of the inner forces of disruption that once more break loose over the Borkman household. In terms of physical actions, the increasingly bitter and vehement confrontation between these two unyielding opponents remained virtually static, played with almost no movement and a minimum of visual contact. It was entirely the corrosive, barely controlled inner tension between them, rather than the naturalistic sound of pacing footsteps, that drove home the point of a pattern repeated – a futile struggle for dominion over Erhart that mirrored their equally desperate struggle over his father long ago. Throughout this long, tense encounter – and even after Fanny Wilton, played by Rita Russek in a gaudy orange evening-dress, had walked in with Erhart in tow – Mrs. Borkman continued to sit rigidly in the same spot, trapped in her own solipsistic world.

In particular, the altered perception of Ella Rentheim that this production yielded represented a radical contrast to the idealized, even sentimentalized view of this character which the play's stage history has perpetuated – basically the "sad old maid of sixty" described by Henry James in his wrongheaded review.[22] The destruction time has wrought on this pale, physically exhausted, mortally ill human being was the key to Bergman's view that "she lives in the total absence of love, and her furious despair that love has gone out of her life is terrifying to witness." In an emphatic departure from tradition, Christa Berndl's interpretation drew a complex and ambiguous picture of Ella as a woman filled with a harrowing sense of futility and loss that has consumed her warmth and her capacity for love, leaving her, as she tells Borkman with bitterness, "cold and barren like a wilderness of ice, inside and outside." Rather than representing the antithesis of her brooding, implacable twin sister, this Ella seemed as blighted a spirit as Gunhild herself. Both women clung with equally selfish desperation to the palpably hollow fiction of Erhart's love, as a last, forlorn hope amidst the wreckage of their hopeless lives. In her subsequent face-to-face encounter with Borkman in the second act, Ella's inner pain and turmoil welled to the surface with virtually explosive force. Her discovery that he had deliberately bartered away her love to gain power and her denunciation of this perfidy (*"That* was double murder! The murder of your own soul and of mine") exposed an aggressiveness and vehemence that brought the scene several degrees closer to Strindberg, in the opinion of many critics. Even more "Strindbergian," meanwhile, was the disquieting and deeply poignant impression Bergman conveyed of characters caught in an existential impasse beyond their control, trapped in a world of deception and delusion in which reality is impossible to grasp. Even a brief glance at the production script reveals the extraordinary plastic eloquence with which the director underscored the complexly orchestrated emotional rhythm of this focal confrontation:

ELLA. Gabriel. (*Pause*) Gabriel, Gabriel. Don't you think there was some sort of curse over our whole relationship?
BORKMAN. Curse?
ELLA. Don't you feel that?
BORKMAN. I do. But why – ? (*He rushes to her, falls on his kness, and buries his head in her lap. Then he looks up, covering his face with his hands.*) Oh, Ella – I don't know any more which of us is right – you or me!
ELLA. (*Takes his hand.*) You're to blame. You killed all human feeling in me.
BORKMAN. Don't say that, Ella!

ELLA. From the day your image began to fade in me, I have lived as though under an eclipse. (BORKMAN *very slowly gets up, retreats to his chair and stands with his back to her*.) All those years I found it harder and harder – at last completely impossible – to love any living being . . .[23]

Yet, as this excerpt also suggests, at the core of Bergman's concept was a totally convincing sense of compassion for Borkman himself and his predicament, that counterbalanced and even overcame Ella's justifiably vehement condemnation of him and his actions. The figure with which Hans Michael Rehberg confronted the audience at the beginning of the second act was thus deliberately unlike the ruthless, autocratic predator which we have been led by Gunhild's descriptions to expect. (In this production it was, in fact, Erhart who stood exposed as the ruthless one, as ready as he is in Munch's garish painting of the reckless sleighride to trample over anyone who might appear to block his path to self-enjoyment.) Nor was Rehberg's Borkman "the mountain-miner's son," professing mystical affinity with the singing ore that "longs to be set free." Like the Napoleonic posturings of stage tradition, these overt symbolic allusions in Ibsen's text were also eliminated in Bergman's *Borkman*. Instead, the actor's performance carved out a passionately human, unexpectedly youthful and vulnerable characterization of a dreamer hopelessly confined – spiritually as well as physically – to the dark prison-world of his own making. "His life consists of silence, of self-justification, of attack. His index-finger is like a raised weapon. His imperative gestures are attempts to break out of a prison of weakness and loneliness," Georg Hensel wrote of Rehberg's profoundly analytical portrayal.[24] This hopelessly divided spirit, trapped between self-assertiveness ("They *must* come! They could be here any day, at any hour") and crippling self-doubt ("The years pass. Life – oh, no – I dare not think of that"), represented a complex union of what had once been irreconcilable opposites in Ibsen's early plays. The heroic "kingly thought" of a Haakon and the self-destructive doubting of a Skule were now amalgamated, as it were, in the single, tormented consciousness of the artist-visionary.

Hence, Bergman's production left no doubt about the reality of Borkman's anguish and the depth of the spiritual suffering and pain he endures in his private inferno. Yet one of its most startling innovations was the manner in which bitter, mocking comedy infiltrated and ultimately reinforced this psychological intensity. In this regard the figure of Foldal, played with wry, Chaplinesque irony by the noted German film actor Heinz Bennent, acquired unusual and crucial significance as Borkman's comic double and grotesque mirror-image. Their two conversations are "so perfect, so precise, so full of black humor," Bergman remarks, that they are "like something you'd expect to find in absurd drama. Or like the dialogue between Lear and Gloucester on the moor." Traditionally, Foldal has almost invariably been played as a sentimental character, the lowly clerk cruelly and repeatedly run over by life, the mild, misunderstood poet *manqué*. In this instance, however, this cherished cliché was treated to a strong dose of trenchant satire. In his long overcoat, black hat, skimpy jacket, and striped trousers, Bennent had Chaplin's eager, whimsical face, his awkwardly dignified walk – and his profound and manifest humanity. Yet all trace of sentimentality was expunged from Borkman's relationship with the faithful Vilhelm, the one person who has not deserted him in his disgrace. Their first scene began as a repetition of the countless previous meetings during which, for the eight long years of Borkman's self-imprisonment, these two dreamers presumably passed the time by feeding one another's illusions. The point was thus not the disparity between them but their grotesque similarity. Borkman's obsessive preoccupation with the power to create a new world ("the obsession of the artist – the imaginative person – with what he really cares about, his own work," Bergman calls it) was seen reflected in the mirror of Foldal's own dogged obsession with the "masterpiece" he has been rewriting for most of his life. Not only did Bennent's Foldal bring his tragedy with him, bound in two thick volumes which he continually handled; he was even permitted to give a short declamatory recitation from it – comprised (to the dismay of some of the more conservative critics) of the opening lines and stage directions from *Catiline*, Ibsen's youthful tragic extravaganza about the disproportion between desire and possibility!

After the prolonged, shocked silence that followed their quarrel and Borkman's cruel snipe ("And you are no poet, Vilhelm"), Foldal, shaken but composed, methodically gathered up his various belongings – umbrella, briefcase, manuscript, and a misplaced hat – in an exquisite Chaplinade. His absurdly dignified parting admission ("I've had doubts of my own now and then – the horrible doubt that I may have squandered my life for the sake of an illusion") was a reflection *in buffo* of a truth that Borkman had begun to recognize all too clearly. Comedy, Ionesco once wrote, "seems more hopeless than tragedy" because it "allows no way out of a given situation." Precisely in this sense, the thrust of this unit of action became, in Bergman's production, the painfully ironic image it conveyed of Borkman's own inevitable defeat and the futility of his situation. The loser in the confrontation was thus not the poetaster but Borkman himself, who, as if he realized that fact, made a clumsy and unsuccessful effort to restore the

38 Vilhelm Foldal, as played by Heinz Bennent, recites his tragedy to the distracted Borkman (Hans Michael Rehberg) in Act II of Ingmar Bergman's production at the Residenztheater, Munich, in 1985.

balance and made amends. From a conspicuously empty purse he took a coin and handed it to his friend for the car fare. At first, out of old habit, Foldal accepted this token of diminished wealth, then reconsidered, and finally handed it back. Having thus regained his full dignity and having found a suitably theatrical cue for his exit, "Catiline" solemnly departed, leaving Borkman to the solitude of his cheerless night-vigil.

The inherently dissonant collision of seriousness and absurdity reasserted itself in the last act, when the dark pattern of the tragedy is pierced by what Bergman calls the "strange *scherzo*" of Foldal's return, after he has been knocked down by the speeding sleigh that carries his daughter away with her "tutor" and Mrs. Wilton. Here again, it was not the potential pathos of the situation ("It's not the first time in your life you've been run over, old friend") but its comic irony that prevailed in this performance. His overcoat now soiled, his umbrella broken, and his glasses lost in the snow, Bennent's Foldal was the awkward and limping but intensely alive refutation of the lifelessness of Borkman himself, who remained virtually motionless throughout the scene. Nearsighted without his glasses and muffled in a scarf to cover his ears from the cold, this comedic casualty of life's heedlessness was figuratively blind and deaf to the personal hardships and sorrows it inflicts. "In other words, in this play about the absence of love, it becomes the fool who carries the theme of love – both in a comic and a tragic sense," Bergman points out. Mindful only of the fine silver bells on the magnificent sleigh that will take "little Frida" into the wide world he himself once dreamed of seeing, Foldal countered Borkman's bitter and disillusioned experience of life with a compelling, profoundly human naivety, and a store of sight gags that included repeated but unsuccessful attempts to shake Borkman's hand. In the end, inevitably finding something positive to say and calling upon his inimitable Catilinean rhetoric for support, he transformed – by magic if not by logic – his own failed poetic vision into an optimistic blueprint for the future: "How strange a man's destiny can be! My – my humble gift of poetry has turned to music in Frida. So I haven't been a poet for nothing after all."

In this way, the pain of knowledge and judgment that Borkman, the "escaped prisoner," comes to endure at the end of the play was accentuated by the spectacle of the happy ignorance of his double. No scene change of any kind intervened to diminish this impression. Borkman simply walked into the deep, encroaching shadows at the rear of the stage, followed closely by Ella. Emerging again into the shadowless white light, taking longer and longer strides, *he* (rather than the scenery) underwent a truly startling transformation, as he cast off hat, cane, gloves, hat, overcoat, and jacket and tore open his collar and cuffs before coming forward to the low, simple bench that had awaited him from the beginning. As Hans Michael Rehberg stood outlined against the totally bare, contourless white space, conjuring up the dream of Borkman's kingdom with an expansive, mantic gesture ("See how the land stretches before us, so spacious and free"), he was no longer weighed down by guilt and doubt but seemed a younger, more vigorous figure. The viewer's thoughts were led back to Ibsen's poetic dramas – and beyond them to their great model. At this virtually hypnotic moment, observed *Die Welt* (3 June), "he achieves a visionary power. We sense that we hear Faust's last words, 'I'd open room to live for millions,' spoken with so much grandeur, so much pride in the face of death."

John Gabriel Borkman, as conceived by Bergman and portrayed by Rehberg, was indeed Faustian in character and dimension, but he was Promethean as well, longing not for personal gain but for the opportunity to "bring light and warmth to thousands upon thousands. *That* is what I dreamed of creating." In this production at least, his aspirations were stretched to embrace, by implication, the vision and calling of the poet as well. Borkman is a man of finance, Halvard Solness is a master builder, Arnold Rubek is a sculptor, but all three of Ibsen's last male protagonists are essentially creative artists, in works that all deal with the relationship of life and art and the spiritual and emotional cost of that art to them and to others around them. Thus, the truly savage condemnation of Borkman delivered by Ella Rentheim in the Bergman version became, for this director, the expression of the "terrible judgment" which the artist himself passes "on his own poetry, his own life's work."

Quite suddenly and brutally in this production, Borkman's brief, emotionally charged vision of his unattainable kingdom and its "bright promise of power and glory" was shattered by Ella's denunciation of the egoist whose life-denying obsession has exacted such an appaling toll in terms of human suffering: "And therefore I tell you this, John Gabriel Borkman – you'll never reap profit from your murder. You will never ride in triumph into your cold, dark kingdom." So unexpectedly violent and even vindictive was this avenging angel's damnation, however, that it became, in its turn, a denial of the balm of human compassion and forgiveness that thrust the reality of Borkman's own pain and despair into the foreground, as the focus of audience sympathy. By rejecting what he regards as an imposed reconciliation of the two sisters at the end of the play, Bergman further deepened the sense

39   "But I'll whisper to you now, in the still of the night": the final image in
Bergman's *Borkman*, 1985.

of unresolved and irresolvable ambivalence inherent in this scene and
in the play as a whole.

At the last, a moment before he slumped forward on the bench,
Borkman passed his hand over his face like a child consoling himself,
whisking away a bad dream. For an instant he became calm, on the
verge of release from his suffering, but the gesture did nothing to
dispel the mood of coldness and desolation that hung heavy over this
last unit of action. Her fury and bitterness spent, Ella rushed forward
to embrace Borkman, passed her hand slowly over his face, and finally
covered his lifeless form with her heavy coat. The few terse lines
exchanged by the sisters in this version provided no conciliatory epilogue, no hint of relief or even receding hostility. Instead, summarized
in the cold, empty, anaesthetized whiteness of the final tableau, the
motionless image of two shadows and a dead man bespoke the fractured, incoherent world reflected in Ibsen's penultimate work more
bleakly than in any of his other plays.

Critics who write about *John Gabriel Borkman* are quite often inclined
to point to an analogue in the self-questioning stanzas of "Bergmanden"
("The Mountain-Miner"), the poem Ibsen wrote when he was only
twenty-three:

Hammer blow by hammer blow
Till the last day of life.
No ray of morning shines.
No sun of hope rises.

Although the intensely dark mood of these lines did find its full
expression in Bergman's *Borkman*, this mood was, however, juxtaposed with an equally emphatic and contradictory sense of the poet's
ultimate vindication. We find it suggested in another of Ibsen's early
poems, "On the Heights," a stanza of which stood in the program as a
more fitting epigraph to this performance of Ibsen's most personal
artist-drama:

Now I am steeled, I heed the command
That bids me wander the peaks!
With lowland life I am finished and done;
Up here on the heights are freedom and God,
Beneath me the others search blindly.

Notes

1 BECOMING IBSEN

1 Quoted in Bernt Lorentzen, *Det første norske teater* (Bergen, 1949), p. 102.
2 For further details, see, for example, Frederick J. Marker and Lise-Lone Marker, *The Scandinavian Theatre: A Short History* (Oxford, 1975), pp. 141f.
3 Lorentzen, p. 106.
4 Lucie Wolf, *Mine Livserindringer* (Christiania, 1898), pp. 182–3.
5 *Cf.* Roderick Rudler, "Ibsens teatergjerning i Bergen," in *Drama och teater*, ed. Egil Törnqvist (Stockholm 1968), p. 61.
6 Daniel Haakonsen, *Henrik Ibsen, mennesket og kunstneren* (Oslo, 1981) contains superb color reproductions for four of Ibsen's own costume designs for *Olaf Liljekrans* (pp. 140–1), as well as samples of his landscape painting (pp. 58, 61).
7 *Cf.* Rudler, p. 66.
8 Craig's production of *The Vikings of Helgeland* is reconstructed in detail in Christopher Innes, *Edward Gordon Craig* (Cambridge, 1983), pp. 83–97.
9 The production history of *The Pretenders*, and in particular Craig's place in it, is the subject of Frederick J. Marker and Lise-Lone Marker, *Edward Gordon Craig and "The Pretenders": A Production Revisited* (Carbondale and Edwardsville, 1981).
10 Emil Poulsen, "Ibsen og Skuespilleren," in *Festskrift til Henrik Ibsen i anledning af hans 70. fødselsdag*, ed. G. Gran (Bergen, 1898), p. 255.

2 IN THE HALL OF THE MOUNTAIN KING: *PEER GYNT*

1 In a speech delivered on 1 April 1898 in Copenhagen; quoted in *Ibsen: Letters and Speeches*, ed. Evert Sprinchorn (New York, 1964), p. 334.
2 Ludvig Josephson, "Om teater-regi," in *Perspektiv på teater*, eds. Ulf Gran and Ulla-Britta Lagerroth (Stockholm, 1971), p. 17.
3 *Cf.* Robert Neiiendam, *Fra Kulisserne og Scenen* (Copenhagen, 1966), pp. 87–8 and Klaus Neiiendam, "The Second Staging of *Peer Gynt*, 1886," *Theatre Research International*, 2 (February, 1977), 104–17. For further details of the collaboration between Grieg and Ibsen, see *The Oxford Ibsen*, ed.

James Walter McFarlane (London, 1972), Vol. 3, pp. 502–4. The prompt-book for this production is in the Danish Theatre Museum in Copenhagen.

4 Quoted in *The Oxford Ibsen*, Vol. 3, p. 498.

5 Ezra Pound, "Mr James Joyce and the Modern Stage," *Drama*, 6:2 (February, 1916), quoted in *Henrik Ibsen*, ed. James [Walter] McFarlane (Harmondsworth, Middlesex, 1970), p. 217.

6 Henrik Ibsen, *Peer Gynt*, trans. Michael Meyer (Garden City, N.Y., 1963), p. xxvii.

7 Quoted in Martin Nag. *Ibsen i russisk åndsliv* (Oslo, 1967), p. 22.

8 Nils Åke Nilsson, *Ibsen in Russland* (Stockholm, 1958), p. 130.

9 Quoted in A. Nicholas Vardac, *From Stage to Screen* (Cambridge, Mass., 1949), p. 219.

10 William Winter, *Life and Art of Richard Mansfield, with Selections from his Letters* (New York, 1910), Vol. 1, pp. 312, 313.

11 *Ibid.*, Vol. 2, p. 207.

12 *Cf.* G. M. Bergman, *Den moderna teaterns genombrott 1890–1925* (Stockholm, 1966), p. 90.

13 Francisque Sarcey, *Quarante ans de théâtre*, (Paris, 1902), Vol. 8, pp. 368–9.

14 Review in *Revue des Deux-Mondes*, 138 (1896), reprinted in Jules Lemaître, *Impressions de théâtre*, (Paris, 1898), Vol. 10, p. 40.

15 Georg Brandes, "Henrik Ibsen en France," *Cosmopolis: An International Monthly Review*, 5 (1897), 120.

16 *Verdens Gang*, 280 (1896), quoted in Kela Nyholm, "Henrik Ibsen på den franske scene," *Ibsen Årbok 1957–9*, ed. Einar Østvedt (Oslo, 1959), pp. 50–1.

17 *Saturday Review*, 74 (21 November 1896), reprinted in George Bernard Shaw, *Our Theatres in the Nineties* (London, 1932), Vol. 2, pp. 231, 233.

18 Sarcey, *Quarante ans*, Vol. 8, p. 369.

19 *Aftenposten*, 785 (1896), quoted in Hans Midbøe, *Peer Gynt: teatret og tiden* (Oslo, 1978), Vol. 1, p. 152.

20 Quoted in *Peer Gynt 1928–1972*, publ. by El Teatro Stabile di Torino (Turin, 1972), p. 37.

21 Review reprinted in Frederick Schyberg, *Teatret i Krig, 1939–1948* (Copen-hagen, 1949), pp. 106–10.

22 "Some Afterthoughts on *Peer Gynt*" appeared in *The Norseman*, 5 (1947). Guthrie's views here correspond directly to those he expresses in his Foreword to Norman Ginsbury's translation of *Peer Gynt* (1946). Both these items are at variance, however, with the opinions contained in Guthrie's "A Message from the Old Vic," published in "Ibsen's *Peer Gynt*: A Souvenir of the Old Vic Production" (London: Royal Norwegian Government In-formation Office, 1944), where the director regrets the fact that war condi-tions prevented him from achieving a *more* faithful and complete rendering of the text and Grieg's score.

The excerpts here are quoted in Midbøe, *Peer Gynt: teatret og tiden*, Vol. 1, pp. 174, 176.

23 Quoted in *ibid.*, Vol. 2 (1976), p. 53.

24 Agne Beijer, *Teaterrecensioner 1925–1949* (Stockholm, 1954), p. 178.
25 Hans Jacob Nilsen, *Peer Gynt: ett anti-romantisk verk* (Oslo, 1948), p. 37. The Nilsen production is treated in exhaustive detail in Midbøe, Vol. 2.
26 Tord Baeckström in *Göteborgs Handels- och Sjöfartstidning*, 9 March 1957.
27 Per Erik Wahlund, *Scenväxling: Teaterkritik 1954–1960* (Stockholm, 1962), p. 130.
28 Baeckström review.
29 Wahlund, p. 128.
30 Werner Egk, *Peer Gynt: Oper in drei akten, in freier Neugestaltung nach Ibsen* (Mainz, 1938, 1966), p. 18.
31 Klaus Wagner in *Frankfurter Allgemeine Zeitung*, 12 June 1968.
32 Quoted in Michael Patterson, *Peter Stein: Germany's Leading Theatre Director* (Cambridge, 1981), p. 74.
33 *Peer Gynt, Ein Schauspiel aus dem neunzehnten Jahrhundert. Dokumentation der Schaubühnen-Inszenierung.* Schaubühne and Hentrich Verlag (Berlin, 1971), p. 97.
34 Günther Rühle, "Was an uns ist noch Peer?" in *Ibsen auf der deutsche Bühne*, ed. Wilhelm Friese (Tübingen, 1976), pp. 133–4.
35 *Dokumentation der Schaubühnen-Inszenierung*, p. 68.
36 *Theater heute*, 1971/13, p. 32.
37 *Dokumentation der Schaubühnen-Inszenierung*, p. 73.
38 *Ibid.*, p. 67.
39 *Ibid.*, p. 146.
40 Rustom Bharucha, "Ciulei's *Peer Gynt*: Under the Sign of the Onion," *Theater*, 15 (Winter, 1983), 70.
41 *Peer Gynt by Henrik Ibsen, in Translation by David Rudkin* (London, 1983), p. 82.

3 ONE NORA, MANY NORAS

1 Herman Bang's analysis is found in his *Kritiske Studier* (Copenhagen, 1880), pp. 220–8. Also of great interest is Bang's illustrated little source-book, *'Et Dukkehjem' paa Nationaltheatret* (Copenhagen, 1880).
2 Edvard Brandes, *Om Teater*, ed. Harald Engberg (Copenhagen, 1947), pp. 151, 177. Brandes' later essays on Hennings first appeared in *Politiken*, 12 March 1928 and 26 October 1935.
3 Maurice Baring, *The Puppet Show of Memory* (Boston, 1922), pp. 210–11.
4 Bang, *Kritiske Studier*, pp. 314–15.
5 Brandes, *Om Teater*, pp. 150–1.
6 A small, black, undated *maskinmesterbog* (pp. 415–21) and the Royal Theatre's *Regieprotokol*, 18 October 1874 (pp. 115–16) provide what evidence we have concerning the staging of this production (Royal Theatre Library).
7 Edvard Brandes, *Fremmed Skuespilkunst: Studier og Portrætter* (Copenhagen, 1881), p. 28.
8 Ove Rode, "Et Teater i Forfald," *Verdens Gang*, 18 October 1882.

9 *The Critic*, 28 December 1889, p. 329.
10 See William Archer, *The Theatrical 'World' for 1893* (London, 1894), pp. 158–9.
11 *Ibid.*, pp. 160–1.
12 Quoted (disapprovingly) in James Agate, *Playgoing: An Essay* (London, 1927), pp. 51–2.
13 Gunnar Heiberg, *Ibsen og Bjørnson paa Scenen* (Christiania, 1918), p. 14.
14 Alfred Polgar, *Brahms Ibsen* (Berlin, 1910), p. 6.
15 In Julius Bab, *Agnes Sorma: Ein Gedenkbuch* (Heidelberg, 1927), pp. 54f.
16 Heiberg, pp. 100–1.
17 William Archer, *World*, 27 April 1892, p. 22.
18 George Bernard Shaw, *Our Theatres in the Nineties* (London, 1932), Vol. 3, pp. 132–3.
19 *Ibid.*, Vol. 2, p. 261. So unsettling was Achurch's performance that she was quickly replaced in the role by Mrs Patrick Campbell, who, Shaw records sarcastically, "succeeded wonderfully in eliminating all unpleasantness from the play" (Vol. 2, p. 272).
20 Lewis Strang, *Famous Actresses of the Day in America* (Boston, 1899), p. 67.
21 "Ibsen versus Humpty Dumpty," *Harper's Weekly*, 49 (1905), p. 161, and Archie Binns, *Mrs. Fiske and the American Theatre* (New York, 1955), p. 139.
22 Francisque Sarcey, *Quarante ans de théâtre* (Paris, 1902), Vol. 8, pp. 361, 359.
23 Herman Bang, *Masker og Mennesker* (Copenhagen, 1910), pp. 176–7.
24 Shaw, *Our Theatres in the Nineties*, Vol. 3, p. 132.
25 Bang, p. 176.
26 Sarcey, pp. 359, 361.
27 Quoted in Kela Nyholm, "Henrik Ibsen paa den franske Scene," *Ibsen-Årbok 1957–9*, ed. Einar Østvedt (Oslo, 1959), p. 59.
28 Quoted in Nikolai A. Gorchakov, *The Theater in Soviet Russia*, trans. Edgar Lehrman (New York, 1957), p. 55.
29 Quoted in Nils Åke Nilsson, *Ibsen in Russland* (Stockholm, 1958). p. 42.
30 A. Bruštejn, *Stranicy prošlogo*, 2md ed. (Moscow, 1956), p. 112.
31 *Meyerhold on Theatre*, ed. and trans. Edward Braun (New York, 1969), p. 30.
32 *Naša zižn'*, 20 December 1906, quoted in Nilsson, p. 46.
33 *Meyerhold on Theatre*, p. 25.
34 Kommisarjevskaya's correspondence with Meyerhold is discussed in some detail in Martin Nag, *Ibsen i russisk åndsliv* (Oslo, 1967), pp. 57–9.
35 Oliver M. Sayler, *Our American Theatre* (New York, 1923), p. 3. Sayler begins his list of "Important Productions on the American Stage 1908–1923" with Kommisarjevskaya's appearance.
36 *Meyerhold on Theatre*, pp. 29–30.
37 Quoted in Konstantin Rudnitsky, *Meyerhold the Director* (Ann Arbor, 1981), p. 287.
38 *Louisville Courier-Journal*, 8 December 1883.
39 "Nora Helmer off to the Antipodes," *Pall Mall Gazette*, 5 July 1889; reprinted in *Ibsen: The Critical Heritage*, ed. Michael Egan (London, 1972), p. 125.
40 Kristian Elster, *Teater 1929–1939*, ed. Anton Rønneberg (Oslo, 1941), p. 56.

41 *Berlingske Tidende*, 6 March 1936; reprinted in Frederik Schyberg, *Ti Aars Teater* (Copenhagen, 1939), pp. 132–5.

42 *Evening Standard*, 4 March 1936 and (London) *Sunday Times*, 8 March 1936.

43 James Agate, *Red Letter Nights* (London, 1944), p. 61.

44 Schyberg, *Ti Aars Teater*, p. 168.

45 *Ibid.*, pp. 168–9.

46 Elster, pp. 235–6.

47 Agne Beijer, *Teaterrecensioner, 1925–1949* (Stockholm 1954), p. 302.

48 Hansgeorg Lenz, "Når det vidunderlige sker," *Information* (Copenhagen), 5 March 1974. As her memoirs imply, Ullmann's English-language performance in *A Doll's House* at the Lincoln Center in New York the following year differed in many respects from the Norwegian production.

49 Helen Dawson in *Plays and Players* (April 1973), p. 42.

50 Quoted in Walter Bilderback, "Beyond Teacups and Wallpaper: The American Ibsen Theater," *Theater*, 16 (Summer/Fall, 1985), 25.

51 Quoted in C. Braad Thomsen, *I Fassbinders spegl* (Copenhagen, 1975), p. 206.

52 Georg Hensel in *Darmstädter Echo*, 5 February 1972.

53 Bergman's *Nora* was first produced as part of a seven-hour thematic cycle of works, christened the Bergman Project by the German critics, which also included his versions of Strindberg's *Miss Julie* and his own film script *Scenes from a Marriage*. The scripts have been published in *Ingmar Bergman: A Project for the Theatre*, edited and introduced by Frederick J. Marker and Lise-Lone Marker (New York, 1983). *Nora* has been performed professionally in English by the Pittsburgh Public Theatre (1984) and the Stratford (Ontario) Shakespeare Festival (1987).

54 *A Project for the Theatre, p.* 94.

4 NATURALISM AND AFTER: *GHOSTS*

1 *Ibsen: Letters and Speeches*, ed. Evert Sprinchorn (New York, 1964), p. 232.

2 The fifth of Ibsen's fragmentary notes on the play, jotted on the back of an envelope, first published after his death in *Efterladte Skrifter*.

3 Quoted in Michael Meyer, *Ibsen* (Harmondsworth, Middlesex, 1974), p. 598.

4 Quoted in Georg Nordensvan, *Svensk teater och svenska skådespelare* (Stockholm, 1918), Vol. 2, p. 351.

5 Archer's letter to his brother Charles about the Lindberg production was first published in *Edda*, 31 (1931), 456–9; reprinted in *The Oxford Ibsen*, ed. James Walter McFarlane (London, 1961), Vol. 5, p. 481.

6 Nordensvan, Vol. 2, p. 351.

7 C. H. Genung, "Ibsen's Spectres," *Nation*, 44 (1887), 116–17.

8 On Mitterwurzer, see Heinz Kindermann, *Theatergeschichte Europas* (Salzburg, 1965), Vol. 7, pp. 186–7. The actor's death in 1897 prompted a famous tribute by the young Ibsen champion Hugo von Hofmannsthal to the protean genius of "der grosse, grosse Gaukler":

Er kroch von einer Larve in die Andere,
Sprang aus des Vaters in des Sohnes Leib,
Und tauschte wie Gewänder die Gestalten.

9 *Bjørnstjerne Bjørnsons brevveksling med danske, 1875–1910*, eds. Øyvind Anker, Francis Bull, and Torben Nielsen (Copenhagen and Oslo, 1972), Vol. 1, 281.

10 Cf. Frederick J. Marker and Lise-Lone Marker, "Early Ibsen Performances in America," *Scandinavian Review*. 66 (December, 1978), 20f.

11 Émile Zola, "Naturalism in the Theatre," in *The Theory of the Modern Stage*, ed. Eric Bentley (Harmondsworth, Middlesex, 1968). p. 351.

12 Quotations are from André Antoine, "Behind the Fourth Wall" in *Directors on Directing*, ed. Toby Cole and Helen K. Chinoy (Indianapolis, 1963), pp. 90, 94, 98, 100.

13 Francisque Sarcey, "Les Revenants" (review dated 2 June 1891), reprinted in *Quarante ans de théâtre*, (Paris, 1902), Vol. 7, p. 331.

14 George Moore's account, "Notes on *Ghosts*," was first published in his *Impressions and Opinions* (London, 1891), pp. 215–26. It is reprinted in *Ibsen: The Critical Heritage*, ed. Michael Egan (London, 1972), p. 185. The subsequent page references in parentheses refer to the Egan anthology.

15 Quoted in *Actors on Acting*, ed. Toby Cole and Helen K. Chinoy (New York, 1970), p. 459.

16 Gunnar Heiberg, *Ibsen og Bjørnson paa Scenen* (Christiania, 1918), pp. 94–5.

17 *Ibid.*, p. 96.

18 Quoted in Gernot Schley, *Die Freie Bühne in Berlin* (Berlin, 1967), p. 43.

19 The respective references are: (for Achurch) James Agate, *The Contemporary Theatre 1923* (London, 1924), p. 65; (for Lehmann) *Punch*, 7 July 1943; (for Robson) *the Observer*, 16 November 1958; (for Worth) *Daily Telegraph*, 18 January 1974.

20 Tracy C. Davis, "Acting in Ibsen," *Theatre Notebook*, 40 (1985), 118.

21 Clement Scott in the *Daily Telegraph*, 14 March 1891; quoted in A. C. Ward, ed., *Specimens of English Dramatic Criticism* (London, 1945), p. 184. George Bernard Shaw in *Our Theatres in the Nineties* (London, 1932), Vol. 3, p. 179.

22 Michael Field diary, quoted in Davies, "Acting in Ibsen," p. 119. The diarist calls this performance "the most complete piece of acting" he has ever seen.

23 Shaw, *Our Theatres in the Nineties*, Vol. 3, p. 183.

24 William Winter's review is reprinted in full in Barnard Hewitt, *Theatre U.S.A.*, *1665 to 1957* (New York, 1959), pp. 291–3.

25 *The Theatre Magazine*, 3 (1903), 100.

26 *Teatret*, 2 (February, 1903), 65.

27 Letter to Sophie Reimers dated 25 March 1887, in *Ibsen: Letters and Speeches*, p. 266.

28 Henri Nathansen, *William Bloch* (Copenhagen, 1928), p. 86.

29 *Ibid.*, p. 48.

30 The handwritten promptbook for this production, marked "*Instruktionsbog*" (325 pp.), is in the Royal Theatre Library in Copenhagen.

31 Nathansen, p. 75.

32 Konstantin Stanislavski, "Director's Diary, 1905," trans. Elizabeth Reynolds Hapgood, in *Stanislavski and America*, ed. Erika Munk (New York, 1966), pp. 38, 32.

33 *Moskovskie vedomostie*, 1905, no. 93, quoted in Nils Åke Nilsson, *Ibsen in Russland* (Stockholm 1958), p. 90. Compare Ibsen's letter to Duke Georg of Saxe-Meiningen (13 November 1886) describing "the interior arrangements of Norwegian country residences" in *Henrik Ibsen*, ed. James [Walter] McFarlane (Harmondsworth, Middlesex, 1970), p. 106.

34 Letter to the Royal Theatre management, quoted in Robert Neiiendam, *Det Kgl. Teaters Historie, 1882–1886* (Copenhagen, 1927), Vol. 4, p. 60.

35 Stanislavski, "Director's Diary, 1905," p. 36.

36 *Vort Land*, 30 January 1903.

37 *Cf.* Ulla Strømberg and Jytte Wiingaard, *Den levende Ibsen* (Copenhagen, 1978), p. 137.

38 *Vort Land*, 30 January 1903.

39 *Teatret*, 2 (February, 1903), 69.

40 Stanislavski, "Director's Diary, 1905," pp. 31, 38.

41 *Teatret*, 2 (February, 1903), 69.

42 Quoted in McFarlane, *Henrik Ibsen*, p. 93.

43 *Politiken*, 30 January 1942, reprinted in Frederik Schyberg, *Teatret i Krig, 1939–1948* (Copenhagen, 1949), pp. 60–4. Schyberg was an expert witness: his father, Robert Schyberg, took over the part of Osvald from Nicolai Neiiendam in the original Royal Theatre production.

44 Program for *Rosmersholm*, Teatro della Pergola, Firenze, 5 December 1906: quoted in Denis Bablet, *Edward Gordon Craig* (London, 1966), p. 87.

45 Alfred Polgar, *Brahms Ibsen* (Berlin, 1910), p. 7.

46 Quoted in *Max Reinhardt and his Theatre*, ed. Oliver M. Sayler (New York, 1968), p. 26.

47 Ernst Stern, *My Life, My Stage*, trans. Edward Fitzgerald (London, 1951), pp. 74–5.

48 Frank E. Washburn-Freund, "The Evolution of Reinhardt," in Sayler, p. 53.

49 In Sayler, p. 324.

50 Polgar, p. 8. See also L. Schönhoff, *Kritische Theaterbriefe* (Berlin, 1900), p. 30: quoted in Schley, p. 131.

51 Quoted in Kela Kvam, *Max Reinhardt og Strindbergs visionære dramatik* (Copenhagen, 1974), p. 45.

52 Quoted in Edda Fuhrich and Gisela Prossnitz, *Max Reinhardt: Eine Dokumentation* (Vienna, 1987), p. 98.

53 Julius Bab, *Das Theater der Gegenwart* (Leipzig, 1928), p. 126.

54 *Süddeutsche Zeitung*, 17 April 1965. Henrichs' comment appeared in the same paper two days before.

55 Klaus Wagner in *Frankfurter Allgemeine Zeitung*, 24 November 1969.

56 Klaus Wagner in *Frankfurter Allgemeine Zeitung*, 7 July 1977.

57 In *The Lady*, 14–21 February 1974.

5 IBSEN'S 'NEW METHOD': *THE WILD DUCK*

1 Letter dated 12 June 1883, in *Ibsen: Letters and Speeches*, ed. Evert Sprinchorn (New York, 1964), p. 220.
2 Letter dated 2 September 1884, in *ibid.*, pp. 236–7.
3 Letter dated 14 November 1884, in *ibid.*, p. 242.
4 Sergei Eisenstein, *Film Sense* (New York, 1942), p. 31.
5 Letter to Leonid Sredin dated 24 September 1901. The Stanislavski production of *The Wild Duck* had opened five days before. See Martin Nag, *Ibsen i russisk åndsliv* (Oslo, 1967), p. 110.
6 "Le Canard sauvage" in *Le Temps* (4 May 1891), reprinted in Francisque Sarcey, *Quarante ans de théâtre* (Paris, 1902), Vol. 8, p. 339.
7 Review in *Journal des Débats* 11 May 1891), reprinted in Jules Lemaître, *Impressions de théâtre* (Paris, 1892), Vol. 6, p. 31.
8 Unsigned review in the *Daily Telegraph* (5 May 1894), reprinted in *Ibsen: The Critical Heritage*. ed. Michael Egan (London, 1972), p. 319.
9 Gunnar Heiberg, *Ibsen og Bjørnson paa Scenen* (Christiania, 1918), p. 47.
10 Quoted in *Ibsen: Letters and Speeches*, p. 243.
11 Quoted in Berit Erbe, *Bjørn Bjørnsons vej mod realismens teater* (Bergen, 1976), p. 196.
12 Letter to Hans Schrøder dated 14 December 1882, quoted in *Ghosts and Three Other Plays*, trans. Michael Meyer (Garden City, 1966), p. 214.
13 Sven Lange, *Meninger om Teater* (Copenhagen, 1929), p. 246.
14 *Berlingske politiske og Advertissements Tidende*, 5 March 1883.
15 Letter to Edvard Fallesen, head of the Danish Royal Theatre, dated 12 December 1882, in *Ibsen: Letters and Speeches*, p. 215.
16 This production and its sources are discussed in detail in Lise-Lone Marker and Frederick J. Marker, "William Bloch and Naturalism in the Scandinavian Theatre," *Theatre Survey*, 15 (March 1974), 85–104. An excerpt from Bloch's holograph promptbook can be found reprinted (without commentary) in Kela Kvam, "William Bloch and Ibsen," *Henrik Ibsen i scenisk belysning*, ed. Jytte Wiingaard (Copenhagen, 1978), pp. 54–99.
17 Quoted in Lise-Lone Marker, *David Belasco: Naturalism in the American Theatre* (Princeton, 1975), p. 10.
18 Bloch's holograph promptbook, signed by him on the title page, is bound together with the printed copy of the play submitted to the Royal Theatre on Ibsen's behalf: København: Gyldendalske Boghandels Forlag, 1884, 244 pp. (Royal Theatre Library). Important corroborating sources are the Theatre's *Regieprotokol*, 17 March 1881, and the handwritten *Maskinmester* journal.
19 *Intelligentssedlerne*, 12 January 1885, quoted in Erbe, p. 198.
20 *Dags-Telegrafen*, 24 February 1885.
21 *Regieprotokol*, 17 March 1881, p. 77 (Royal Theatre Library).
22 Erbe, p. 200.
23 Quoted in Carla Rae Waal, *Johanne Dybwad, Norwegian Actress* (Oslo, 1967), p. 147.

24 William Bloch, "Nogle Bemærkninger om Skuespilkunst," *Tilskueren* (1896), Vol. 14, p. 447.

25 Vilhelm Møller, *Ude og Hjemme* (March, 1885), quoted in Elisabeth Davidsen, *Henrik Ibsen og Det Kongelige Teater* (Copenhagen, 1980), p. 95. One cannot agree with Davidsen's assertion that this remark can be taken as evidence of an inherent lack of unified ensemble playing in Bloch's performance. What it *is* evidence of is a common contemporary reaction to the novelty of Ibsen's multiple focus in the play and to its consequent realization in performance.

26 Excerpt from Bloch's holograph promptbook, pp. 158–9 (Royal Theatre Library). The directions are all Bloch's; the translation is by the present authors.

27 *Berlingske politiske og Advertissements Tidende*, 23 February 1885.

28 *Dagens Nyheder*, 24 February 1885.

29 Only reportedly: in an account by P. A. Rosenberg of a conversation with Ibsen that took place more than thirteen years later (3 April 1898). Only Betty Hennings satisfied Ibsen completely: "Fru Hennings *is* Hedvig," he said. See Ibsen's *Samlede Værker, Hundreårsutgave*, ed. Francis Bull, Halvdan Koht and Didrik Arup Seip (Oslo, 1928–57), Vol. 10, p. 38.

30 *Politiken*, 24 February 1885, reprinted in Edvard Brandes, *Om Teater*, ed. Harald Engberg (Copenhagen, 1947), p. 19.

31 Thomas B. Krag, "Ibsen-Fortolkning paa Scenen," *Teatret*, 1 (November-December, 1901), 57.

32 Vilhelm Møller, *Ude og Hjemme* (March, 1885).

33 *Politiken*, 30 October 1942, reprinted in Frederik Schyberg, *Teatret i Krig, 1939–1948* (Copenhagen 1949), p. 75.

34 *Göteborgs Handels- och Sjöfartstidning*, 14 May 1949, reprinted in Agne Beijer, *Teaterrecensioner* (Stockholm, 1954), p. 546.

35 Sjöberg's interleaved script, marked *Regiexemplar* (246 pp.), is in Kungliga Dramatiska teatern. The remarks quoted are from the end of the second act (p. 86) and the end of the play.

36 Desmond MacCarthy, *The Court Theatre 1904–1907* (London, 1907), pp. 37–8.

37 James Agate, *The Contemporary Theatre, 1925* (London, 1926), p. 75.

38 Kenneth Tynan *Curtains* (London, 1961), p. 112.

39 Tord Bæckström in *Göteborgs Handels- och Sjöfartstidning*, 18 March 1972.

40 Björn Samuelsson in *Folket* (Eskilstuna), 24 March 1972.

41 *Ideskisse "Vildanden"* 1965 P.R. *Gauguin – Pål Løkkeberg/II.-V. akt* (Universitetsbibliotek, Oslo).

42 Jens Kistrup in *Berlingske Tidende* (Copenhagen), 27 April 1972.

43 "Talking about Theatre," in Lise-Lone Marker and Frederick J. Marker, *Ingmar Bergman: Four Decades in the Theatre* (Cambridge, 1982), p. 20.

44 Karl-H. Sandberg in *Arbetarbladet* (Gävle), 18 March 1972.

45 Vera Nordin in *Östgöta Correspondenten* (Linkjöping), 21 March 1972.

46 All information about cuts is taken from the prompter's copy, marked *Sufflörexemplar*, 161 pp. (Kungliga Dramatiska teatern).

47 Kistrup in *Berlingske Tidende*, 27 April 1972.
48 From an unpublished script of the Bergman version, as translated by the present authors.
49 Yvonne Shafer, "Interview with Harold Clurman," *Ibsen News and Comment*, 1 (Spring, 1980), 12.
50 William A. Henry III in *Time*, 127 (7 April 1986).
51 Review reprinted in Friedrich Luft, *Stimme der Kritik* (Frankfurt am Main, 1982), Vol. 2, pp. 318–19.
52 Alfred Polgar, *Brahms Ibsen* (Berlin, 1910), pp. 16–17.
53 *Ibid.*, pp. 15–16.
54 "Ibsen Triumphant," *Saturday Review*, 22 May 1897, reprinted in George Bernard Shaw, *Our Theatres in the Nineties*, (London, 1932), Vol. 3, p. 138.

6 MESSENGER FROM A CLOSED COUNTRY: *HEDDA GABLER*

1 The complete run of Ibsen's notes is printed in *The Oxford Ibsen*, ed. James Walter McFarlane (London, 1966), Vol. 7, pp. 476–97.
2 *Ibid.*, p. 486.
3 *Fortnightly Review*, XLIX NS, 289 (1 January 1891).
4 Jules Clarétie, then administrator of the Comédie Française, quoted in Kela Nyholm, "Henrik Ibsen på den franske scene," *Ibsen Årbok* 1957–9, ed. Einar Østvedt (Oslo, 1959), p. 53.
5 Henry James, "On the Occasion of *Hedda Gabler*," *New Review*, 4 (June, 1891), reprinted in James' *The Scenic Art*, ed. Allan Wade (New York, 1967), pp. 245–6.
6 *Illustrated London News*, 25 April 1891, reprinted in *Ibsen: The Critical Heritage*, ed. Michael Egan (London, 1972), p. 227.
7 Justin McCarthy, "Pages on Plays," *Gentleman's Magazine* (June, 1891), p. 638. McCarthy had a personal axe to grind, however, in that he had originally hoped to produce the play himself.
8 Elizabeth Robins, *Ibsen and the Actress* (London, 1928), pp. 53–4. Subsequent references to this work are given in parenthesis.
9 James, *The Scenic Art*, p. 250.
10 *The Oxford Ibsen*, Vol. 7, pp. 485, 502.
11 George Bernard Shaw, *Collected Letters* (New York, 1965), p. 292.
12 The script is preserved in the Elizabeth Robins collection at the Fales Library, New York University. It has been studied in detail in Rita E. Much, "The Staging of Ibsen's Modern Plays in England," unpublished dissertation, University of Toronto, 1981.
13 For a comment on the stock set borrowed by Robins, see Gay Gibson Cima, "Elizabeth Robins: The Genesis of an Independent Manageress," *Theatre Survey*, 21 (1980), 152. See also the Robins sketch entitled "Working at Hedda" in the Fales Library.
14 Tracy C. Davis, "Acting in Ibsen," *Theatre Notebook*, 40 (1985), 121. Archer's letter to Robins, dated 25 April 1891, is in the Fales Library.

15 A documentary account of this production is found in Randolph Goodman, *From Script to Stage: Eight Modern Plays* (New York, 1971), pp. 57–62.
16 Charles Marowitz, *Hedda*, in *Sex Wars: Free Adaptations of Ibsen and Strindberg* (Boston and London, 1982), p. 97. The collage was first performed in Bergen, Norway, in 1978, and was revived at the Round House in London in 1980.
17 Quoted in Archie Binns, *Mrs. Fiske and the American Theatre* (New York, 1955), pp. 139, 161.
18 The Suzman lecture, "*Hedda Gabler*: the Play in Performance," is published in *Ibsen and the Theatre* (proceedings of a conference held at the University of British Columbia in 1978), ed. Errol Durbach (London, 1980), pp. 83–104.
19 Sheridan Morley in *Punch*, 22 June 1977.
20 The respective references in this paragraph are: (for Fiske) William Winter, *The Wallet of Time* (New York, 1913), Vol. 2, p. 297; (for Nazimova) Walter Prichard Eaton, *The American Stage of To-day* (Boston, 1908), p. 133; (for Campbell) James Agate, *Red Letter Nights* (London, 1944), pp. 77, 78; (for Nansen) *Politiken*, 13 January 1924; (for Robertson) *The Sketch*, 31 January 1951; (for Ashcroft) Kenneth Tynan in the *Observer*, 12 September 1954. For Ashcroft's statements, see "An English Hedda: Interview with Peggy Ashcroft" in Goodman, *From Script to Stage*, pp. 64–5.
21 Cf. Jean-Paul Sartre, "Forgers of Myths" (1946), in *Theatre Arts Anthology*, ed. Rosamond Gilder, Hermine R. Isaacs and others (New York, 1951), pp. 135–42.
22 All of Craig's statements are from his program article for *Rosmersholm*, Teatro della Pergola, Firenze, 5 December 1906: quoted in Denis Bablet, *Edward Gordon Craig* (London, 1966), pp. 87–8.
23 For Vakhtangov's notes on his *Rosmersholm* production, see *Evgeny Vakhtangov*, compiled by Lyubov Vendrovskaya and Galina Kaptereva (Moscow, 1982), pp. 43–55.
24 Pavel Yartsev's notes on Meyerhold's *Hedda Gabler* are reprinted in *Meyerhold on Theatre*, ed. and trans. Edward Braun (New York, 1969), pp. 65–8.
25 In M. V. Alpatov and E. A. Gunst, *Nikolai Nikolaevic Sapunov* (Moscow, 1965), p. 23.
26 *Ibid.*, quoted in Martin Nag, *Ibsen i russisk åndsliv* (Oslo, 1967), p. 49. A somewhat different version of this description is quoted in Nikolai A. Gorchakov, *The Theater in Soviet Russia* (New York, 1957), p. 56.
27 Georg Fuchs, *Revolution in the Theatre*, condensed and adapted by Constance Connor Kuhn (Ithaca, N. Y., 1959), p. 74.
28 *Meyerhold on Theatre*, p. 68.
29 *Teatr i iskusstvo*, 1908/16: cf. Nils Åke Nilsson, *Ibsen in Russland* (Stockholm, 1958), p. 109.
30 Siegfried Melchinger in *Theater heute*, 10 (1967), 8. Melchinger saw the production when it was revived at Dramaten (and also played in Berlin) in 1967.
31 See Lise-Lone Marker and Frederick J. Marker, *Ingmar Bergman: Four Decades in the Theatre* (London and New York, 1982), p. 179.

32 Peter Cowie's *Ingmar Bergman: A Critical Biography* (London, 1982) reproduces (on p. 225) the original drawing-room set which Mago designed along traditional lines, and which Bergman rejected (though Cowie does not say so).

33 *Time*, 96 (20 July 1970).

34 In an addition to his early draft version of the play, Ibsen let Hedda refer to Løvborg as being "like a messenger from a closed country" (*The Oxford Ibsen*, Vol. 7, p. 492). Is it unreasonable to speculate that he discarded the line again because the phrase is so strikingly applicable to Hedda herself?

35 *Cf.* Alan Dent, *Mrs. Patrick Campbell* (London, 1961), p. 216.

36 In addition to personal observation, the sources of information for this and other scenes in Bergman's productions of *Hedda Gabler* are the director's own script, the script of his German *regieassistent* Johannes Kaetzler, and the Swedish stage-manger's script, marked *Scenen* (247 pp., Kungliga Dramatiska teatern).

37 Reprinted in Per Erik Wahlund, *Avsidesrepliker: Teaterkritik 1961–1965* (Stockholm, 1966), p. 190.

38 The caricature of depraved sensuality served up by Robert Stephens in the London revival ("bloody mouthed and half-delirious with his fly-buttons undone," as *The Times* put it) destroyed whatever was left of Bergman's intentions in this unrepresentative production.

39 *Cf.* Francis Fergusson, *The Idea of a Theatre* (New York, 1953), p. 93.

40 As the last seven lines of the scene were condensed in the German version (translated by Heiner Gimmler) at the Residenztheater.

41 Quoted in *Kvällsposten* (Malmö), 18 October 1964.

42 *Guardian*, 29 June 1972. John Osborne's capricious rewriting of *Hedda Gabler* was published by Faber and Faber in 1972.

43 Charles Marowitz, *Confessions of a Counterfeit Critic* (London, 1973), p. 170.

44 Letter to Moritz Prozor, dated 4 December 1880.

7 ON THE MOUNTAIN TOP: *JOHN GABRIEL BORKMAN*

1 Letter to Olaf Hansson in Bergen, dated 2 January 1897, quoted in *The Oxford Ibsen*, ed. James Walter McFarlane (London, 1977), Vol. 8, p. 342.

2 *Nationaltidende* (Copenhagen), 1 February 1897.

3 Particularly ironic when one remembers that a plank of Sverdrup's platform was the elimination of Swedish domination over Norway – and Lindberg's troupe was Swedish.

4 *Sunday Times* (London), 2 February 1975.

5 *Vort Land*, 1 February 1897.

6 Quoted remark by Jack Tinker in the *Daily Mail*, 29 January 1975.

7 Alfred Polgar, *Brahms Ibsen* (Berlin, 1910), p. 42.

8 *Saturday Review*, 75 (8 May 1897), reprinted in George Bernard Shaw, *Our Theatres in the Nineties* (London, 1932), Vol. 3, 122.

9 For further details, see Rune Johansen, *Teatermaler Jens Wang: Dekorasjonskunst og sceneteknikk* (Oslo, 1984), pp. 72–7.

10 Henrik Ibsen, *John Gabriel Borkman*, English version and Introduction by Inga-Stina Ewbank and Peter Hall (London, 1975), p. 10.

11 James Agate, *Red Letter Nights* (London, 1944), p. 88. For readers puzzled by Agate's learned allusion, see Coleridge's "The Rime of the Ancient Mariner," lines 488–91.

12 Kristian Elster, *Teater, 1929–1939* (Oslo, 1941), p. 296.

13 Sjöberg's marked script and work photos of the settings are in the library of Kungliga dramatiska teatern.

14 Agne Beijer, *Teaterrecensioner, 1925–1949* (Stockholm, 1954). p. 513.

15 *Ibid.*, p. 514.

16 Lise-Lone Marker and Frederick J. Marker, "Bergman's *Borkman*: An Interview," *Theater*, 17 (Spring 1986), 51, 50.

17 In *Ibsen auf der deutsche Bühne*, ed. Wilhelm Friese (Tübingen, 1976), p. 132.

18 *Ibid.*, p. 133.

19 Most of Bergman's statements about the production are found in the interview published in *Theater*. Apart from personal observation during the rehearsal period, information about the production itself is based on the director's own script, the script of his *regieassistent* Annette Gassmann, and the authors' own unpublished rehearsal log.

20 Gerhard Pörtl in *Südwestpresse*, 3 June 1985.

21 Interview in *Theater*, 51.

22 Henry James, *The Scenic Art*, ed. Allan Wade (New York, 1957), p. 294.

23 From an unpublished English script of the Bergman version, by the present authors.

24 *Frankfurter Allgemeine Zeitung*, 3 June 1986.

Select bibliography

References to unpublished sources and to reviews and articles in newspapers and periodicals are found only in the Notes.

Agate, James. *The Contemporary Theatre, 1923*. London, 1924
  The Contemporary Theatre, 1925. London, 1926
  Playgoing: An Essay. London, 1927
  Red Letter Nights. London, 1944
Archer, William. *The Theatrical 'World' for 1893*. London, 1894
  The Theatrical 'World' for 1894. London, 1895
Bab, Julius. *Agnes Sorma: Ein Gedenkbuch*. Heidelberg, 1927
  Das Theater der Gegenwart. Leipzig, 1928
Bang, Herman. *'Et Dukkenhjem' paa Nationaltheatret*. Copenhagen, 1880
  Kritiske Studier. Copenhagen, 1880
  Masker og Mennesker. Copenhagen, 1910
Bang-Hansen, Kjertil, Erik Piersdorff and Önjan Wiklund. *Når det kommer til stykket*. Oslo, 1972
Baring, Maurice. *The Puppet Show of Memory*. Boston, 1922
Beijer, Agne. *Teaterrecensioner, 1925–1949*. Stockholm, 1954
Bergman, Gösta M. *Den moderna teaterns genombrott, 1890–1925*. Stockholm, 1966
Binns, Archie. *Mrs. Fiske and the American Theatre*. New York, 1955
Blanc, T. *Henrik Ibsen og Christiania Theater, 1850–1859*. Christiania, 1906
Borg, Mette. *Sceneinstruktøren Herman Bang*. Copenhagen, 1986
Brandes, Edvard. *Dansk Skuespilkunst*. Copenhagen, 1880
  Fremmed Skuespilkunst: Studier of Portrætter. Copenhagen, 1881.
  Om Teater, ed. Harald Engberg. Copenhagen 1947
Davidsen, Elisabeth. *Henrik Ibsen og Det Kongelige Teater*. Copenhagen, 1980
Dent, Alan. *Mrs. Patrick Campbell*. London, 1961
Durbach, Errol, ed. *Ibsen and the Theatre*. London, 1980
Eaton, Walter Prichard. *At the New Theatre and Others*. Boston, 1910
  The American Stage of To-day. Boston, 1908
Egan, Michael, ed. *Ibsen: The Critical Heritage*. London, 1972

Eller, William H. *Ibsen and Germany, 1870–1900*. Boston, 1928
Elster, Kristian. *Teater, 1929–1939*, ed. Anton Rønneberg. Oslo, 1941
Erbe, Berit. *Bjørn Bjørnsons vej mod realismens teater*. Bergen, 1976
Fergusson, Francis. *The Idea of a Theater*. Garden City, N. Y., 1953
Friese, Wilhelm, ed. *Ibsen auf der deutsche Bühne*. Tübingen, 1976
Gjesdahl, Paul. *Premierer og portrætter*. Oslo, 1957
Godman, Randolph. *From Script to Stage: Eight Modern Plays*. New York, 1971
Grein, J. T. *Dramatic Criticism, 1903–1904*, Vol. 5. London, 1905
Haakonsen, Daniel. *Henrik Ibsen, mennesket og kunstneren*. Oslo, 1981
Heiberg Gunnar. *Ibsen og Bjørnson paa Scenen*. Christiania, 1918
Henrik Ibsens brevveksling med Christiania Theater, 1878–1899. Oslo, 1965
Ibsen, Henrik. *Samlede Værker, Hundreårsutgave*, ed. Francis Bull, Halvdan
     Koht, and Didrik Arup Seip. 21 vols. Oslo, 1928–57.
James, Henry. *The Scenic Art*. ed. Allan Wade. New York, 1957
Johansen, Rune. *Teatermaler Jens Wang: Dekorasjonskunst og sceneteknikk*. Oslo,
     1984
Josephson, Ludvig. *Ett och annat om Henrik Ibsen och Christiania Teater*. Stock-
     holm 1898
Kerr, Alfred. *Teaterkritiken*. Stuttgart, 1971
Kindermann, Heinz. *Theatergeschichte Europas*, Vols. 7–9. Salzburg, 1965, 1968,
     1970
Koht, Halvdan, *Henrik Ibsen: Ett diktarliv*. 2 vols. Oslo, 1928–9
Kvam, Kela [Nyholm]. "Henrik Ibsen paa den franske Scene,' *Ibsen-Årboken*,
     1957–59, ed. Einar Østvedt, Oslo, 1959, pp. 7–78.
   Max Reinhardt og Strindbergs visionære dramatik. Copenhagen, 1974
Lange, Sven. *Meninger om Teater*. Copenhagen, 1929
Lemaître, Jules. *Impressions de théâtre*, Vols. 5–10. Paris, 1894–8
Luft, Friedrich. *Stimme der Kritik*, 2 vols. Frankfurt am Main, 1982
Lugné-Poë, A. M. *Ibsen i Frankrike*. Oslo, 1938
Lund, Audhild. *Henrik Ibsen og det norske teater*. Oslo, 1925
MacCarthy, Desmond. *The Court Theatre, 1904–1907*. London, 1907
Marker, Frederick J. and Lise-Lone Marker. *The Scandinavian Theatre: A Short
     History* Oxford, 1975
   Ingmar Bergman: A Project for the Theatre. New York, 1983
Marker, Lise-Lone and Frederick J. Marker. *Ingmar Bergman: Four Decades in the
     Theatre*. Cambridge, 1982
Marowitz, Charles. *Confessions of a Counterfeit Critic*. London, 1973
McFarlane, James Walter, ed. *Henrik Ibsen: A Critical Anthology*. Harmonds-
     worth, Middlesex, 1970
   The Oxford Ibsen. 8 vols. London, 1960–77
Melchinger, Siegfried. *Theater der Gegenwart*. Frankfurt am Main, 1956
Meyer, Michael. *Henrik Ibsen*. 3 vols. London, 1967–71
Meyerhold on Theatre, ed. and trans. Edward Braun. New York, 1969
Midbøe, Hans. *Max Reinhardts iscenesættelse av Ibsens Gespenster i Kammerspiele
     des Deutschen Theaters Berlin 1906*. Videnskabers Selskab Skrifter. Trond-
     heim, 1967

Peer Gynt, teatret og tiden. 2 vols. Oslo, 1976–8

Munk, Erika, ed. *Stanislavski and America*. New York, 1966

Nag, Martin. *Ibsen i russisk åndsliv*. Oslo, 1967

Nathansen, Henri. *William Bloch*. Copenhagen, 1928

Neiiendam, Robert. *Det kgl. Teaters Historie, 1882–1886*, Vol. 4. Copenhagen, 1927

    Fra Kulisserne og Scenen. Copenhagen, 1966

Nilsen, Hans Jacob. *Peer Gynt: ett anti-romantisk verk*. Oslo, 1948

Nilsson, Nils Åke. *Ibsen in Russland*. Stockholm, 1958

Nordensvan, Georg. *Svensk teater och svenska skådespelare*. 2 vols. Stockholm, 1918.

Northam, John. *Ibsen's Dramatic Method*. London, 1953

Næss, Trine. *Arne Walentin, teatermålar og scenograf*. Oslo, 1978

Patterson, Michael. *Peter Stein: Germany's Leading Theatre Director*. Cambridge, 1981

Peer Gynt, Ein Schauspiel aus dem neunzehnten Jahrhundert: Dokumentation der Schaubühnen-Inszenierung. Berlin, 1971

Polgar, Alfred. *Brahms Ibsen*. Berlin, 1910

Robins, Elizabeth. *Ibsen and the Actress*. London, 1928

Rudler, Roderick. "Ibsens teatergjerning i Bergen," *Drama och teater*, ed. Egil Törnqvist, Stockholm, 1968, pp. 59–68

Rudnitsky, Konstantin. *Meyerhold the Director*. Ann Arbor, 1981

Sarcey, Francisque. *Quarante ans de théâtre*, Vol. 8. Paris, 1902

Sayler, Oliver M., ed. *Max Reinhardt and his Theatre*. New York, 1968

Schley, Gernot. *Die Freie Bühne in Berlin*. Berlin, 1967

Schönhoff, L. *Kritische Theaterbriefe*. Berlin, 1900

Schyberg, Frederik. *Teatret i Krig, 1939–1948*. Copenhagen, 1949

    Ti Aars Teater. Copenhagen, 1939

Shaw, George Bernard. *Collected Letters*. New York, 1965

    Our Theatres in the Nineties. 3 vols. London, 1932

Sjögren, Henrik. *Ingmar Bergman på teatern*. Stockholm, 1968

Sprinchorn, Evert, ed. *Ibsen: Letters and Speeches*. New York, 1964

Stern, Ernst, *My Life, My Stage*, trans. E. Fitzgerald, London, 1951

Strømberg, Ulla and Jytte Wiingaard. *Den levende Ibsen*. Copenhagen, 1978

Tennant, P. F. D. *Ibsen's Dramatic Technique*. Cambridge, 1948

Thomsen, C. Braad. *I Fassbinders spegl*. Copenhagen, 1975

Tynan, Kenneth. *Curtains*. London, 1961

Vardac, A. Nicholas. *From Stage to Screen*. Cambridge, Mass., 1949

Waal, Carla Rae. *Johanne Dybwad, Norwegian Actress*. Oslo, 1967

Wahlund, Per Erik. *Avsidesrepliker: Teaterkritik, 1961–1965*. Stockholm, 1966

    Scenväxling: Teaterkritik, 1954–1960. Stockholm, 1962

Ward, A. C., ed. *Specimens of English Dramatic Criticism*. London, 1945

Wiingaard, Jytte, ed. *Henrik Ibsen i scenisk belysning*. Copenhagen, 1978

Winter, William. *Life and Art of Richard Mansfield, with Selections from his Letters*. 2 vols. New York, 1910

    The Wallet of Time. 2 vols. New York, 1913

Chronological index of Ibsen plays and productions

This chronological index provides a guide to the principal references to Ibsen plays and performances found in the present study. It is not intended as a substitute for the more comprehensive Ibsen production calendars available elsewhere. In the case of the English-speaking theatre, for example, one is extremely fortunate to have the detailed lists of productions compiled by Michael Meyer (in the hardback editions of his translations, 1960–5), by James Walter McFarlane (in *The Oxford Ibsen*), and (for U.S. theatre) by Rolf Fjelde (in his collected translation of Ibsen's prose plays, 1978).

General index

Printed in the United Kingdom
by Lightning Source UK Ltd.
107400UKS00001BA/166-207